Across the world, democracy is under threat from the wealth and power that is ever more concentrated in the hands of the few. But the rule of the few over the many rests on very shaky ground. When we have both the ideas and the power, and when we unite, we can overcome these crises and build a world of peace and justice.

This volume provides a space for campaigners from different places and different traditions to discuss, refine and share ideas, which is essential to building movements that can provide hope and real change.

Jeremy Corbyn, former leader of the UK Labour Party, Member of Parliament and founder of the Peace and Justice Project

The democratic rights won under capitalism have always been limited yet crucial to gaining some control over our lives and allowing vital space for challenging capitalism itself. The volume poses neoliberalism's polarisation of this dichotomy. On the one hand, the various authors agree, neoliberalism represents an authoritarian turn; on the other, they argue, that threat poses the necessity and promise of deepening substantive democracy.

Sam Gindin, former Research Director of the Canadian Auto Workers

Contributors draw on Marxist theoretical tools to expose deep tensions between neoliberal capitalism and democracy while determinedly refusing repressive alternatives inspired by orthodox Marxism. Their project is one of democratic and ecological socialism. This book will constitute a stimulating and valuable resource to the many who are committed to that project.

Daryl Glaser, Professor of Political Studies, University of the Witwatersrand, Johannesburg

This volume makes a compelling case for why fascist populist movements are manifestations of broad crises at the heart of modern globalising capitalism. Williams and Satgar have assembled an impressive range of scholars who have spent years reflecting on these issues. The book is timely and deserves to be read widely.

Gilbert M. Khadiagala, Professor of International Relations, University of the Witwatersrand, Johannesburg

A significant volume of wide-ranging scholarship that unpacks the two key phenomena that democracy faces today – fascism and neoliberal capitalism. With experiences from South Africa, India, the USA and Latin America, the authors address the paradox posed by the fact that institutionalised democracy now produces outcomes that run counter to the interests of the people.

Nivedita Menon, Professor in the School of International Studies, Jawaharlal Nehru University, New Delhi

T0317766

DEMOCRATIC MARXISM

DEMOCRATIC MARXISM SERIES

Series Editor: Vishwas Satgar

The crisis of Marxism in the late twentieth century was the crisis of orthodox and vanguardist Marxism associated mainly with hierarchical communist parties, and imposed, even as state ideology, as the 'correct' Marxism. The Stalinisation of the Soviet Union and its eventual collapse exposed the inherent weaknesses and authoritarian mould of vanguardist Marxism. More fundamentally vanguardist Marxism was rendered obsolete but for its residual existence in a few parts of the world, including within authoritarian national liberation movements in Africa and in China.

With the deepening crises of capitalism, a new democratic Marxism (or democratic historical materialism) is coming to the fore. Such a democratic Marxism is characterised by the following:

- Its sources span non-vanguardist grassroots movements, unions, political fronts, mass parties, radical intellectuals, transnational activist networks and parts of the progressive academy;
- It seeks to ensure that the inherent categories of Marxism are theorised within constantly changing historical conditions to find meaning;
- Marxism is understood as a body of social thought that is unfinished and hence challenged by the need to explain the dynamics of a globalising capitalism and the futures of social change;
- It is open to other forms of anti-capitalist thought and practice, including currents within radical ecology, feminism, emancipatory utopianism and indigenous thought;
- It does not seek to be a monolithic and singular school of thought but engenders contending perspectives;
- Democracy, as part of the history of people's struggles, is understood as the basis for articulating alternatives to capitalism and as the primary means for constituting a transformative subject of historical change.

This series seeks to elaborate the social theorising and politics of democratic Marxism.

Published in the series and available:

Michelle Williams and Vishwas Satgar (eds). 2013. *Marxisms in the 21st Century: Crisis, Critique and Struggle*. Johannesburg: Wits University Press.

Vishwas Satgar (ed.). 2015. *Capitalism's Crises: Class Struggles in South Africa and the World*. Johannesburg: Wits University Press.

Vishwas Satgar (ed.). 2018. *The Climate Crisis: South African and Global Democratic Eco-Socialist Alternatives*. Johannesburg: Wits University Press.

Vishwas Satgar (ed.). 2019. *Racism after Apartheid: Challenges for Marxism and Anti-Racism*. Johannesburg: Wits University Press.

Vishwas Satgar (ed.). 2020. *BRICS and the New American Imperialism: Global Rivalry and Resistance*. Johannesburg: Wits University Press.

DESTROYING DEMOCRACY

NEOLIBERAL CAPITALISM AND THE RISE OF AUTHORITARIAN POLITICS

Edited by Michelle Williams and Vishwas Satgar

WITS UNIVERSITY PRESS

Published in South Africa by:

Wits University Press
1 Jan Smuts Avenue
Johannesburg 2001

www.witspress.co.za

Compilation © Michelle Williams and Vishwas Satgar 2021
Chapters © Individual contributors 2021
Published edition © Wits University Press 2021

First published 2021

http://dx.doi.org.10.18772/22021086994

978-1-77614-699-4 (Paperback)
978-1-77614-700-7 (Hardback)
978-1-77614-701-4 (PDF)
978-1-77614-702-1 (EPUB)
978-1-77614-704-5 (Open Access PDF)

The publication of this volume was made possible by funding from the Rosa Luxemburg Stiftung and through a grant received from the National Institute for the Humanities and Social Sciences.

Project manager: Inga Norenius
Copyeditor: Lee Smith
Proofreader: Lisa Compton
Indexer: Margaret Ramsay
Cover design: Hothouse
Typeset in 10 point Minion Pro

CONTENTS

ACKNOWLEDGEMENTS

This volume owes a special debt to the Rosa Luxemburg Foundation (RLF). Without the support given by RLF it would have been impossible to hold a contributors' workshop in South Africa and ensure the manuscript was prepared for publication. We are also grateful for the support given by the Co-operative and Policy Alternative Centre (COPAC), which played a central role in organising the workshop convened with contributors and activists from various social movements and community organisations. The support given by the National Institute for the Humanities and Social Sciences (NIHSS) has enabled the series to be published open access. Moreover, it is important to acknowledge the editorial assistance provided by Jane Cherry from COPAC. Her efforts were crucial for keeping things on track. The efforts and inputs from Courtney Morgan, Awande Buthelezi and William Shoki are also appreciated. Finally, our sincerest appreciation to the team at Wits University Press, particularly Veronica Klipp, Roshan Cader and Corina van der Spoel, for supporting this volume and the Democratic Marxism series.

ACRONYMS AND ABBREVIATIONS

ANC	African National Congress
ANCYL	African National Congress Youth League
ARRA	American Recovery and Reinvestment Act
BEE	Black Economic Empowerment
BJP	Bharatiya Janata Party
Cosatu	Congress of South African Trade Unions
DA	Democratic Alliance
EFF	Economic Freedom Fighters
EU	European Union
GDP	Gross Domestic Product
GEAR	Growth, Employment and Redistribution
GHG	Greenhouse Gas
GS	Goldman Sachs
IMF	International Monetary Fund
IPCC	Intergovernmental Panel on Climate Change
JCPS	Justice, Crime Prevention and Security
KKK	Ku Klux Klan
LARR	Land Acquisition, Rehabilitation and Resettlement Act
Nafta	North American Free Trade Agreement
Nato	North Atlantic Treaty Organization
NDR	National Democratic Revolution
NGO	Non-governmental Organisation
NPA	National Prosecuting Authority
Numsa	National Union of Metalworkers of South Africa
OECD	Organisation for Economic Co-operation and Development
PAIA	Promotion of Access to Information Act
PCB	Communist Party of Brazil (*Partido Comunista do Brasil*)
PT	Worker's Party (*Partido dos Trabalhadores*)
RDP	Reconstruction and Development Programme
RTI	Right to Information Act
SABC	South African Broadcasting Corporation
SACP	South African Communist Party
Saftu	South African Federation of Trade Unions
SAPS	South African Police Service
SRWP	Socialist Revolutionary Workers Party
SSA	State Security Agency

TPP	Trans-Pacific Partnership
TTIP	Transatlantic Trade and Investment Partnership
UK	United Kingdom
UN	United Nations
UPA	United Progressive Alliance
US	United States of America
USSR	Union of Soviet Socialist Republics
WMC	White Monopoly Capitalism
WTO	World Trade Organization

PREFACE

Neoliberal Capitalism in the Time of Covid-19: Destroying Democracy and Rising Authoritarianism

Michelle Williams and Vishwas Satgar

The novel coronavirus changed the world in unimaginable ways. Weeks before the virulent virus – about 8 000 times smaller than a grain of salt – went global in February 2020, no one imagined that our highly globalised world was so fragile. In a matter of weeks, nearly all countries in the world closed their borders, locked down their inhabitants, stopped economic activity, shut down domestic and international travel, implemented massive state-led economic relief programmes, highlighted the importance of public health, and recognised glaring inequalities, hunger and poverty that have increasingly characterised neoliberal capitalism. With oil prices collapsing and crucial supply chains disrupted, the world as we knew it ceased to exist. While many scholars have written about capitalism's crises (including volumes two, three and five in the Democratic Marxism series), no one dreamed that the entire globalised economic system would grind to a halt in a matter of weeks. One microbial virus among the many quadrillion that exist on Earth has brought human civilisation to its knees as scientists, epidemiologists, medical professionals, governments, corporations and publics scramble to react to the devastation. Nature has disrupted, at least temporarily, fossil fuel capitalism and all our lives that are so integrally intertwined with it.

The hardships this has entailed span the global North and South, with nearly two million deaths as of January 2021, record-breaking unemployment levels, millions going hungry, collapsing health systems, rising inequality, astronomical private indebtedness, and psychological strain from months of lockdown isolation. The one clear silver lining is that the stalling of economic activity has given Earth a moment to breathe, to begin to heal itself. The crisis has made clear that capitalism rests on 'background' conditions such as our capacity to act as social beings, the vital role of social reproduction, human interconnection with human and non-human nature, the importance of public goods such as public health systems, and the essential role of political power (Fraser 2018).

Governments, scientists and publics responded variously to the spread of Covid-19. Political leaders in some countries made decisions based on scientific evidence and medical professionals' advice. Others engaged their publics in a joint response enlisting the publics' support for behaviour change and collective goods. Yet others used top-down technocratic state responses to combat the virus, often curtailing civil and political rights and freedoms, with some intensifying authoritarianism, power grabs and neo-fascist populism. These different state approaches triggered varying responses from citizens, including publics engaging a range of issues, deepening democratic practices and institutions, promoting solidarity within communities, mounting court challenges, protesting exclusionary politics and state violence, and challenging rising authoritarianism. While Covid-19 intensified these countervailing tendencies coursing through polities across the world, they have been long in the making.

While the authors do not directly engage with the world-changing effects of the Covid-19 pandemic, the analyses in the volume anticipate many of the threats to democracy and rising authoritarianism that Covid-19 accentuated. The forces destroying democracy intensified in the three international cases included in the volume (India, Brazil and the US), while South Africa's contestation over democracy deepened as the state used the Disaster Management Act to curtail constitutionally protected rights and freedoms. The politics of hate, exclusion and violence raged through the social fabric of India, Brazil and the US, while Modi, Bolsonaro and Trump ramped up their attacks on democratic institutions of the state. The storming of the US Capitol on 6 January 2021 shocked and horrified citizens and elected officials across the world, yet the antipathy towards democratic institutions was a consistent refrain throughout Trump's presidency. These once vibrant democracies were placed in jeopardy. Through it all, some mega-corporations, especially in information technology and telecommunications, experienced windfall profits, becoming wealthier and more powerful. The chapters presented here were written during the Trump administration, and although Trump is no longer the president of the US, the analyses and arguments in the volume remain valid as the underlying conditions and neoliberal forces that gave rise to the authoritarian politics of Trump and his administration have not changed.

The chapters in this volume all speak to the various threats to democracy, and provide a compass as to how we can reclaim and rebuild democracy from within.

Part One begins with an introductory chapter that frames the threats to democracy and rising authoritarianism. Michelle Williams traces democracy's ambivalent relationship to capitalism, showing how neoliberal capitalism has generated particular crises for democracy. Williams argues that democracy requires particular components – administrative capacity and state legitimacy – together with the principles of equality and liberty. She shows that neoliberal capitalism eroded both the administrative capacity and state legitimacy of democratic states as well as invoked equality of opportunity and liberty as non-interference, both of which undermine deeply democratic systems. Williams suggests that, along with effective state administration to regulate large and powerful corporations, strong publics with the capacity to articulate public interests and ensure that states act in the public interest, are the cornerstone to reclaiming democracy.

In chapter two, Vishwas Satgar focuses on the major threat of neoliberal times: the rise of eco-fascism. Using metabolic rift analysis to show how the metabolising of fossil fuels provides the basis for the climate crisis, Satgar offers an understanding of how ecological crises are part of the second coming of fascism. He explains that the eco-fascist threat can only be countered by democratising democracy and 'building mass subaltern power to also lead system change from below'. The only hope for humanity to achieve transformative change is to develop climate justice movements through 'resistance, defence and systemic alternatives'.

Part Two of the volume explores the undoing of three democracies – the US, Brazil and India – through the lens of neoliberal capitalism and its concomitant ecological devastation.

Narrowing our gaze to fascism in the US, Linda Gordon outlines the long history of the dangers of populism and fascism by tracing the history of the Ku Klux Klan in order to investigate the degrees to which the Klan and the US polity have harboured fascism. According to Gordon, populism 'refers to regimes, political parties and social movements that use demagoguery to promote bigotry and often reject the rule of law and the classic liberal guarantees of due process and civil liberties'. Moreover, Gordon's analysis highlights the Klan's fascist use of mysticism to discount evidence that challenged their claims to destiny and tradition similar to the way in which today's secular populists may discount evidence as fake news. Gordon's chapter reads as a warning of the rising fascistic tendencies emerging in the world.

Ingar Solty looks at what right-wing authoritarianism does once in power, in the heart of the neoliberal order – the US. Solty shows how Trump's 2016 election victory reflects the crisis of representation in the US. His presidential election campaign had two main critiques of the establishment: a critique of 'free trade' capitalism, and the imperial politics of previous US administrations. Solty argues that while Trump's trade wars had elements of protectionism and represented partial imperial retreat, his economic and foreign policies embodied a neo-Reaganite approach to intensifying world market integration. Bilateral transactionalism was the strategy to achieve this goal. Ultimately, what Trump represented was a continuation of US foreign economic policy that reinforced a 'competitive austerity approach'.

Saad-Filho provides a chilling account of how neoliberalism resulted in the rise of authoritarianism in Brazil through homing in on Bolsonaro's 2018 election. Saad-Filho shows how three primary modalities converged to lay the basis for authoritarian neoliberalism to take root in Brazil: the worldwide rise of the Right and the diffusion of neoliberal rationality; the Brazilian Left's recent decline stemming from mistakes within the approach of the Workers' Party to economic development and redistribution; and the global rise of authoritarian politics based on a new elite alliance. Saad-Filho draws important lessons for the Left in Brazil that also serve as lessons for progressive forces seeking to build expansive democracy in many contexts.

Taking us to India's version of authoritarian (and increasingly fascist) neoliberalism, Alf Nilsen shows how the right-wing Hindu nationalist Bharatiya Janata Party's 2019 general election victory paved the way for the consolidation of the authoritarian populism of Prime Minister Narendra Modi, leaving India's democracy in free fall. Nilsen argues that Modi's success is not a departure from neoliberalism, but fuses market-based development with a coercive majoritarianism that resonates across caste and class divides among the country's Hindu majority. Recent developments in India suggest that Nilsen's warning is fast becoming a reality: 'we live in an age where populism fuels fascism, and India under the authoritarian populism of Modi 2.0 might very well prove to be an example of precisely this'. One thing is certain – Modi's government is antithetical to democracy, even in its liberal form.

As we look at these cases in other parts of the world, the empirical evidence clearly paints a picture of rising and consolidated threats to actually existing democracies. All the cases highlight neoliberalism's destructive role in democratic polities. The different terms to describe these developments – authoritarian populism (Hall 1988; Nilsen, this volume), authoritarian neoliberalism (Saad-Filho, this volume), fascistic tendencies and fascism (Gordon, this volume) and eco-fascist (Satgar, this volume) – converge in highlighting the rise of anti-democratic rationality. The world is witnessing the consolidation of authoritarian, exclusionary, life-threatening (human and non-human life) politics within neoliberal rationality and globalised capitalism. Covid-19 has exacerbated many of these tendencies towards authoritarianism and the concentration of power and wealth in a very small number of global corporations and elite. It is in this context that we turn to Part Three, to see how South Africa negotiates its spatial and historical location within a globalised neoliberal rational order.

Devan Pillay investigates contending political narratives (liberalism and nationalist-populist) and the working-class responses to them: Marxist–Leninism and popular-democratic, or what Pillay calls democratic eco-socialism. Pillay shows the important democratising role of the labour movement, but notes that the very same movement helped bring Jacob Zuma and his allies to power in 2007/2008. Pillay argues that 'the organised Left, in particular the trade union movement, today stands as transfixed as a deer caught in the headlights, while right-wing nationalist-populists steal aspects of their discourse to ride the wave of discontent'. He suggests that left alternatives are being articulated by social movements, non-governmental organisations and a small number of unions. This is critical as part of a longer-term vision of building an alternative working-class politics that draws on the popular-democratic promises of the 1980s, and combines it with a renewed emphasis on democratic eco-socialism.

Dale McKinley looks at post-apartheid South Africa's reluctant commitment to the right to information, a fundamental democratic right. He argues that by locating this right within the state's security and intelligence apparatus, the state has curtailed democracy by hobbling informed popular participation and citizen voices. While the right to information is enshrined in the constitution, it has generally been viewed as a secondary human right. As a result, the state does not prioritise transparency, information-sharing and accountability, but rather relies on 'enclosed structures, invited spaces, securitised politics, secretive deals and unilateral decision making'. McKinley reminds us of the paramount importance of access to information for a robust and expansive democracy, as the 'commoning of, and public access to, information is the lifeblood of any meaningful democratic participation'.

Mandla Radebe situates his analysis within the central democratising role the media plays as the fourth estate, but shows how ownership patterns of media houses threaten to undermine this role. Radebe historicises his analysis by pointing out that some sections of the media played a significant role in the struggle for democracy, and while the post-apartheid constitution enshrines media freedoms, advances are limited by the way in which the media has been configured along liberal theories and concentrated ownership patterns. He shows how commercialisation has narrowed the democratic space for subalterns through the demise of left-leaning alternative media. Ultimately, Radebe argues that the post-apartheid media has continuities with the authoritarianism of apartheid and 'a decommodified alternative media must be reimagined'. Radebe's and McKinley's chapters provide a powerful analysis of the threats to democracy found in the private sector's control of the media and the state's control of information, respectively. While social media is ostensibly open to multiple sources of news, it still concentrates control in corporate hands and presents other threats in terms of misinformation, opinions rather than fact-based news, and sensationalism.

Jane Duncan explores the increasing trend towards securitising protests in response to rising levels of anti-austerity unrest in South Africa, as well as globally. With high levels of unemployment and poverty, the state has opted for a 'law-and-order' approach rather than democratising society, dismantling inequality and ensuring security of existence. Duncan claims that the global trend has shifted to 'modes of social control . . . transmitted as purported security "best practices" around the world'. She shows that this turn to greater securitisation threatens democracy. Duncan focuses on protest waves since 2015 and illustrates how the state identifies 'domestic instability as a major security threat alongside other serious crimes', laying the basis for the state to justify anti-democratic practices of invasive surveillance and securitisation. Reflecting the depth of neoliberal rationality, these practices are not seen as undermining fundamental democratic rights, but are instead framed as a 'good state' protecting the nation.

Gunnett Kaaf turns our attention to finding spaces for left renewal in crises-ridden times. Kaaf argues that building a renewed left project requires both the ability to imagine a different future (a vision) and ideas about how to concretely realise the vision (political strategy). He provides a powerful critique of the current political parties in South Africa and argues for the need to envision a future outside these parties. He locates renewal in mass movements that are not afraid to think beyond our current realities to envision realistic, radical possibilities. Avoiding blueprints requires thinking, debating and experimenting with possibilities that do not simply hark back to bygone eras of imagined better times. Kaaf offers an important reflection on possible ways to rebuild a left project.

The chapters collectively and individually raise important warnings about the ways in which neoliberal capitalism erodes democracy and enables its capture by corrupt, authoritarian and in some instances neo-fascist forces. Neoliberal capitalism is destroying democracy. Democratic forces are facing a difficult world but the future is still contested and has not yet been written.

REFERENCES

Fraser, N. 2018. 'Democracy's crisis: On the political implications of financialised capitalism'. Public lecture. Accessed 15 January 2019, https://web.facebook.com/WCFIA/videos/vb.144673958897100/269566100364576/?type=2&theater.

Hall, S. 1988. *The Hard Road to Renewal: Thatcherism and the Crisis of the Left*. London: Verso Books.

NEOLIBERAL CAPITALISM'S DESTRUCTION OF DEMOCRACY

1

THE CRISIS OF DEMOCRACY: NEOLIBERAL CAPITALISM, AUTHORITARIANISM AND RECLAIMING DEMOCRACY

Michelle Williams

The crisis of democracy is undeniable, registering in rising authoritarianism, the politics of hate and exclusion, right-wing populist movements, distrust of fact-based information and news, and the withering of accountable state institutions. Less obvious is that democracy's destruction is not simply a problem of politics requiring political solutions. Fixing politics, restoring democratic sensibilities (including fact-based decision making), enhancing democratic publics and overcoming a politics of hate will not save democracy – though these are all important and worth restoring – because the sources of democracy's destruction lie in systemic, intersecting crises combining four strands: the economy, ecology, social reproduction and politics. Democracy's destruction is one manifestation of the broader crisis created by neoliberal capitalism.[1] By neoliberal capitalism I am not only referring to economic liberalisation, including privatising state assets, liberalising markets (including labour markets), deregulating financial institutions, the ascendancy of transnational regulatory agencies and dismantling state welfare support systems. I am also referring to what Wendy Brown (2015: 15) calls neoliberal rationality, assigning economic metrics to all aspects of life, including non-human life, where the state, non-human nature, society and social reproduction are valued in terms of their contribution to economic interests.

It is commonplace to say that capitalism experiences periodic crises. History is testament to this. It is less common to acknowledge that capitalism actually generates these crises through the way in which it organises economic activity (what Marxists call the contradictions within production). It is even less common to see the crises generated in capitalism's contradictions in what Nancy Fraser (2018) calls the interrealm boundaries – that is, the economy's relation to non-human nature, to the necessary conditions of social reproduction, and to political power and the state. Similar to the contradictions within production that Marx highlighted, these interrealm contradictions are inherent to capitalism, as it has self-destabilising dynamics across the social matrix of capitalist society. When crises occur simultaneously in all four realms, they combine into a systemic crisis, and, as history has shown, capitalism is vulnerable to structural transformations that result in new ways of organising production and in the economy's relation to nature, polities and social reproduction (see Fraser 2014, 2018). Each of capitalism's four major historical periods[2] has established particular forms of organising social relations, with each resulting in particular contradictions. Democracy's fate is thus tethered to the larger social matrix that includes the organisation of social relations in the economy and the interrealm spaces between the economy and nature, the economy and social reproduction, and the economy and polities. Yet, the crisis of democracy demands our attention because democratic political power is essential to resolving the crises in the other realms. In fact, democracy is essential for any transformative politics that seeks social, ecological, economic and political justice. How democracy's crisis is resolved is linked to the capacity of society and the state to push for new forms of organising our social world and hence limiting the economy's power over these other realms.

This chapter looks at the crisis of democracy and highlights that the ways in which it is resolved have important implications for finding prefigurative alternatives beyond capitalism. I question whether democracy is an ideal worth fighting for by interrogating what it is, and then show the ways in which democracy's current crisis manifests in polities. I conclude by suggesting the necessity of prefigurative initiatives reconstituting democratic power by building anti-capitalist social relations in the interstitial spaces within and beyond capitalism.

CONTESTATION WITHIN/OVER DEMOCRACY

On 12 December 2019, the Hindu fundamentalist government in India under the leadership of Prime Minister Narendra Modi and his Bharatiya Janata Party (BJP) passed a Citizenship Amendment Act that offers refuge and possibly citizenship to persecuted religious minorities, except for Muslims, in some neighbouring countries. When this Act is placed alongside the proposed National Register of Citizens, it will require many Indian Muslims to prove that they qualify as Indian citizens, effectively dismantling the secular foundations of India's democracy.

On 15 December, three days after passage of the Citizenship Amendment Act, and in the shadow of growing police brutality against students protesting the Act, a large group of primarily women and children began a sit-in in an area of Delhi known as Shaheen Bagh. As the sit-in grew, it became a site for rehearsing a new vision of citizenship – the women were collectively redefining fundamental democratic notions of freedom, equality and solidarity.

These two simultaneous and ongoing episodes in Indian politics capture what is at stake in the bifurcated politics coursing through polities across the world. These developments reflect in the election of exclusionary neo-fascist political leaders in places such as the US,[3] Poland, Hungary, Turkey, Brazil and India. Populist (and fascist) movements in western Europe such as the Alternative für Deutschland in Germany and the League Party in Italy, and the Economic Freedom Fighters in South Africa, raise exclusionary appeals that resonate with large numbers of precarious people abandoned by traditional political parties. The rise of these movements through electoral democratic systems raises questions about the merits of democracy. At the same time, the second decade of the twenty-first century witnessed unprecedented pro-democracy protests across the world. While protests have been an important component of democratic claims-making for well over two centuries, the recent protests in Brazil, Chile, India, Egypt, Hong Kong and the US share a common thread in their resistance to the rise of authoritarian politics. The rise of authoritarian politics and the robust defence of democratic spaces simultaneously articulate narrow and exclusionary appeals as well as more expansive and inclusive notions of democracy, and are responses to capitalism's multiple crises unravelling societies' capacities to sustain life and flourish. How can such opposing forms of political practices, visions and understandings arise within and make claims to democracy?

What is democracy?

The contestation over democracy is partly because it is an ideal that allows for many permutations – radical, participatory, liberal, bourgeois – each emphasising different principles, values, procedures and institutional arrangements. Democracy is the only form of rule that sees people collectively ruling themselves. It is fundamentally different from all other forms of rule, such as plutocracy (rule by and for the rich), aristocracy, monarchy, dictatorship, fascism, vanguardism (rule by an elite within a political party) or 'corporatocracy' (rule by corporations) (George 2015: 6). When we speak of democracy, we implicitly refer to necessary components for practising democracy and aspirational principles of democracy. Democracy has at least two essential components (administrative capacity and public legitimacy) and two primary principles (equality and liberty). Shortcomings in administrative capacity and public support weaken democracy, and understandings of equality and liberty shape the degree to which democracy can be realised.

Democracy for and by the people refers to the institutional arrangement of the state (for the people) and mechanisms for participation (by the people). Institutionally, a capable democratic state is able to develop and implement laws and public policy that reflect the broader interests of the public, including steering economic activity in the interests of society, protecting the natural world, supporting social reproduction and ensuring democratic public institutions for people's participation. The state must have the capacity to ensure that private interests, such as large corporations and the economic and political elite, comply with state regulation in the interest of the public, as well as financial accountability of public funds. Without strong, efficacious, and accountable administrative capacity within all levels of the state, democracy is undermined and eroded. Democracy also requires arenas and mechanisms for civil society and publics to engage the state around public interest and to voice public opinions about the state's regulations. State legitimacy is secured through public engagement around what constitutes the public interest and translating these interests into state policy and action. A robust, organised, engaged and informed citizenry is essential to ensuring efficacious public engagement as democracy is realised through practising it concretely. Consent of the governed is thus achieved through democratic means such as active political participation by a wide range of constituents through civil society organisations, local governmental institutions, participatory forums, and an open, free and fair media. These must ensure financial accountability and transparent and participatory budgeting, policy making and implementation processes. Thus, democracy requires both state capacity and state legitimacy (Fraser 2014).

The varied meanings of the foundational principles of equality and liberty are fundamental to the contestation within democracy. The concept of liberty ranges from non-interference to a more robust notion of independence from arbitrary power and non-domination by others. On the one side, the emphasis on liberty as non-interference sets the basis for free markets as the state should not interfere to regulate markets.[4] Similarly, liberty as non-interference lays the basis for minimal state support in social welfare as individuals are responsible for their own development. Liberalism promotes significant universal rights such as universal suffrage, education, human rights, civil rights, and freedom of association, speech and the

5

press. When married to liberty as non-interference, these rights are interpreted through the lens of possessive individualism, elevating individuals above the common good. On the other side – usually associated with social justice, egalitarian liberals and republicans – law and policy can enhance freedom by curtailing the arbitrary power of others. Thus, a 'liberty-protecting state' ensures that no institution (including the state, corporations and markets), person or other entity has 'arbitrary power over any citizen' (Pettit 1997: 67). For a more expansive notion of democracy, this second idea of liberty and freedom is central as it allows state intervention to ameliorate and protect against inequalities of power and wealth, and protects citizens from arbitrary power and domination. This also implies that democratic decision making is not limited to the political sphere, as a liberty-protecting state regulates the economy and redefines the interrealm boundaries between the economy and social reproduction and non-human nature. While it too promotes universal rights, it emphasises the relativity of rights in relation to others and the collective good. Thus, the importance of a liberty-protecting state for a robust and expansive democracy cannot be overstated.

The other contested notion is equality. Liberal democracy foregrounds equality of opportunity, which assumes everyone starts from the same conditions and ignores pre-existing inequalities. Equality of opportunity together with liberty as non-interference limits state involvement in protecting the population and the natural world from the market and minimises state-supported social welfare. In this framework, individuals are free to compete equally to achieve their life choices. A more expansive notion of democracy, by contrast, defines equality in terms of outcomes and recognises the necessity for state intervention in achieving equality. The creation of high-quality public goods such as public transportation, schools, health systems and spaces for recreation and enjoyment is central to achieving equality of outcomes, as is the social wage – both income distribution and the distribution of goods and services, including forms of government support such as grants, and subsidised housing and food systems. Redistributive programmes seeking equality of outcomes by a liberty-enhancing state are essential for achieving social justice. To do this requires state administrative capacity and active citizens, and simultaneously yields state legitimacy. Thus, if a robust and expansive democracy focuses on equality of outcomes by a liberty-protecting state that ensures institutional arrangements, engaged publics, laws and policy to realise this goal, why do we not live in such a democracy?

Modern liberal democracy has largely promoted liberty as non-interference by the state and equality of opportunity. It came of age in the eighteenth century with the development of capitalism, which has charted its trajectory and governed much of the Euro-Atlantic world (i.e. the centres of capitalism) for nearly two centuries. Liberal democracy in capitalist centres promoted the illusion of a virtuous cycle between democracy and capitalist development. Central to this relationship was the need to narrow democracy from an expansive understanding of rule by and for the people, by separating politics from the economy and limiting political participation to representation of the people by elected officials voted for in elections. Separating the economic and political spheres limits political and public oversight and state 'interference' in economic activity. As a result, a defining measure of democracy became synonymous with electoral procedures ensuring elections are transparent, accountable and inclusive of all qualified voters based on competition (i.e. equitable opportunity to compete in the election).

Limiting democratic decision making to the political realm allows corporations to operate under limited control and amass enormous power and wealth at the expense of other social realms. Fraser explains that capitalism's three fundamental divisions – the separation of production from social reproduction, the separation of humans from the non-human natural world, and the separation of economics and politics – create the illusion of spheres outside of capitalism (Fraser 2018; Fraser and Jaeggi 2018). These three spheres are the 'background' on which capitalism operates. By separating the economic from these 'decommodified' background spheres, capitalism mystifies the productive foundation on which it operates and exempts it from paying the actual costs of capitalist production.

Modern liberal democracy's imbrication with capitalism laid the basis on which capitalist markets were ensured the freedom to act in the pursuit of profits, allowed private property to become a primary site of capitalist accumulation, set the parameters for the commodification of nature, guaranteed 'free' labour to populate the factories and farms, devalued social reproduction, and justified disciplinary state order and security in the service of non-interference in the market. Democracy's liberal instantiation with capitalism gained widespread acceptance as the centres of capitalism venerated it as the 'best' form of government, while an increasing number of countries incorporated into capitalist markets. As a result, by the second decade of the twenty-first century over 100 countries claimed to be liberal democracies within the global capitalist economy.

Commonplace understandings often assume that democracy will survive no matter what, and that democratic capacities are inherent to the human condition. Both assumptions are patently untrue. For democracy in any form to thrive it must be engendered, nurtured and sustained in the institutions, practices and laws that uphold it as well as in the individuals that share in its rule. The point is worth emphasising: people must be educated into the values and practices of democracy; the institutions, laws and policies that uphold democracy must be enacted, respected and supported; and the political parties and states that represent aggregate interests must be accountable, transparent and responsive to their public duty.

The chequered history of democracy also lies in another conceptual knot: who are 'the people'? History demonstrates that the people can be exclusively conceived – men who own property, men, whites, educated – or inclusively conceived – all citizens, all residents living in a territory, all people on Earth. Who is defined as 'the people' has important implications for what constitutes public interests and who is elected to represent them. These are essentially classification struggles, which, for Pierre Bourdieu (1984, 2000), are engaged in by the elite and the state. Yet democratic forces also challenge fundamental understandings of citizenship, work, gender, relations to nature, social reproduction, equality, economy and who counts as a citizen or worker. For example, by demystifying the background conditions on which capital-ism depends, democratic forces ensure that the three inherent divisions in capitalism are laid bare in the interest of human well-being and substantive equality. Expansive democracy provides the possibility for embedding economic activity in social repro-duction, the natural world (planetary boundaries) and the polity. Through recal-ibrating the interrealm boundaries between the economy and social reproduction, non-human nature and politics, economic activity is reimagined (and retooled) in the service of public interest and society. In other words, an expansive democracy unteth-ered from capitalism can integrate economic activity in the entire social-ecological matrix. To do this requires direct forms of deliberation and decision making over the entire social-ecological matrix – including the economic arena – and an expansive notion of liberty that ensures the state acts to promote social, ecological and eco-nomic justice (substantive equality, inclusivity, fairness, planetary boundaries). Thus, a robust and expansive democracy reclassifies public power by extending into the economic sphere and providing the possibility for developing anti-capitalist alterna-tives that challenge the divisions inherent to capitalism. Throughout capitalism's his-tory, there have been episodic attempts to do this.

Classification struggles also link to the way in which notions of inclusion and solidarity are constructed. Whether solidarity is framed in narrow, exclusionary terms or in expansive, inclusionary terms has a significant impact on the imagined community, who belongs in it and the nature of the democracy. It also has important implications for the types of struggles that cross interrealm boundaries. Negative solidarity is built on exclusionary categories of race, ethnicity, gender, nationality, religion, unions and work, and narrow issues that reinforce boundaries. These cat-egories divide people, hierarchise groups against each other and focus on differ-ence as bounded categories of exclusion. Solidarities built on exclusion reinforce unequal power relations and powerful institutions that regulate our lives, such as the economy, religion, politics, patriarchy, inequality and access to economic livelihoods. It is the source of femicide, eco-cide, racism, genocide and xenophobia. The BJP's Citizens Amendment Act is a contestation over narrowing who counts as an Indian citizen by preparing the ground to disenfranchise millions of Muslims.

Another, more powerful form of solidarity, built on principles of a shared humanness, equality of all, and socio-economic and ecological justice, rejects the othering of people based on nationality, gender, race, religion, union affiliation or culture and connects interrealm boundaries across spheres of economy, polity, nature and social reproduction, as well as across capitalist centres and peripheries. It builds common ground among diverse groups and interrealm boundaries through reconstituting social relations and finding our common humanity. This requires moving beyond social categories and particular issues, to a willingness to embrace difference and expand solidarity across boundary struggles and national scales. This sort of solidarity was seen on the 20 September 2019 Global Day of Climate Action when millions of people and organisations across the planet protested for systemic change in response to the climate emergency, directly making links across boundaries of economy, democracy, care work and climate change. This is also the struggle that the women sitting in at Shaheen Bagh are waging. A robust and expansive democracy requires an inclusionary notion of the people, expansive notions of interrealm boundaries and the connections across them, and across geographical regions.

We now look at how we got to this crisis, this place of undemocratic, market democracy, before turning to the possibilities for renewing democracy.

CRISIS OF DEMOCRACY UNDER NEOLIBERAL CAPITALISM

The crisis of democracy is the political crisis generated by neoliberal capitalism. By turning everything into a potential commodity, neoliberal capitalism has elevated corporate interest within the economy and pushed into the background conditions on which capitalism depends – social reproduction, non-human nature and public power – transmogrifying them through neoliberal rationality. While particular articulations are unique to local contexts, extant cultures and political traditions, neoliberal capitalism has succeeded in framing all aspects of life in economic terms, undermining state administrative capacity and eroding state legitimacy.

There is excellent academic work cataloguing the effects of neoliberalism on the economy and the background realms of political power, social reproduction and non-human nature. Studies show polarising inequality and the rise of consumer debt (Ferguson 2006; Krugman 2003, 2012, 2013; Piketty 2013; Reich 2010; Sachs 2012; Sen 1999; Stiglitz 2012; Williams and Satgar 2020); the commodification and destruction of human and non-human habitats (Burawoy 2013; Sachs 1999; Saito 2017; Satgar 2013, 2018); the link between fossil fuel capitalism and climate change (Malm 2016; Mann and Kump 2015; Moore 2015; Satgar 2020); the crisis of social reproduction (Cock and Luxton 2013; Elson 2012; Fraser 2016); the new constitutionalism and the power of transnational regulatory bodies and corporations over territorial states (Gill 1998); economic instability, growing numbers of permanently unemployed and increased precarity of working and middle classes (Habib and Padayachee 2000; Harvey 2005; Hudson 2012; Mirowski 2013; Smith 2010; Standing 2011, 2016); the insidious creep of neoliberal rationality on human subjectivity (Brown 2015); and the rise of corporate power (Dörre 2019; Fraser and Jaeggi 2018; George 2015; Hacker and Pierson 2011; Streek 2011; Wolin 2008).[5]

Collectively, this work demonstrates the crises generated by neoliberal capitalism in the economy, polity, social reproductive realm and non-human nature. Public and common interests have been supplanted by the supremacy of private interests, states have been reduced to instruments of security with minimal interference in the market, and citizens are consumers of commodities. It is now commonplace to see our interests and education as investments in ourselves. Individuals are good citizens if they develop their human *capital* to make themselves more marketable in the world of work. Similarly, the state's primary role is tethered to its capacity to create the conditions for economic growth, including passing laws in the interests of corporations. Economic growth is both a primary goal and the means to state legitimation. Even the natural world is ascribed economic value – countries and corporations trade clean air with carbon credits. Pollution clean-up is measured in costs to GDP, although causes of pollution are not. Even the oceans are sites for capital accumulation. In short, the state is seen to be doing a good job if it steers the economy into positive economic growth and increasing commodification (Brown 2015), even if its citizens are growing poorer, more marginalised, unhappier and unemployed, and its natural environment unliveable. States' administrative capacity to act in the public interest has been systematically dismantled. In this way, neoliberal capitalism has remade the state and changed the conditions under which we live. After 30 years of creeping into the rationality of institutions, neoliberalism has engendered a market democracy in which the interests of corporations are elevated into national interests. This neoliberal transfiguration of democracy into 'de-democratised' (Dörre 2019) or undemocratic democracies in which states are not accountable to their populations, acting on the dictates of external corporate powers, spans the centres and peripheries of capitalism.

Transnational corporations have used corporate power to promote their interests and displace public interests through influencing state action (George 2015: 12). They exercise their power through lobbies, transnational agencies, and directly influencing governments by 'convincing elected officials to pass this law or that one, but also through obscure "expert committees" or ad hoc bodies' behind closed doors (George 2015: 1). Through such actions, transnational corporations undermine the 'legitimate authority' of elected governments: 'A broad spectrum of shadowy non-elected people is entrenching neoliberal values and doctrine, orienting government decisions and standing against democracy' (George 2015: 17).

The power of corporations is demonstrated in the many countries passing laws that service the interest of corporations rather than people or the public good. To take one example, the US Supreme Court ruled in favour of Monsanto,[6] making it virtually impossible for farmers to save seeds to reuse or sell to other farmers. They are thus forced to buy seeds every year from Monsanto, which has sewn up the market in seeds. Another example is the European Commission's adoption of the rules of the International Accounting Standards Board (IASB) as official parameters within which European governments can collect taxes (George 2015: 17). With more and more of these sorts of laws, states slowly shift from legitimate power (accountable to the electorate) to illegitimate power (accountable to corporations) that is concentrated in the hands of the political and economic elite. Neoliberal rationality makes states more concerned with creating the conditions for capitalist accumulation, enhancing the country's competitive edge in the global marketplace and improving credit ratings than with human well-being or ecological sustainability. For the elite (and increasingly it has become commonplace understanding), democracy is about liberty as non-interference, about the freedom to choose in the marketplace.

Another example of neoliberal rationality's insidious creep is the way in which corporations, supranational bodies and national states refer to citizens as stakeholders, consumers and clients. Corporations adopted 'stakeholders' – who are distinct from shareholders – to denote people who have an interest in the corporation's activity but do not have power in the hierarchy. For corporations, their fiduciary duties are limited to 'increase shareholder value. This distinctive requirement leaves out what a company may do to its workers or to the environment in order to attain that end' (George 2015: 7). Thus, the effects of increasing shareholder value can be detrimental to 'stakeholders', such as massive job losses, the decimation of local economies or destruction of the natural environment. In other words, stakeholders have an interest but no power, whereas shareholders have both an interest and power. Governments have adopted similar language, reflecting a shift in their role.

Providing government services to citizens implies a particular relationship between the state and citizens based on the state's public function. This is very different from a state that sees its role as selling services to stakeholders and clients. An equally worrying trend is the use of 'corporate citizens' to refer to corporations. For example, in a 2019 court affidavit by the South African parastatal Eskom, Deloitte is repeatedly referred to as a 'corporate citizen' (Comrie 2020). These are not innocent turns of language but reflect a shift in the locus of power away from the people, away from democratically accountable states.

The amalgamation of corporate power and state power, especially in the US, unleashed a particular type of corporate democracy that represented 'the *political* coming of age of corporate power and the *political* demobilization of the citizenry' (Wolin 2008: xviii, italics in original). In effect, states' goals have increasingly aligned to and are indistinguishable from those of modern firms, especially as firms adopt elements of 'justice', redistribution and sustainability through corporate social responsibility, public relations campaigns and 'green' initiatives. Remaking the state into an apparatus that prioritises economic health sublimates equality, liberty, inclusivity and constitutionalism to this goal. In this way, neoliberal rationality has undermined democratic demands for justice and inclusion and turned the state into an entity modelled on the modern firm with techniques of 'governance' that highlight best practices, performance management and quantitative deliverables.

Under these conditions, freedom has been reduced to consumer choice, dizzying degrees of information widely accessible through social media, networked platforms and advertisements. Brown (2015: 41) explains the implications for liberty: 'As liberty is relocated from political to economic life, it becomes subject to the inherent inequality of the latter and is part of what secures that inequality … Liberty itself is narrowed to market conduct, divested of association with mastering the conditions of life, existential freedom, or securing the rule of the demos.' Freedom to participate in self-rule has been turned into freedom to compete and consume in the unregulated market. Neoliberal capitalism has not only made corporations more powerful than states and citizens, but has turned states and entire populations into economic entities in the service of markets. Neoliberal rationality has also reinforced the idea that social forces shaping the world, such as structural unemployment, are personal troubles in an individual's milieu (Mills 1959), isolating individuals from broader social and collective communities. Zygmunt Bauman (2001: 106) captures the tendency to look at individual problems rather than the social forces that created them: 'With eyes focused on one's own performance and thus diverted from the social space where the contradictions of individual existence are collectively produced, men and women are naturally tempted to reduce the complexity of their predicament.' Reducing social issues into personal troubles further undermines democracy as forms of collective action and associational power are weakened.

Neoliberal rationality's slow creep into common language is further reflected in the increasing use of 'governance' instead of 'government' (George 2015). While the meaning of government refers to directing and administering the state, the meaning of governance shifts the emphasis away from democratic control. Governance is often referred to as 'the art of governing without government' as states manage citizens through non-state means and enforce compliance through state security apparatus such as the police (see Duncan, this volume).

Thus, the dramatic rise in corporate power and the withering of state capacity to challenge corporate domination has meant that states have increasingly lost (or sold) their capacity to act in the interests of their electorates. Neoliberal capitalism has smothered democracy with the loss of state sovereignty, violations to the basic rule of law, and erosion of political freedoms in many longstanding democracies such as Greece, the USA and India. The Greek electorate rejected the 2015 referendum on the European Union's (EU's) austerity approach to Greece. The left-leaning prime minister, Alexis Tsipras, ultimately agreed to an EU deal that was in direct contravention of the interest of the people expressed in a democratic referendum. Greece's attempts to stand up to the EU and the 'concessions' ultimately forced on the country demonstrate the power of illegitimate authority and neoliberal rationality. The Greek citizens are merely stakeholders – as opposed to citizens directing their government – in the European Commission's language (George 2015: 7–8).

Similarly, in the US, the capture of the state by corporate power is seen in the money spent by mega-lobbies. Lobbies have been around for well over 150 years and, until recently, registered their activities in an official registry. But with government attempts to further regulate their power, lobbies have found loopholes in legislation with many deregistering and shifting their activities to more opaque forms of control, and through coordinating efforts into highly financed, industry-centred mega-lobbies that influence the allocation of fiscal resources (George 2015: 19–21). To illustrate the enormous amount of money mega-lobbies spend, the pharmaceutical industry and other industries in health products spend the largest lobbying budget in Washington: by the third quarter of 2019, they had spent US$228 million on lobbying. The US has the most expensive healthcare system in the world with many people unable to afford any healthcare coverage, but these industries make enormous profits and shape government policies through their lobbying. Similarly, gas, oil and other energy and 'natural' resources have consistently spent over US$91 million on lobbying, while the financial sector, including securities and investment, commercial banks and real estate collectively, spent well over US$200 million on lobbying in Washington.[7] The US financial sector's lobbying efforts resulted in a political coup for the industry. From the 1980s, the sector (banking, securities, insurance and accounting) employed around 3 000 people and spent nearly US$5 billion to dismantle New Deal era legislation (passed in the 1930s under Franklin Roosevelt) that protected the US economy from crisis for nearly 60 years. Repealing the Glass-Steagall Act of 1933, which separated commercial (retail) banking from investment banking, was a significant victory of these lobbying efforts. President Clinton repealed the Act in 1999, allowing investment banks to 'hide' asset losses from their balance sheets and place them in 'shadow' accounts. These 'toxic derivative products' based on huge consumer debt were bundled together and traded without regulation and oversight (George 2015: 22–25) and laid the basis for the 2007 financial crisis.

Under President Trump's administration the influence of corporate power deepened as he regularly undermined state legitimacy through anti-state rhetoric of the 'deep state' and the appointment of corporate elites to key positions within the government. In 2019, Trump's cabinet included 17 millionaires, two centi-millionaires and one billionaire. Three key cabinet positions were held by three of the richest: billionaire Betsy DeVos as secretary of education, centi-millionaire Wilbur Ross as secretary of commerce and centi-millionaire Steven Mnuchin as secretary of the Treasury. Appointing the super-elite was an overt approach by Trump, who announced to supporters at an election victory speech, 'I want people who have made a fortune' (Tindera 2019). Trump also nominated corporate elites to crucial positions within the state, though he was not always successful in these nominations. For instance, the National Oceanic and Atmospheric Administration (NOAA) is a respected scientific agency within the Department of Commerce that focuses on oceans, major waterways and the atmosphere. NOAA provides detailed information to citizens, scientists, government agencies and countries around the world about weather, changing climatic conditions and threats to the planet's climate. In 2017, Trump nominated AccuWeather CEO Barry Meyers to head NOAA, which would constitute a direct conflict of interest. After two years of attempting to get Meyers appointed amid strong resistance, Trump eventually withdrew the nomination in December 2019.[8] Trump's June 2020 appointment of logistics and shipping businessman and Republican Party mega-donor Louis DeJoy to the post-master general position[9] demonstrates the insidious creep of corporate control over a myriad of taken-for-granted state entities. It also demonstrates the importance for democracy of accountable administrative capacity in all sectors of the state. The US Postal Service dates back to the 1770s and is one of the most loved US brands[10] and most reliable state services, though it has faced challenges with the declining mail volume due to online communications. It was particularly vital for the 2020 presidential election as many states opted for mail-in ballots due to the Covid-19 pandemic. In this context, DeJoy announced new rules that would effectively slow down the mail delivery system, and possibly disenfranchise millions of people as their ballots would not arrive in time to be counted. His actions coincided with Trump's derision of the postal service and accusations that mail-in ballots were illegitimate.

In South Africa, neoliberalism has taken on a particularly local character that combines with corruption of public officials and elected leaders. The term 'state capture' characterises the way in which the state has been used to enrich political leaders, especially former president Zuma and his faction in the African National Congress (ANC) and their link to the nefarious Gupta family business empire (see Pillay, this volume). Enormous amounts of public funds have gone into the coffers of political elites and public officials through these corrupt relations. However, there is another threat to hollowing out the state that receives far less attention but is equally detrimental: corporate influence.

Corporations encourage the state to outsource functions that have either historically been in-house or are created as new needs. For example, the 2020 auditor-general's report found that municipalities spent R1.26 billion on consultants in preparing their financial statements, a function that they should be able to do in-house. In another example, a 2020 report by the amaBhungane Centre for Investigative Journalism[11] claimed that Eskom (the state-owned energy company in charge of generation, transmission and distribution) awarded tenders to Deloitte for services in which it appears Deloitte influenced the decision-making processes. According to amaBhungane, the dubious relationship between Eskom and Deloitte surrounds a number of contracts that were stacked in favour of Deloitte by high-ranking internal Eskom officials. In 2019, Eskom's then chairperson, Jabu Mabuza, lamented in a court affidavit that the relationship with Deloitte 'indicates the extent to which processes and procedures at state institutions … can be manipulated so that pre-determined outcomes can be achieved by abuse and improper use of power by those in senior positions [within the state]' (Comrie 2020). Here again, corporate influence and neoliberal rationality combine to shape the performance of a crucial state institution.

Eskom provides approximately 95 per cent of the electricity consumed in South Africa and is a key state asset, but corporate influence together with maladministration, corruption and fraud within the state have undermined its capacity to deliver energy and remain solvent. The efforts to clean up Eskom are proving extremely difficult as powerful vested interests within the ANC, the state and corporations are deeply embedded in Eskom.

The ANC's 26 years of rule have been marked by its obsession with markets, economic growth and maintaining credit ratings instead of ensuring the politically and constitutionally mandated goals of redistribution, justice and radical democratic forms of rule (see Pillay, Duncan, McKinley, Radebe and Kaaf, this volume). As corruption becomes endemic within the party–state nexus, it threatens the survival of once-crucial state-owned enterprises (e.g. Eskom) and delivery of social services such as education and healthcare. In response, the ANC increasingly combines a dangerous ethnic, nationalist and race-based populism with a renewed commitment to neoliberal rationality. Thus, it ensures freedom for footloose corporations to pollute, exploit and relocate; it focuses the state on managing the population through disciplinary techniques and increasing surveillance; and it passes myriad anti-people laws such as the Traditional Leadership and Governance Framework Amendment Act 2 of 2019, which reinforces patriarchal traditional leadership in rural areas. The police force has returned to a law-and-order approach characteristic of apartheid, rather than the community policing and public safety approach widely endorsed in the 1990s. As a result, citizens are often met with aggressive policing that undermines the crucial role of voicing discontent in a robust democracy. At the same time, it takes on increasingly xenophobic rhetoric, blaming foreigners and racial minorities (who have lived in South Africa for hundreds of years) for the failures of development.

In addition to the ANC's dysfunctional state, the Economic Freedom Fighters' (EFF's) destructive tactics also undermine key institutions of democracy.[12] For example, democracy requires free and reliable communication through freedom of assembly, press and speech. The EFF undermines these freedoms through threatening critical journalists and independent voices, employing trolls to wreak havoc on social media against critics, threatening protestors and critical voices, and silencing and intimidating alternative views. It has adopted militaristic, male chauvinistic rhetoric for its internal party structures: the leadership structure uses military language, referring to the party leader, Julius Malema, as commander-in-chief and wearing military-style clothing. The other opposition party, the Democratic Alliance (DA), has a deeply pro-market approach that reinforces neoliberal rationality and fails to speak to the interests of the majority of South Africans. It too prioritises creating the conditions for neoliberal markets to thrive, focusing on liberty as non-interference.

These examples show how states have been influenced, shaped and remade. Reducing democracy to liberty as non-interference and participation to voting in elections, and by dismantling the democratic and accountable administrative capacity of state institutions, the basis was laid for neoliberalism to hollow out democracy from within and enable corporate capture to turn it into 'market democracy'. Slowly eating away at the foundations of democracy, neoliberalism is increasingly showing its violent, intolerant and exclusionary side. In a growing number of places in the world, market democracy has created the conditions for anti-democratic forces to rise, such as right-wing authoritarian leaders and neo-fascist movements that dismantle democracy through its very mechanisms (see Satgar, this volume). We see this in the US with Trump's assault on the basic institutions of democracy (see Gordon and Solty, this volume), in Brazil with Bolsonaro's dismantling of key democratic protections (see Saad-Filho, this volume) and in India with Modi's attack on citizen rights (see Nilsen, this volume). Politics absent strong democratic institutions and democratic publics provides ample ground for states to become authoritarian while maintaining the veneer of democracy. These trends have become more pronounced due to the coronavirus pandemic.

Finally, neoliberal capitalism has also converged with revolutionary changes in information and communications technology (ICT) – through social media, internet sites and the dark web – garnering vast amounts of personal information used to shape public opinion. Rather than enhancing democracy, ICT often undermines it through manipulating elections, undermining democratic debate, spreading misinformation, providing greater space for corporate intrusion into everyday lives and amplifying right-wing voices. In an expansive and robust democracy, democratic deliberation and political decisions can be contested, and are not based on faith or conviction. Reducing fact-based critique to opinions and false information vanquishes the possibility of shared norms and universals that define a democracy. According to Habermas (1991), deliberation among participants engenders legitimacy, fosters shared norms and nurtures democratic capacities. It is also crucial in developing an understanding of issues, and the capacity to contest ideas and build confidence. The circulation of opinions on social media subsumes engaged discussion, and creates conditions for elected leaders to engage the public through sensational messages. Social media takes this to new levels – all that matters is the number of 'shares' and responses messages get, and the more sensational, the more shares. Whether or not the content is true is irrelevant. Trump's claims to alternative facts and the dark web's promotion of conspiracy theories perhaps best represent this phenomenon, but it has been the basis of right-wing propaganda, populist appeals and climate denialism. Reducing politics to communicative acts through social media feeds into the illusion of political efficacy, when in fact it unhinges political practice. Democratic engagement tries to understand issues and not simply proffer an opinion or sow doubt. Deliberation is aimed at understanding, whereas communicative acts are aimed at broadcasting opinions. Traditional forms of media are also compromised through concentration in ownership and control of the major media houses (see Radebe, this volume), which reinforces the importance of free, accessible, reliable and critical forms of information and media (see McKinley, this volume).

Democracy is clearly not perfect: it can be captured, it can fail, it can be remade, it can promote an anti-democratic ethos. Nevertheless, the ideal of people ruling themselves is worth fighting for if for no other reason than the alternative – rule by others, such as the economic elite – is a ghastly option. Only robust and expansive democracy holds the potential to create a better world in which there is universal human thriving, justice, equality, liberty, inclusion of all people and living within our planetary boundaries. Only robust and expansive democracy allows for redefining the interrealm boundaries between the economy, social reproduction, non-human nature and politics. The task of our times is to engender 'democracy shorn of its imbrication with capitalism' (Brown 2015: 12) as the basis on which to build more radical forms of democracy. The foundational rights that ensure freedom – of assembly, speech and the press, as well as the impartiality of the law to treat all people equally – were victories won through people's struggles and are central to social, economic and ecological justice. Our task is not to discard liberal democracy, but to recognise its limits and build on its foundational pillars. The question is, how do we remake – democratise – democracy?

RECLAIMING DEMOCRACY

While some on the Left argue that democracy is a liberal invention and highlight the failure of 'actually existing democracy' (Dean 2009; Žižek 2004), the critique ends by rejecting democracy as radical ideal, as political practice and as a basis for law and easily slides into authoritarianism. It ignores the history of struggle over democracy. While democracy has been transmogrified through its instantiation with capitalism, democratic struggles have won important universal rights: suffrage, education, human rights, civil rights, and freedom of association, speech and the press. For over 200 years, these rights were fought for and won by working classes, the excluded, the racially oppressed, women, sexual minorities and ordinary people.

The industrial working classes made democratic claims for a greater share in the economic and political structures of society. Workers pushed for more redistributive demands and increased egalitarianism. The Swedish working class registered its interests through the Social Democratic Party, US workers were instrumental in redistributive gains in the early and mid-twentieth century, and studies show that strong labour movements produce more redistributive outcomes (Ahlquist 2017; Pontusson 2013; Webster and Englert 2020). In South Africa, labour was a crucial democratising force ensuring many of the democratic victories of the 1990s. Redistributive gains and public goods such as security of employment, maternity leave, working hours, paid holidays, pension funds, public education, transport and health were victories of working-class people. Many of these struggles envisioned and demanded more robust forms of democracy that sought justice (substantive equality) and a broader conception of liberty (protection from arbitrary power).

Yet, today we live in market democracies. Most are narrow democracies in which corporations have enormous power to shape national agendas and laws and have systematically rolled back many democratic victories. Political parties that once fought for the interests of working classes, the poor and marginalised, slowly eroded their resistance to neoliberalism, adopting euphemisms like Blair and Clinton's 'Third Way social democracy' and the ANC's 'deracialising of capitalism'. It is no surprise that the Labour Party in the UK, the Democratic Party in the US, the Social Democratic Party in Germany, the Congress Party in India and the ANC in South Africa are in crisis.

Karl Polanyi (1944) captured the pendulum of history in *The Great Transformation*, in which he discusses the continual tension between the self-regulating market and society's attempts to protect itself from the ravages of the market. Polanyi shows how the social destruction caused by the self-regulating market can lead to fascism. His work reads like a warning for our times. While Polanyi does not frame it in terms of democracy per se, his analysis can also be seen as the struggle between two types of democracy. In the one, the state restricts popular forces and ensures power is concentrated in the hands of the ruling classes. In the other, the state protects society from the market and facilitates democratic deepening by creating spaces for popular control over the commons and public goods. While market democracy is certainly the overarching arc of history, there continue to be extraordinary experiments looking to reclaim democracy through more expansive notions of liberty, equality and justice. What would Polanyi's double movement entail if it were to reflect a more expansive democracy?

Robust and expansive democracy that overcomes the economic and political divide, that foregrounds social reproduction and non-human nature allows for human existence to move beyond the 'realm of necessity' by laying the basis for the 'realm of freedom' (Marx 1972: 441). In other words, expansive democracy offers the potential to resolve the interrealm boundary struggles and create the conditions for new social relations based on social, economic and ecological justice. In the 1970s the Marxist Left elaborated some of the most important debates about the state and the role of democracy (Althusser 1971; Hall 1980, 1982; Jessop 1990; Miliband 1969; Poulantzas 1972, 1978). By the late twentieth century, much of the Left neglected to think about the changing nature of the state and its relationship to capital, subaltern classes and social transformation. Rosa Luxemburg warned against neglecting the importance of democracy in her debate with the anti-democratic position of Lenin and Trotsky, who advocated for dissolving the Russian constituent assembly in the early twentieth century. Luxemburg argued instead for more democracy:

> And the more democratic the institutions, the livelier and stronger the pulse-beat of the political life of the masses, the more direct and complete is their influence … To be sure, every democratic institution has its limits and shortcomings, things which it doubtless shares with all other human institutions. But the remedy which Trotsky and Lenin have found, the elimination of democracy as such, is worse than the disease it is supposed to cure; for it stops up the very living source from which alone can come correction of all the innate shortcomings of social institutions. That source is the active, untrammeled, energetic political life of the broadest masses of the people. (Luxemburg 2004: 310)

We must learn from the limits of liberal democracy, but we must also heed Luxemburg's warning against jettisoning the idea of people's rule. While modern liberal democracy has always been realised in conjunction with capitalism and imbued by certain capitalist values and powers, it has nevertheless provided 'the language and promise of inclusive and shared political equality, freedom, and popular sovereignty' (Brown 2015: 44). Democracy is the only form of rule in which people can collectively rule and share in the powers of governing.

The more expansive form of democracy continues to find its mooring in local communities, social movements and popular struggles for a more egalitarian world. Democratic experiments are happening around the world in cooperative forms of production, consumption and finance, participatory budgeting, local community-owned energy grids, alternative currencies, transition towns and local food movements. There are calls to strengthen state accountability to citizens' demands and increase capacity to deliver public goods. Taken together these experiments are developing prefigurative practices involving new forms of power, the reproduction of the commons, democratic self-management and democratising state institutions. They are recalibrating the inter-realm boundaries between the economy and social reproduction, the natural world and public power in order to retool economic activity in the service of society.

The history of democracy makes clear that it is an ongoing process, an ongoing struggle. It is time to reclaim democracy to become genuinely people-centred, to create a better, more just, more egalitarian world. Democracy is not perfect, but it remains the only form of government where people collectively govern themselves. As South African scholar-activist Rick Turner (1972) wrote over 40 years ago, building a robust democracy requires utopian thinking.

NOTES

1   I use neoliberal capitalism and neoliberalism interchangeably to mean the latest variant of capitalism. For discussion of the varieties of capitalism, see Soskice and Hall (2001).

2   Mercantile capitalism in the seventeenth and eighteenth centuries, laissez faire capitalism of the nineteenth century, state-managed monopoly capitalism of the second half of the twentieth century, and neoliberal capitalism – the latest variant of capitalism's organisation of social relations – that began in the 1980s.

3   While Trump is no longer in power in the US, the argument in this chapter (and in the volume as a whole) remains valid as the underlying conditions of neoliberal financialised and globalised capitalism remain in place. The threat of authoritarian politics remains very real in the US as indicated by the fact that 73 million people voted for Trump.

4   This is the position of classical liberal democracy. There is a long history within liberalism with important and significant differences among the different strands (classical liberals, egalitarian liberals, social justice liberals, republicans). Here I primarily refer to the classical liberal tradition.

5   George (2015: 8) highlights key aspects of legitimate power in democracies: 'free and fair elections for designating officials to represent the people, constitutional government, the rule of law, equality before the law, separation of executive, legislative and judicial powers, checks and balances to prevent any one part of government from becoming too powerful, the separation of church and state. All these are crowned by the general notion of the "consent of the governed".'

6   See https://www.nytimes.com/2013/05/14/business/monsanto-victorious-in-genetic-seed-case.html. Monsanto was bought by Bayer in 2018.

7   All the data on lobbying in 2019 are from Open Secrets, https://www.opensecrets.org/news/2019/10/big-pharma-continues-to-top-lobbying-spending/andhttps://www.opensecrets.org/industries/lobbying.php?cycle=1998&ind=F03 (accessed 19 August 2020).

8   In September 2020 Trump succeeded in appointing climate science denier David Legates as NOAA's deputy assistant secretary of commerce.

9   Postmasters general have typically come through the ranks of the postal system. DeJoy's appointment therefore diverges from historical practice. There was speculation that Trump intended to privatise the US Postal Service, and DeJoy's appointment appears to be in line with this.

10   See https://morningconsult.com/most-loved-brands-2020/ (accessed 23 November 2020).

11   The information in this section is from amaBhungane's report by Susan Comrie (2020).

12   The EFF is an opposition party formed in 2013 by expelled and disgruntled ANC members, most notably the former leader of the ANC Youth League. For an excellent analysis of the neo-fascism of the EFF, see Satgar (2019) and Habib (2019).

REFERENCES

Ahlquist, J. 2017. 'Labor unions, political representation, and economic inequality', *Annual Review of Political Science* 20: 409–432.

Althusser, L. 1971 [1970]. 'Ideology and ideological state apparatuses (notes towards an investigation)'. *In Lenin and Philosophy and Other Essays*. New York: Monthly Review Press. Accessed 17 November 2020, http://www.csun.edu/~snk1966/Lous%20Althusser%20Ideology%20and%20Ideological%20State%20Apparatuses.pdf.

Bauman, Z. 2001. *The Individualized Society*. Cambridge: Polity.

Bourdieu, P. 1984. *Distinction: A Social Critique of the Judgement of Taste*. Conclusion. Cambridge: Harvard University Press.

Bourdieu, P. 2000. *Pascalian Meditations*. Palo Alto, CA: Stanford University Press.

Brown, W. 2015. *Undoing the Demos: Neoliberalism's Stealth Revolution*. New York: Zone Books.

Burawoy, M. 2013. 'Marxism after Polanyi'. In M. Williams and V. Satgar (eds), *Marxisms in the 21st Century: Crisis, Critique and Struggle*. Johannesburg: Wits University Press, pp. 34–52.

Cock, J. and Luxton, M. 2013. 'Marxism and feminism: "Unhappy marriage" or creative partnership?' In M. Williams and V. Satgar (eds), *Marxisms in the 21st Century: Crisis, Critique and Struggle*. Johannesburg: Wits University Press, pp. 116–142.

Comrie, S. 2020. 'The dirt on Deloitte's consulting deals at Eskom, part one', *Daily Maverick*, 15 January. Accessed 19 November 2020, https://www.dailymaverick.co.za/article/2020-01-15-the-dirt-on-deloittes-consulting-deals-at-eskom-part-one/?utm_medium=email&utm_campaign=First%20Thing%20Wednesday%2015%20January%202020%20Summer%20Place&utm_content=First%20Thing%20Wednesday%2015%20January%202020%20Summer%20Place+CID_e6850c1ef9e45b0c2da878c59f-12b590&utm_source=TouchBasePro&utm_term=The%20dirt%20on%20Deloittes%20consulting%20deals%20at%20Eskom%20Part%20One.

Dean, J. 2009. *Democracy and Other Neoliberal Fantasies: Communicative Capitalism and Left Politics*. Durham: Duke University Press.

Dörre, K. 2019. 'Democracy, not capitalism, or expropriate Zuckerberg!' In H. Ketterer and K. Becker (eds), *What's Wrong with Democracy? A Debate with Klaus Dörre, Nancy Fraser, Stephan Lessenich and Hartmut Rosa*. Berlin: Suhrkamp Taschenbuch Wissenschaften, pp. 21–51.

Elson, D. 2012. 'Social reproduction in the global crisis: Rapid recovery or long-lasting depletion?' In P. Utting, S. Razavi and R.V. Buchholz (eds), *The Global Crisis and Transformative Social Change*. London: Palgrave Macmillan, pp. 63–80. https://doi.org/10.1057/9781137002501_4.

Ferguson, J. 2006. *Global Shadows: Africa in the Neoliberal World Order*. Durham: Duke University Press.

Fraser, N. 2014. 'Democracy's crisis'. Lecture presented at Erasmus University, Rotterdam, Netherlands, 7 November.

Fraser, N. 2016. 'Contradictions of capital and care', *New Left Review* 100: 99–117.

Fraser, N. 2018. 'Democracy's crisis: On the political implications of financialised capitalism'. Public lecture. Accessed 15 January 2019, https://web.facebook.com/WCFIA/videos/vb.144673958897100/269566100364576/?type=2&theater.

Fraser, N. and Jaeggi, R. 2018. *Capitalism: A Conversation in Critical Theory*. Cambridge: Polity Press.

George, S. 2015. *Shadow Sovereigns: How Global Corporations Are Seizing Power*. Cambridge: Polity Press.

Gill, S. 1998. 'New constitutionalism, democratisation and global political economy', *Pacifica Review: Peace, Security & Global Change* 10 (1): 23–38, doi: 10.1080/14781159808412845.

Habermas, J. 1991 [1981]. *Theory of Communicative Action: Reason and Rationalization of Society*. Cambridge: Polity Press.

Habib, A. 2019. 'No country for appeasers as fascism rises in South Africa', *Daily Maverick*, 18 December.

Habib, A. and Padayachee, V. 2000. 'Economic policy and power relations in South Africa's transition to democracy', *World Development* 28 (2): 245–263.

Hacker, J.S. and Pierson, P. 2011. *Winner-Take-All Politics: How Washington Made the Rich Richer – and Turned Its Back on the Middle Class*. New York: Simon and Schuster.

Hall, S. 1980. 'Nicos Poulantzas: "State, Power, Socialism"', *New Left Review* 1/119, Jan.–Feb.

Hall, S. 1982. *Policing the Crisis: Mugging, the State, and Law and Order*. London: Macmillan.

Harvey, D. 2005. *A Brief History of Neoliberalism*. New York: Oxford University Press.

Hudson, M. 2012. *Finance Capitalism and Its Discontents*. Dresden: Islet Verlag.

Jessop, B. 1990. *State Theory: Putting the Capitalist State in Its Place*. University Park: Penn State Press.

Krugman, P. 2003. *The Great Unraveling: Losing Our Way in the New Century*. New York: Norton.

Krugman, P. 2012. *End This Depression Now!* New York: Norton.

Krugman, P. 2013. 'Hunger games, U.S.A.', *New York Times*, 15 July. Accessed 31 December 2020, http://www.nytimes.com/2013/07/15/opinion/krugman-hunger-games-usa. html.

Luxemburg, R. 2004 [1918]. 'The Russian Revolution'. In P. Hudis and K.B. Anderson (eds), *The Rosa Luxemburg Reader*. New York: Monthly Review Press, pp. 281–311.

Malm, A. 2016. *Fossil Capital: The Rise of Steam Power and the Roots of Global Warming*. London: Verso.

Mann, M. and Kump, L.R. 2015. *Dire Predictions: Understanding Global Warming* (second edition). New York: DK.

Marx, K. 1972 [1894]. 'On the realm of necessity and the realm of freedom'. In R. Tucker (ed.), *Marx Engels Reader*. New York: W.W. Norton and Company, pp. 439–441.

Miliband, R. 1969. *The State in Capitalist Society*. London: Weidenfeld & Nicolson.

Mills, C.W. 1959. *The Sociological Imagination*. Oxford: Oxford University Press.

Mirowski, P. 2013. *Never Let a Serious Crisis Go to Waste: How Neoliberalism Survived the Financial Meltdown*. New York: Verso.

Moore, J.W. 2015. 'Putting nature to work: Anthropocene, Capitalocene, and the challenge of world ecology'. In C. Wee, J. Schönenbach and O. Arndt (eds), *Supramarkt: A Micro-Toolkit for Disobedient Consumers, or How to Frack the Fatal Forces of the Capitalocene*. Gothenburg: Irene Books, pp. 69–117.

Pettit, P. 1997. *Republicanism: A Theory of Freedom and Government*. Oxford: Clarendon Press.

Piketty, T. 2013. *Capital in the 21st Century*. Cambridge, MA: Harvard University Press.

Polanyi, K. 1944. *The Great Transformation: The Political and Economic Origins of Our Times*. Boston: Beacon Press.

Pontusson, J. 2013. 'Unionization, inequality and redistribution', *British Journal of Industrial Relations* 51 (4): 797–825.

Poulantzas, N. 1972. 'The problem of the capitalist state'. In R. Blackburn (ed.), *Ideology in Social Science: Readings in Critical Social Theory*. New York: Pantheon Books, pp. 238–262.

Poulantzas, N. 1978. *State, Power, Socialism*. London: New Left Books.

Reich, R. 2010. *The Next Economy and America's Future*. New York: Vintage.

Sachs, J. 2012. *The Price of Civilization: Reawakening American Virtue and Prosperity*. New York: Random House.

Sachs, W. 1999. 'Sustainable development: On the political anatomy of an oxymoron'. In *Planet Dialectics: Explorations in Environment and Development*. New York and London: New Internationalist.

Saito, K. 2017. *Karl Marx's Ecosocialism: Capital, Nature, and the Unfinished Critique of Political Economy*. New York: Monthly Review Press.

Satgar, V. 2013. 'Transnationalising Gramscian Marxism'. In M. Williams and V. Satgar (eds), *Marxisms in the 21st Century: Crisis, Critique and Struggle*. Johannesburg: Wits University Press, pp. 53–81.

Satgar, V. (ed.). 2018. *The Climate Crisis: South African and Global Democratic Eco-Socialist Alternatives*. Johannesburg: Wits University Press.

Satgar, V. 2019. 'Black neofascism? The Economic Freedom Fighters in South Africa', *Canadian Review of Sociology* 56 (4): 580–605.

Satgar, V. 2020. 'Where have all the flowers gone? A final climate crisis warning', *Daily Maverick*, 7 September. Accessed 8 September 2020, https://www.dailymaverick. co.za/opinionista/2020-09-07-where-have-all-the-flowers-gone-a-final-climate-crisis-warning/.

Sen, A. 1999. *Development as Freedom*. New York: Random House.

Smith, Y. 2010. *ECONned: How Unenlightened Self Interest Undermined Democracy and Corrupted Capitalism*. New York: Palgrave Macmillan.

Soskice, D. and Hall, P.A. 2001. *Varieties of Capitalism: The Institutional Foundations of Comparative Advantage*. Oxford: Oxford University Press.

Standing, G. 2011. *The Precariat: The New Dangerous Class*. Oxford: Bloomsbury Academic.

Standing, G. 2016. *The Corruption of Capitalism: Why Rentiers Thrive and Work Does Not Pay*. London: Biteback Publishing.

Stiglitz, J. 2012. *The Price of Inequality: How Today's Divided Society Endangers Our Future*. New York: Norton.

Streek, W. 2011. 'The crisis of democratic capitalism', *New Left Review* 71 (September–October): 5–29.

Tindera, M. 2019. 'The definitive net worth of Donald Trump's cabinet', *Forbes*, 25 July. Accessed 8 January 2021, https://www.forbes.com/sites/michelatindera/2019/07/25/the-definitive-net-worth-of-donald-trumps-cabinet/#4616d8806a15.

Turner, R. 1972. *The Eye of the Needle: Towards Participatory Democracy in South Africa*. South African History Online. Accessed 4 January 2020, https://www.sahistory.org.za/archive/eye-needle-rick-turner.

Webster, E. and Englert, T. 2020. 'New dawn or end of labour? From South Africa's East Rand to Ekurhuleni', *Globalizations* 17 (2): 279–293.

Williams, M. and Satgar, V. 2020. 'Transitional compass: Anti-capitalist pathways in the interstitial spaces of capitalism', *Globalizations* 17 (2): 265–278.

Wolin, S. 2008. *Democracy Incorporated: Managed Democracy and the Specter of Inverted Totalitarianism*. Princeton: Princeton University Press.

Žižek, S. 2004. *Iraq: The Borrowed Kettle*. London: Verso.

2

THE RISE OF ECO-FASCISM

Vishwas Satgar

INTRODUCTION

All human and non-human life faces the prospect of extinction in a heating world, despite scientific warnings, almost three decades of multilateral negotiations and at least two cycles of global climate justice struggles. The climate crisis is worsening through extreme weather shocks such as floods, droughts, heatwaves, tornadoes, wild fires and sea level rise. However, according to current climate science, we have not overshot 1.5°C yet and climate breakdown has not happened. The science is telling us that we can and must act now. The global political economy can still be ecologically restructured through deep just transitions to draw down carbon, build adaptive systems, prepare for climate shocks and ultimately prevent catastrophic climate change. Human and non-human life has a chance of surviving and dealing with the consequences of locked-in climate change. Those most vulnerable and least responsible for the problem do not have to pay the price for climate harms. Of course, this means class and popular struggles for climate justice are essential, now more than ever.

Given how high the stakes are, critical social science, including Marxist ecology, has the crucial task of explaining this situation. We have to ask why carbon capitalism is destroying planetary life, and how it is doing so. This chapter tackles these questions through historicising the political economy of climate crisis, identifying the class project and social forces it aggregates to accelerate the climate crisis, the relational class practices of such forces, the limits of an emerging eco-fascist project and the implications of such an analysis for climate justice forces. The premise for such an analytical approach is the new conjuncture of worsening capitalist crisis (2007–present) and the emergence of new hard-right neoliberals. This new hard Right is directly implicated in the second coming of modern fascism, within the context of globalised monopolies, the deepening authoritarianism of neoliberalism and worsening climate crisis. This chapter argues the new hard Right is in essence an eco-fascist Right at the forefront of exterminating human and non-human life.

FROM FASCISM TO ECO-FASCISM

Fascism in the interwar years of the twentieth century was not only engendered by structural crisis and crises of European subjectivity. According to Karl Polanyi (1944), the countermovement of fascism, the New Deal and Soviet planning emerged as a response to marketisation. Western-centred capitalism did not learn the lessons of market-driven economics from the late nineteenth century and how it contributed to World War I. Instead, it repeated the same mistake in the 1920s and reinstated the market-centred gold standard as the basis for international trade and finance. This led to World War II. In 2007, almost three decades of marketisation produced the worst financial crash in modern history. After massive bailouts to the US-centred financial system and Obama in the White House, it was business as usual. The poor were declared 'big enough to fail', homelessness shot up due to repossessions, and stabilisation and austerity policies became the norm in a volatile global financial system. Neoliberalism (as a class project of financial and transnational capital) took its next big leap from market democracies (hegemonic from 1980 to 2000 and co-optive from 2000 to 2007) in the liberal world to authoritarian market democracies in the global North and South: Trump's USA, Poland, Turkey, Israel, Italy, Brazil (largest democracy in Latin America), Philippines, Australia and India (largest democracy in the world). Hard-right parties and movements have also broken into the mainstream in countries such as France and Germany. In Bolivia a coup in 2019 deposed a democratically elected indigenous president and US-supported destabilisation of Venezuela continues by right-wing forces.

In March 2019, a mass shooter in Christchurch, New Zealand, killed 51 people and declared he was an eco-fascist. Similarly, on 28 July 2019 a man killed three people at California's Gilroy Garlic Festival motivated by environmental concerns, and on 3 August 2019 a gunman killed 22 people at an El Paso, Texas, Walmart and provided a link to environmentalism in his manifesto. These killings by hard-right extremists break with the climate crisis denialism of the Trump current within hard-right neoliberalism, but at the same time share a conception of migration as a problem. For these more eco-conscious fascists, population causes environmental problems and hence migrants/immigrants are objects of hate (Achenbach 2019; Hansman 2019).

This idea as part of white nativist nationalism dates back in the US to the late nineteenth century, when conservationists believed that race purity was also about purity of the land, and hence Native Americans could not be part of conservation spaces. Hitler and the Nazis also had romantic conceptions of 'blood and soil' and romanticised the agrarian past. Their relationship to modernity was also contradictory, rejecting aspects but also embracing the technological and scientific side of it. The 'greening of hate' has historical roots but is also expressing itself ideologically in a new context.

A new contemporary fascism is on the march in the world, different from twentieth-century fascism. It has continuities and discontinuities and sometimes expresses itself in unprecedented ways, thus posing a methodological challenge in how it is analysed. The dominant understandings of fascism in historical sociology and political science are derived from the interwar years of the twentieth century. These definitions, ideal types and models are blunt instruments to understand contemporary fascism. Instead, it is crucial to historicise and situate contemporary fascism to appreciate its specificity. The approach adopted in this chapter is based on three methodological premises (Satgar 2019: 588–591). First, contemporary fascism can be understood not through transhistorical definitions but rather through a definitional approach that does not define fascism but situates it in relation to capitalism. This means: 'It is a tendency within the monopoly and contemporary transnational techno-financial stages of capitalism, enabled by particular conditions of crisis and takes on an organized form as part of the struggle to achieve a monopoly on state power' (Satgar 2019: 589). A new fascism has to be studied in context to explicate its features. Such studies include case studies of long histories and conjunctural analyses. Also, comparative studies assist with highlighting similarities and differences but, given the new context and conditions, historical case studies of specific right-wing forces are also useful.

Second, while the historiography of fascism focuses on it as a Western phenomenon manifested in the interwar years, a decolonial perspective recognises a second moment of fascism after World War II, as expressed through the emergence of US-supported military dictatorships mainly in the global South. These regimes married authoritarianism and the defence of key institutions of capitalism. In places like Chile, Brazil and Bolivia these historical forces are still present and shaping the direction of their societies. Methodologically, these histories have to be taken into account to understand the return of fascism in these societies.

Third, the new wave of fascism globally has to be located in the context of the specific dynamics of the general crisis of contemporary capitalism. While financialised instabilities and inequalities expressed themselves sharply from 2007 in the global political economy with the financial crash, this has converged with worsening climate crises, resource constraints and food crises. In this context a shift to a more authoritarian neoliberalism and worsening ecological crises have to be studied more closely. This chapter elaborates specifically on how a neo-fascism in the early twenty-first century, enabled by the total socio-ecological crisis of capitalism, engages with the most dangerous ecological contradiction, the climate crisis, which poses a threat to all life on Earth. It highlights how the new hard-right neoliberals are rising as an eco-fascist Right.

CLIMATE CRISIS, THE METABOLIC RIFT AND PLANETARY ECO-CIDE

Since 1988, National Aeronautics and Space Administration (Nasa) scientist James Hansen made the climate crisis a public issue by reporting to the US Congress. The Intergovernmental Panel on Climate Change (IPCC) was established thereafter by the UN, and the UN Framework on Climate Change was set up in 1992 to find a global solution to the climate crisis. Carbon emissions have, ironically, doubled since 1988. In 2018 the UN IPCC put out a global warming report which drew attention to risks of failed action. The report highlighted the world has until 2030 to prevent catastrophic climate change by cutting global emissions by 45–50 per cent at 2010 levels and then ensuring net zero carbon targets by 2050. Emissions have to drop by 15 per cent per annum to prevent a 1.5°C overshoot in the next decade (Hausfather 2019). Additionally, countries must increase their ambitions threefold to achieve a well below 2°C target and fivefold to achieve the 1.5°C (UNEP 2019).

A Marxist ecology perspective explains the climate crisis by focusing on the divide between capitalism and nature. For Marx, this began with industrial agriculture and the devastation it wrought on the fertility of soils (Foster 1999). This metabolic rift had negative implications for energy and resource flows, mediated by labour, but was also damaging for social and spatial relations. The techno fixes of industrialising nature produced hunger and widened the urban/rural divide. For Foster et al. (2010), this extends to a host of other ecological rifts constituted through capital's domination of nature. Extraction, energy, production and consumption have all impacted on the metabolic rift with nature. In this context the carbon cycle of Earth is also driven by this rift based on carbon extraction, processing, burning and use. The more capitalism continues its fossil fuel addiction, the worse the climate metabolic rift. Currently, ten per cent of Earth has already been lost to 2°C warming, making socio-ecological reproduction extremely difficult, and threatening to make parts of Earth uninhabitable. At 4°C, scientists estimate massive biodiversity loss, food system collapses and mass die-offs of the human population. The carbon logic of contemporary capitalism is best understood as eco-cide, or the extermination of life on Earth. How eco-fascism locks this in is explored further below.

THE CLASS PROJECT OF ECO-FASCISM

Carbon capital (coal, gas, oil) has been at the heart of capitalist accumulation for 150 years. Over the past three decades, with peak oil production registering around the mid-2000s, carbon capital intensified its efforts to secure complex hydrocarbons – tar sands, offshore extraction and fracking. This coincided with the restructuring of global capitalism through neoliberalisation as a class project of transnational and finance capital. In this process of economising everything, liberal democracy has been constitutionalised to limit subaltern power and remake the state, while locking in the sovereignty of capital over society. Market democracy took root with Reagan's declaration that the 'state was the problem' and Thatcher's notion that there is 'no such thing as society'. This unleashed a libertarian version of the market as freedom and equated financialised reason to progress such that social democracy was co-opted (particularly its Third Way variants), and today hard-right neoliberal forces are the beneficiaries of market democracies (see Williams, this volume).

Hard-right neoliberal forces end the pretence of 'green neoliberalism' with its emphasis on treating nature as capital and using the market to address the climate problem through carbon markets, carbon offset mechanisms and using forests as carbon sinks (Bassey 2012). While these have been unworkable solutions, they nonetheless provided 'green cover' for centre-right neoliberals. For instance, Obama deepened the fracking boom in the US, making it rival Russia and Saudi Arabia in terms of gas and oil output. Justin Trudeau, in Canada, also defends and promotes the tar sands extractive industry there. Ramaphosa in South Africa publicly defends the building of the largest coal-fired power stations in the world, a coal-dominated energy mix and offshore carbon extraction. Yet all these centre-right neoliberals have been committed to the Paris climate agreement.

Trump's withdrawal from the climate agreement, support for fossil fuel interests and dismissal of climate science have been major setbacks for the world and have engendered a deep fault line between dominant centre-right neoliberals and hard-right neoliberals, ultimately pushing the neoliberal ideological spectrum further to the Right. The Trump effect gave licence to and engendered the rise of leaders and social forces globally that are authoritarian populists, committed to global financialised accumulation, champion reactionary and exclusionary nationalisms, and are committed to carbon interests at any cost. Such forces are post-hegemonic, remaking national political blocs and exploiting the weaknesses of market democracies. This authoritarian phase of neoliberalism is centrally also about the future of US leadership of the world order. A US-led eco-fascism is on the rise, underpinned by a nexus of class forces involving various fractions of global carbon capital (extractive, productive, financial, digital, military), the global power structure and local carbon ruling classes in national formations. While this creates tensions, realignments and global rivalries, there are relational class practices, domestically and globally, that congeal a degree of coherence to how eco-fascism is constituted in the context of a worsening climate crisis. Centre-right neoliberalism is also remade in this context and pushed further to the Right in its reaction to eco-fascism.

Accelerating carbon capitalism and the climate metabolic rift

According to the UN Environment Programme's Emissions Gap Report, current planned oil, gas and coal investments up to 2030 are going to accelerate global heating and the climate metabolic rift. We are heading for planetary heating beyond 1.5°C, moving us closer to 2°C in the coming decade (UNEP 2019). Since Hansen made the climate crisis a public problem in 1988, why has global heating accelerated, carbon emissions increased and extraction continued? Even now, when there is greater global awareness, climate shocks are registering and the science is clear about the dangers ahead, why is the world prolonging the use of fossil fuels and widening the climate metabolic rift?

These questions can only be answered by scrutinising the role of fossil fuel corporations and of the US eco-fascist state and China. In the case of liberal US democracy, the relationship between fossil fuel corporations, a crucial fraction of carbon capital, and the state is crucial. Exxon has understood the climate science and the carbon problem since the 1970s. Yet this did not inform policy choices. By 1979 the top US scientists, policy makers, President Carter, social thinkers and the fossil fuel industry understood the climate problem and recognised the need for action. The Charney report, *Carbon Dioxide and Climate: A Scientific Assessment,* was released in 1979 and clinched a consensus amongst all these constituencies (Rich 2019: 36). Carter also passed the Energy Security Act in June 1980, which directed the National Academy of Sciences to prepare a detailed and multi-year study on changing climate (Rich 2019: 51). With Reagan in the White House after Carter, this all changed and a rollback began. Even the National Academy report and its messaging slowed momentum massively on the climate problem. Hansen's 1988 public intervention brought this issue back and prompted a serious offensive against climate science by fossil fuel corporations. Exxon chose a public relations approach together with the American Petroleum Institute, which then expanded rapidly to include the National Association of Manufacturers, the US Chamber of Commerce and 13 other industry associations (Rich 2019: 182–183). This crystallised into the Global Climate Coalition, which successfully shifted public discourse in the US and amongst ruling classes.

Various strategies were used by fossil fuel corporations and the Coalition to ensure the fossil fuel industry was not hampered by a regulatory approach to the climate problem (Mann 2015). The strategies included propagating doubt about climate science, discrediting climate science and scientists, strategic lobbying and dishonest marketing. Every American president since George Bush senior has refused to lock the US into a binding global treaty, under the UN Framework Convention on Climate Change, to share its responsibility for the climate problem, both as the major historical emitter and the country with the highest per capita carbon emissions. Obama's 'pledge and review' mechanism, at the heart of the Paris agreement, has also not seen the light of day in the US. With the public completely subverted on the urgency of the climate crisis and pliant political leadership and, in the case of George Bush junior, overtly supportive of fossil fuel interests, the Global Climate Coalition had won and by 2002 had disbanded.

Obama oversaw the fracking boom but Trump went further and withdrew from the Paris climate agreement. Currently, all the evidence about fossil fuel extraction in the US and the global North confirms increased extraction in coming decades with disastrous consequences for the climate metabolic rift, particularly human and non-human life. Recent research shows that 157 new or expanded projects linked to the fracking boom will push up US emissions by 30 per cent by 2025. This is an additional 227 tons of carbon emissions (the equivalent of 50 coal-fired power stations) on top of the 764 million tons from these industries in 2018 (Corbert 2020). According to Carbon Tracker (2019), the major oil corporations in the global North, including the US – Exxon, Shell, Chevron, BP, Total, ENI and ConocoPhillips – have to cut emissions from oil and gas production by 40 per cent over the next two decades compared to 2019 levels, to ensure the world does not overshoot climate agreement commitments. At the same time, the actual commitments from these oil and gas majors are far from breaking with a business-as-usual trajectory. Shell, for instance, while adopting the climate problem more explicitly in its public relations rhetoric, has planned up to US$300 billion in fossil fuel investments and has a mere eight per cent of its capital budget allocated for renewables (McCarthy 2020).

Currently, 78 per cent of greenhouse gas (GHG) emissions are from G20 member countries. Together with fossil fuel corporations, the policy choices made by these countries also impact directly on the climate metabolic rift. However, leading in terms of aggregate emissions is China, at about 13 billion gigatons (UNEP 2019). China has some of the largest coal reserves, while it is also supporting the development of one of the largest renewable energy industries in the world and transitioning rapidly to mass public transit systems. At the same time, China's industrial export orientation and mass consumption society is also increasing demands for the efficiencies of fossil fuel energy. Currently, the per capita emissions of China are almost equivalent to those of the EU (UNEP 2019). China is also skewing the global energy mix towards fossil fuels, and its state-based fossil fuel corporations invest heavily in fossil fuel resources. Currently, China is backing over half of global coal power capacity domestically and internationally, in countries such as South Africa, Pakistan and Bangladesh (Ambrose 2019). It has a coal energy capacity (147 GW) that is more than all the coal energy plants in the EU and almost 50 per cent higher than all new coal plants (105 GW) planned on the planet. In short, the UN multilateral process has not been able to provide global leadership to solve the climate metabolic rift. Instead, for almost three decades, carbon emissions have gone up, climate shocks have intensified and the climate problem demands ever more ambitious transformative interventions requiring complete system change. Eco-fascist forces – carbon-addicted states, fossil fuel corporations, hard-right neoliberals – are standing in the way of such necessary transformations.

Securitising climate chaos and advancing imperial control

Since 9/11, US liberal democracy has increasingly securitised. Homeland Security has become a crucial institution for governing 'risks'. In 2005, when Hurricane Katrina battered New Orleans, the US response was a militarised one, with citizens treated as criminals and threats to national security (Buxton and Hayes 2016a). These actions were largely aimed at the already vulnerable African American population in New Orleans. A security-led approach to climate crisis is profoundly eco-fascist. It turns citizens into enemies of the state, profit making and market democracy. Moreover, it creates the basis for the state's monopoly of violence to be unleashed.

As the climate crisis worsens, carbon capital refuses to unplug from fossil fuels. Militarising the crisis is a crucial strategy of eco-fascism, and has been happening in parallel to the failed UN climate negotiations. Buxton and Hayes (2016b) argue that, given this failure, military and corporate power focuses on securitising the future rather than solving the climate crisis by systemic transformation, including transitioning the world beyond fossil fuel systems. In 2007 the Pentagon officially defined its position on the climate crisis in a document titled *National Security and the Threat of Climate Change*. Such thinking has continued to be elaborated for over a decade in various policy frameworks in the US and various Department of Defense policy documents. The climate problem is now understood as a 'threat multiplier' and a threat to national security (Klare 2019: 15–39). The US military officially understands climate change will engender state collapse, internal unrest and chaos abroad as basic needs like water, food and shelter are not met. Many American allies, including the UK, Europe, North Atlantic Treaty Organization (Nato), G7/8, G20, World Bank and the World Economic Forum, have followed in lockstep with regard to the climate security agenda. For the US armed forces, climate change is also a direct threat to its own infrastructure, which has a massive footprint inside and outside the country. This is despite Trump's official rejection of climate-change science, policy and concern. He has actively reversed any focus on climate change, including removing mention of it from official government documents and rescinding Obama's 2009 executive order instructing all government departments to develop plans to reduce GHG emissions. Despite this climate denialism, the military has maintained serious concerns about climate impacts on its operations (Klare 2019).

Treating climate change as an 'apocalyptic future' and a 'threat multiplier' has implications for climate politics and democracy. This easily elides into elite panic and greater securitisation of the climate problem (Hayes 2016). Ultimately, securitising climate change means citizens are a threat to stability and order. Adaptation is on the terms of those who benefit from the status quo. The root causes of the problem and those responsible are unimportant, including governance and policy failures. Hence, more Katrina-like responses are very likely towards any citizen-based 'threat'. This converges with another authoritarian dynamic of corporate-controlled market democracies: increasing securitisation since 9/11. Mass surveillance, technologies of control and invasions of privacy, as Edward Snowden highlighted, are on the increase.[1] Coupled with this is a willingness by many Western governments to copy the Homeland Security boilerplate. In 2004 the UK parliament passed the Civil Contingencies Act which provides for the government to declare a state of emergency even without a parliamentary vote and potentially even without declaring it to the public. For Ahmed, Hayes and Buxton (2016), this proliferation of complex emergency thinking in which various systems can be disrupted by a threat, and the obsession with mitigating 'manufactured risk' which has been caused by not dealing with the root causes, provide the basis for full-blown securitisation of market democracies in the context of worsening climate crises. Canada and Australia have also copied this approach.

Feeding into this climate security paradigm has been the growth of a global high-tech security industry, worth billions of dollars. It has been on full display in the detention centres and control systems put in place across Europe to deal with the 'refugee crisis' and when state and corporate power converge against threats from 'citizens'. For activism generally, but particularly environmental justice politics, this growing trend is proving to be licence for authoritarian state and corporate intervention. In the US, various tactics have been documented: law-enforcement agencies partnering with private corporate security to monitor activists and control protests, FBI informants infiltrating movements, creating 'no-fly zones' during police crackdowns, blanketing out media coverage, categorising activism as 'domestic terrorism', passing laws to prevent undercover investigations of agricultural issues like poor treatment of animals, and attempting to secure affidavits to search social media tools like Facebook (Bittar 2018). In the UK, the non-violent Extinction Rebellion and Greenpeace have been placed on a list of extremist ideologies by counterterrorism police (Dodd and Grierson 2020a, 2020b). Global Witness has observed an increase in violent murders and attacks on activists, with 2017 registering 201 killings, six more than in 2016.[2] Killings by agribusiness and the extractives industries topped the charts.

This all adds up to a conception of risk that is about protecting the status quo, while being blind to those who are vulnerable and ignoring how to reduce their vulnerability. For the Pentagon, the logic of climate security means climate change contributes to state failure and chaos among poorer countries. In other words, climate change becomes an all-encompassing explanation rather than a deeper appreciation of the historical political economy dynamics shaping a country. For a very poor country like Mozambique, debt-ridden and beholden to the International Monetary Fund (IMF) and World Bank before cyclones Idai and Kenneth hit in 2019, infrastructure losses running into about US$1 billion due to these cyclones created a fiscal crisis.[3] This was followed by more loans from the IMF and World Bank. The debt trap for Mozambique has been exacerbated by the worst cyclonic devastation in the history of the global South, with 2.2 million people in need. At the same time, Mozambique is facing an incursion of Muslim fundamentalist extremists in the north and is locked into gas extractivism, a resource curse. Following the logic of the Pentagon's understanding of climate change as a threat multiplier, Mozambique is a failing state and a threat. It is a security risk like many other African countries in a similar situation. The Africa Command of the US military would read and understand most African countries in this way. Again, if the UN multilateral process prioritised the phase-out of fossil fuels, rather than emissions, in the negotiations, and if Western governments contributed to the green climate fund, as promised, countries like Mozambique could manage a deep just transition from fossil fuels and make the necessary adaptations to protect its people from further climate harms.[4] Instead, many African and poor countries are driven into a state of climate chaos by the eco-fascist class project dominating global climate politics.

Yet while the US military understands climate change as a threat multiplier, it also has a massive responsibility for causing the problem. It has been excluded from accounting for its emissions since the Kyoto Protocol, but is one of the largest users of petroleum on the planet and the single largest producer of GHG in the world. In the invasions and wars in Afghanistan and Iraq it emitted 1 212 million metric tons of GHG by the end of 2017 (Crawford 2019). The most powerful military in the world, it has been engaged in uninterrupted warfare since 1991. At the same time, the 'war on terror' is proving to be one of the longest wars in modern history. The US military is thus also a threat multiplier of climate change given its carbon footprint. More war means more carbon emissions. With its global reach, strategic footprint and formidable power, the US military has been central to advancing US imperial interests in the name of defending national security. It has secured sea lanes, American investments, including in fossil fuel extraction, and commercial supply lines. The geopolitics of this is most starkly expressed in the Arctic, both as a zone of climate catastrophe for those who inhabit it and for the world, given the rapid methane release from permafrost, but also as a zone of resource extraction for carbon ruling classes. The perverse logic of eco-fascism has translated the Arctic's receding ice, methane release and shoreline erosion as a crucial site of carbon accumulation and for the reproduction of the global fossil fuel economy. Today a complex alignment of military resources by various countries has made the Arctic an explicit theatre of geopolitical rivalry between the US, Canada, Norway, Nato, Russia and China (Klare 2019: 120–139). The next big war might be fought over more oil and gas, but ironically in a rapidly heating world.

Exclusionary nationalism, patriarchy and eco-cide

Climate shocks are already displacing people and contributing to one of the world's largest migrations of humans. In 2017, about 258 million people lived outside their country, up from 173 million in 2000 (Hill 2018). In Syria, drought has been a serious factor contributing to the conflict and displacing people. Similarly, in Central America, a severe drought has devastated agriculture in countries such as Honduras, forcing many to leave the land and some to march to the US border (Philips 2019). In Europe, the response has been 'fortress Europe' and the assertion of an exclusionary nationalism (Georgi 2019). Extreme right-wing forces, including ruling parties, have used nationalism in Italy, Germany, France and Poland, for instance, to vilify refugees and migrants. The 'war on terror' and Islamophobia have given a fillip to racist stereotyping in Europe. At the same time, Trump's call to 'Make America Great Again' is really about making white, male, supremacist America great again. His white nationalism articulated consistently with racism and sexism. His support for extreme right-wing elements and his history of misogyny allowed him to weaponise identity politics in deeply reactionary ways. His obsession with building a wall around 'lifeboat' America and incarcerating undocumented migrants and refugees reinforced his binaries, such as good white male American versus bad Mexican (Phillips 2017).

'Fortress Europe' and Trump's border incarceration complex, combined with racist and sexist exclusionary nationalism, have become crucial for the global agenda of the new hard neoliberal Right. Essentially, with Trumpism, the class project of Trump and his class allies, the US standard of liberal democracy has been plunged into crisis and its self-serving universals are now implicated in the making of global eco-fascism. In India the ruling Bharatiya Janata Party (BJP), led by Narendra Modi, gradually unleashed a full-blown Hindu nationalist assault on the Muslim minority (see Nilsen, this volume). The most recent measure is the passing of the Citizenship Amendment Act (CAA), which legalises discrimination on the basis of religion and undermines the secular foundations of India's constitution. The CAA allows those living in India prior to 2014 who are from neighbouring Afghanistan, Bangladesh and Pakistan to have Indian citizenship, but not if they are Muslim. Moreover, there is a strong attack aimed at India's 200 million Muslim population through the passing of the National Register of Citizens Act, tested in the province of Assam to discriminate against Muslims, and now to be used to disenfranchise Muslims across India. Floods, droughts and heatwaves in India will further marginalise India's Muslim minority and add to their vulnerability. In countries like Bangladesh, which is also at the frontline of sea level rise in its southern parts, the displacement that has and will continue to happen with sea level rise means big parts of its 150 million Muslim population face a militarised and hostile Indian border regime. The Islamophobia of the Modi government is also consistent with the geopolitics of the war on terror and its racism. These dynamics essentially give greater control to an eco-fascist USA and its allies in the unending war on terror.

In 2019 in Brazil, 87 000 forest fires – set by vested interests such as loggers, ranchers, mining – raged for months in the Amazon. These fires were encouraged by President Bolsonaro, who has a visceral antipathy for environmentalism similar to Trump's. He supports illegal mining, deforestation and agricultural interests but also has strong ties to the Brazilian military. Bolsonaro is openly racist and against the 400 indigenous tribal groups in the Amazon (about one million people). His rhetoric gives licence to further violence against these communities and support for brazen dispossession. The burning of the Amazon is part of a larger vision to industrialise it and deepen a financially globalised Brazil (see Saad-Filho, this volume). As the Amazon burns, it releases carbon and becomes a feedback loop for more accelerated warming on a planetary scale. The climate metabolic rift is also widened by this destruction – which has now reached about 20 per cent – of the greenest lung on Earth (absorbing a quarter of carbon dioxide released from fossil fuel combustion), the largest rainforest (5.5 million square kilometres) and one of Earth's most biodiverse spaces – over three million species of animals and plants, more than half the species on the planet. As global heating increases, with more droughts and drier conditions, about 85 per cent of the Amazon could be wiped out, with disastrous consequences for the global climate.

The bushfires that raged in Australia in 2019 revealed a regime deeply pro coal mining and fossil fuel exports, and, like Trump, the Scott Morrison government did not have any serious commitments to deal with the worsening climate crisis. Prior to the fires his government actively vilified environmentalists, and he also ensured the enactment of a law targeting protestors to limit non-violent resistance tactics (Feder 2020). The epicentre of the fires was New South Wales, home to most of the indigenous peoples in Australia. Already brutalised by the ongoing coloniality in Australia, the fires destroyed indigenous homes, cultural sites and historical archives (Funes 2020). An estimated billion animals were lost in the bushfires, affirming the eco-cidal logic of carbon capitalism. The Morrison government also manages a racist exclusionary border with an incarceration complex on numerous islands for refugees trying to reach Australia from conflicts elsewhere, including from the Middle East.

Trump's racist and exclusionary lifeboat approach to America and the border incarceration complex are consistent with the populationist racism that has been central to some variants of deep ecology and the white nationalist Right. Populationists and deep ecologists such as Paul Ehrlich (1968) have made specious and racist arguments about population since the 1960s. According to Angus and Butler (2011: 12), Ehrlich's bestseller, *Population Bomb*, not only blamed too many people for environmental crises but also called on the US government to impose population reduction measures on other countries. As the populationist argument gained traction within elite environmentalism, then deep ecology in the 1980s, Ehrlich's position on the population, environmental and migration challenge became more exclusionary. In the early 1990s he became a founding patron of the Optimum Population Trust (OPT), the leading environmental charity and think tank in the UK dealing with population growth and environment. While the OPT wants better birth control, its main proposal for reducing population growth is severe immigration restrictions to curb the population explosion, limit GHG emissions, limit crowding, congestion and development, and reduce pressure on green resources and spaces (Angus and Butler 2011: 29). James Lovelock, the progenitor of the Gaia hypothesis and also on the board of the OPT, has even more extreme views. He believes population and climate catastrophe is inevitable and therefore it is crucial to preserve 'islands of civilisation' in a ruined world, using military force to fend off climate refugees (Angus and Butler 2011: 30).

In the US, the white nationalist Right has over decades built up a racist perspective on population and racial purity and against inward migration. During the 1970s, John Tanton, a white nationalist, combined his concerns with overpopulation and environmental destruction with a strong anti-immigration position. He wanted to curb non-white immigration into the US and took these positions into the Sierra Club, an environmental organisation. Moreover, he set up a network of anti-immigration organisations, including the Federation for American Immigration Reform (FAIR) and the Center for Immigration Studies. The FAIR was extremely influential in the Trump administration in terms of border control (Kovensky 2019). Attributing causality to population growth in the context of climate change is disingenuous and central to discourses on exclusionary racism. In micro contexts, more people will impact on resources and ecological limits. However, on a global scale, both in terms of land use and climate change, using population as a causal factor is spurious. Numbers do not add up to causality. A critical global political economy perspective brings into view history, resource use, corporate control, resource inequalities and carbon debt by the global North to explain the current ecological crisis, including climate crisis. The bottom line is that the average American has an extremely intensive carbon and resource footprint. The reproduction of this way of life would require at least five planet Earths, according to National Geographic's Human Footprint project.[5] The problem is not people but rather the imperial mode of living (Brand and Wissen 2018).

In 2019, the impacts of climate shocks on the African continent were devastating. According to an international disasters database, compared to 2018, there was a 195 per cent increase in the number of Africans impacted by extreme weather events, 56 extreme weather events were registered compared to 45 in 2018, and 16.6 million people were affected in climate-related disasters in 29 African countries, compared to 5.6 million in 2018 (Pandy 2019). Trump was brazenly oblivious to these realities in what he deemed to be a 'shithole'. Central to these climate disasters have been impacts on women and children. Aid organisations operating in Mozambique in the aftermath of cyclones Idai and Kenneth made this observation:

> For example, they [women and children] are often at a greater distance from water collection points, sanitation facilities and health centres, which may be in unsafe locations, exposing them to additional protection threats such as sexual and gender-based violence (SGBV). With the destruction of health facilities, pregnant women have limited access to support for delivering their babies safely. It is estimated that more than 75,000 cyclone-affected women are pregnant, with more than 45,000 live births expected in the next six months; 7,000 of those could experience life-threatening complications. Girls are more likely to miss out on school following the damage wrought to schools and learning materials following the cyclones. Though their vulnerabilities are both extensive and multi-sectoral, funding to address the complex needs of women and girls falls far short. (CARE, Oxfam and Save the Children 2019)

Prior to the worst drought (2014–2016) in South African history, 14 million people went to bed hungry. Anecdotal evidence illustrates that hunger has worsened during this climate-change-induced drought, although the state has not tracked it adequately. African working-class and poor women have been at the frontlines of the crisis through skipping meals, rationing food to their children, providing cheap unhealthy food to their households and borrowing food. South African hunger has produced racialised and gendered climate inequalities (Satgar and Cherry 2019). Such climate harms intersect with the lived realities in one of the most unequal countries in the world, due to over two decades of deep globalisation and financialised neoliberalisation. An unviable society is becoming more so in the context of the worsening climate crisis.

Geoengineering the future

The plutocratic carbon ruling classes have the means to buy themselves out of the short-term disruptions and stresses of a heating world: from insurance to bunkers, Mars exploration, creating exclusionary 'safe zones' and buying property in 'safe' parts of the world. In the long run, however, the plutocrats will also face catastrophic climate change, resulting in the need to reach for techno fixes such as geoengineering. Simply, geoengineering is about using technology to manipulate Earth's climate system to reduce global heating. Climate-altering technologies are used to control Earth's thermometer. There are controversial aspects to the definitional remit of geoengineering (Wetter et al. 2016): whether to include weather-altering interventions, such as cloud seeding, or to limit it to technologies that deflect sunlight away from Earth, also known as solar radiation management (such as continuously spraying sulphur dioxide into the stratosphere to reflect more of the sun's rays outward), and technologies that remove, capture and/or store carbon dioxide, such as ocean fertilisation with iron, nitrogen or bio char. Wetter and colleagues (2016) argue for definitional aspects which include intentional or deliberate activity (despite unintended consequences); global or large-scale effects, even if it has local deployment; and a high-technology approach involving unknown risk to the environment.

Playing with Earth's thermometer is a harder task than we think but also has grave consequences for human and non-human life. If these technologies are in private hands, we are all at the mercy of these profiteers. Moreover, if wealthy countries control these technologies, the implications for North–South geopolitics are nothing short of colonial. But there are also democracy deficits and the dangers of unintended consequences on a planetary scale. Klein (2019: 107) argues that

> the truth is that geoengineering is itself a rogue proposition. By definition, technologies that tamper with ocean and atmospheric chemistry on a planetary scale affect everyone. Yet it is impossible to get anything like unanimous consent for these interventions. Nor could any such consent possibly be informed, given that we don't, and can't, know the full risks involved until these planet-altering technologies are actually deployed.

Funding, research and modelling of geoengineering has taken off. In 2010, the US House Committee on Science, Space and Technology recommended more research on geoengineering, giving momentum to a British government research agenda and to millions spent by the Gates Foundation to experiment and develop geoengineering solutions (Klein 2019: 106–107). Scientists such as Paul Crutzen, Nobel Prize winner for his work on the ozone layer, supports it, as does the widely read magazine *Science*. By 2008 Republican politicians like Newt Gingrich were calling on the American public to reject legislation that led to fossil fuel reductions and instead called on them to support geoengineering of the atmosphere through sulphates as a better solution. Since then numerous neoconservative think tanks have openly come out in support of geoengineering: the American Enterprise Institute, Cato, Hoover, the Competitive

Enterprise Institute and the International Conference on Climate Change, the main-stay of climate denialists and sceptics (Wetter et al. 2016). In 2013, the UN IPCC included geoengineering as a solution in its report *Climate Change: The Physical Science Basis*.[6] While the UN has not given full endorsement for such technologies, it has not consistently rejected geoengineering as part of the scientific research agenda. As it stands, powerful carbon states, philanthropic capital, carbon capital, some scientists and academics, and the UN IPCC are churning the tide of geoengineering, rather than phasing out fossil fuels and advancing resourcing for deep just transitions and for capacity building to deal with climate shocks. The techno fixes of eco-fascism are irrational and undemocratic. They express elite panic and reflect a capitalist techno-topia, a worldview that has failed to emancipate humanity.

LIMITS OF ECO-FASCISM

Increasing planetary heating due to carbon extraction and use takes the world into an unprecedented place in human history. In 2019 alone the costs of hurricanes, floods and wildfires cost the world US$150 billion (Ziady 2020). Climate shocks are already costing the US billions of dollars annually, including over the past decade with droughts, hurricanes, floods, wild fires, freezes and severe storms. According to McKibben (2019: 28), climate costs in the US are at $240 billion per year and the world at $1.2 trillion annually, wiping out 1.6 per cent of the global GDP. No country is going to be immune from its impacts and consequences. Eco-fascists cannot use incarceration, walls and powerful militaries to manage this planetary crisis. The US military itself is concerned about overstretch in a permanent crisis in which its own operations will be seriously constrained. All of humanity will be tested and the divisions and rivalries of a new eco-fascism will be difficult to sustain.

Planetary awareness of the climate emergency and the need for decisive action is growing. In 2019, several important scientific studies issued by UN agencies dealing with land use, climate hot spots, planetary heating and its implications for agriculture, and climate-change impacts on our oceans, as well as an emission gaps report, were made available to policy makers and publics. At the same time, many media outlets have started mainstreaming climate news. The informed global public is growing, including inside the US, where 72 per cent of Americans affirm it is important (Revkin 2019), and the list of countries committing to transitions to net zero carbon targets is increasing.[7]

Climate justice politics has also gone through two cycles of resistance. Between 2007 and 2015 climate justice forces successfully developed a critique and ideological discourse around climate justice alternatives, as the basis of systemic change. The high point of this cycle of resistance was the Cochabamba People's Summit in 2010, hosted by the only climate justice state in the interstate system, Bolivia. From 2016 onwards a new cycle of resistance began with the Standing Rock struggle against the Dakota Access Pipeline. In the wake of this iconic struggle, Extinction Rebellion, Greta Thunberg's #FridaysForFuture, the US-based Sunrise Movement and the Climate Justice Charter process in South Africa have all emerged as '1°C movements'. These initiatives have played a crucial role in shifting public discourse and register in policy debates from below. These forces will grow on a planetary scale as the climate crisis worsens and the eco-fascist class project stands in the way of fundamental transformation to prevent a 1.5°C overshoot.

CHALLENGES FOR CLIMATE JUSTICE FORCES

Eco-fascism is the fundamental challenge to climate justice forces but also more generally to human and non-human life. It has to be defeated through national and global mass resistance. Climate justice forces have to resist the expansion of carbon capital, fight against the new conjunctural racisms and exclusionary nationalist regimes that are rising, defend the most vulnerable who are least responsible for the climate crisis, and champion deep just transitions. While raising the alarm and disruption will be crucial in this phase of resistance, more fundamental is the challenge of building mass subaltern power to also lead system change from below. This has implications for how mass and electoral power are conceived strategically to enable transformative class projects to come to the fore. Governments committing to net zero targets have to be pushed hard to deliver on these commitments. Climate justice forces must have answers for the transformative change required now. Green new deal agendas, 'green manifestos', just transition programmes and climate justice charters are all crucial to define the trajectories of mass and electoral power. Climate justice struggles are now about resistance, defence and systemic alternatives to achieve transformative change in the coming decade. As 1°C movements grow, they have to be harbingers of a new transformative politics, constructing system change alternatives from below such as food sovereignty, commoning, solidarity economies, climate jobs and democratic planning. Counterhegemonic alliance building in national contexts, to deepen mass convergences around climate justice political projects, is going to be crucial to determine the possible futures of climate justice politics beyond the limits of symbolic protests, lobbying and changing narratives.

While climate politics has had a shot in the arm from the #FridaysForFuture movement and Extinction Rebellion, this is not enough to strengthen climate justice politics. These are examples of crowd politics that have been downloaded into national contexts, but do not always translate into mass-based alliance building given the different contexts, political traditions and social conditions. The world needs a global climate justice movement to tackle the climate crisis. In this regard, proposals for a post World Social Forum convergence are crucial, such as Samir Amin's (2020) call for a Fifth International of Workers and Peoples. This is not about an old-style authoritarian vanguardist politics but rather about building a coordination mechanism for movements, parties and projects to learn critical lessons from earlier experiences of internationalism and to shift the balance of global power. The world's working class, peasantry and precariat are central to such an attempt at realignment. Other proposals, including for a new World Party and a new vessel for the Left, also have to be debated and engaged with (Chase-Dunn 2020). The time has come for climate justice politics to also be about a new internationalism that is democratically institutionalised on a global scale. It has to take on board these debates and concerns.

Fossil fuel corporations are at the heart of the challenge. While inspiring struggles have been waged against extractivism over the past years to gridlock carbon, including in the Niger Delta, Germany and Standing Rock, this has not stopped the onward march of fossil fuel corporations. Divestment campaigns have important but limited impacts. While calls to keep fossil fuels in the ground and for phase-out will be intensified in coming years, mainly in national contexts, added pressure will also come from attempts to ensure the UN Conference of Parties process directly addresses the end of fossil fuels. In South Africa, the Climate Justice Charter process has called for an 'End Fossil Fuels Treaty', echoed by one of Africa's leading climate justice activists, Nnimmo Bassey, who has more recently supported a similar approach which he terms a 'Fossil Fuel Non-Proliferation Treaty' (Bassey 2020). Attempts at climate justice 'lawfare' have to complement such initiatives. Fossil fuel corporations have to be criminalised in national jurisdictions, and even internationally, using constitutional rights. Eco-fascism has to be hauled before international courts in something akin to a climate justice version of the Nuremberg trials.

Moreover, the time has come for climate justice sanctions against eco-fascist regimes that are accelerating the climate metabolic rift. Bond (2019) makes this argument based on the experience of the anti-apartheid movement's success of boycott, divestment and sanctions and the adoption of such a campaign by Palestinian solidarity groups in 2006. This message has to be amplified in national climate justice movements across the world and asserted through governments embracing climate justice. In this way, the US, China and other eco-fascist regimes can be isolated. The time is now.

NOTES

1   Currently the US is no longer meant to be spying on its own citizens, but the rest of the world is fair game.
2   Global Witness, '2017 – the global trends', https://www.globalwitness.org/en/campaigns/environmental-activists/their-faces-defenders-frontline/#chapter-1/section-1 (accessed 18 January 2020).
3   See https://www.worldvision.org/disaster-relief-news-stories/2019-cyclone-idai-facts#damage (accessed 18 January 2020).
4   Western governments were meant to contribute about US$100 billion per annum to the UN climate fund. The contributions have been dismal.
5   See https://www.schooltube.com/media/t/1_octv5jyj (accessed 18 January 2020).
6   See https://www.ipcc.ch/report/ar5/wg1/ (accessed 24 November 2020).
7   See https://climateaction.unfccc.int/views/cooperative-initiative-details.html?id=94 (accessed 8 January 2019).

REFERENCES

Achenbach, J. 2019. 'Two mass killings a world apart share a common theme', *Washington Post*, 18 August. Accessed 18 January 2020, https://www.washingtonpost.com/science/two-mass-murders-a-world-apart-share-a-common-theme-ecofascism/2019/08/18/0079a676-bec4-11e9-b873-63ace636af08_story.html?fbclid=IwAR3r3nq0e_TnboagW8G1m8ZaJFkESptPlWzSfEYaV2_K9NnQJek3rKtf3Ns.

Ahmed, N., Hayes, B. and Buxton, N. 2016. 'A permanent state of emergency: Civil contingencies, risk management and human rights'. In N. Buxton and B. Hayes (eds), *The Secure and Dispossessed*. London: Pluto Press, pp. 87–110.

Ambrose, J. 2019. 'China's appetite for coal power returns despite climate pledge', *The Guardian*, 20 November. Accessed 18 January 2020, https://www.theguardian.com/world/2019/nov/20/china-appetite-for-coal-power-stations-returns-despite-climate-pledge-capacity.

Amin, S. 2020 [2006]. 'Towards the Fifth International?' In V. Satgar (ed.), *BRICS and the New American Imperialism*. Johannesburg: Wits University Press, pp. 148–166.

Angus, I. and Butler, S. 2011. *Too Many People? Population, Immigration and the Environmental Crisis.* Chicago: Haymarket Books.

Bassey, N. 2012. *To Cook a Continent: Destructive Extraction and the Climate Crisis in Africa.* Cape Town: Pambazuka Press.

Bassey, N. 2020. '2019: Year of record climate disasters in Africa', *Enviro News Nigeria*, 8 January. Accessed 18 January 2020, https://www.environewsnigeria.com/2019-year-of-record-climate-disasters-in-africa-nnimmo-bassey/.

Bittar, J. 2018. '6 ways government is going after environmental activists', *ACLU Speech*, 6 February. Accessed 18 January 2020, https://www.aclu.org/blog/free-speech/rights-protesters/6-ways-government-going-after-environmental-activists.

Bond, P. 2019. 'Shifting the balance of forces through sanctions against Trump and U.S. carbon capital'. In J. Foran, D. Munshi, K. Bhavani and P. Kurian (eds), *Climate Futures: Re-Imagining Global Climate Justice*. London: Zed Books, Ebook, pp. 545–580.

Brand, U. and Wissen, M. 2018. *The Limits to Capitalist Nature: Theorizing and Overcoming the Imperial Mode of Living*. London: Rowman & Littlefield.

Buxton, N. and Hayes, B. 2016a. 'Introduction: Security for whom in a time of climate crisis?' In N. Buxton and B. Hayes (eds), *The Secure and Dispossessed: How the Military and Corporations Are Shaping a Climate-Changed World*. London: Pluto Press, pp. 1–22.

Buxton, N. and Hayes, B. (eds). 2016b. *The Secure and Dispossessed: How the Military and Corporations Are Shaping a Climate-Changed World*. London: Pluto Press.

Carbon Tracker. 2019. 'Balancing the budget: Why deflating the carbon bubble requires oil and gas companies to shrink'. Accessed 18 January 2020, https://www.carbontracker.org/reports/balancing-the-budget/.

CARE, Oxfam and Save the Children. 2019. 'From cyclone to food crisis: Ensuring the needs of women and girls are prioritized in the Cyclone Idai and Kenneth responses', *Reliefweb*, 12 July. Accessed 18 January 2020, https://reliefweb.int/report/mozambique/cyclone-food-crisis-ensuring-needs-women-and-girls-are-prioritized-cyclone-idai.

Chase-Dunn, C. 2020. 'The vessel: An alternative strategy for the global left'. In V. Satgar (ed.), *BRICS and the New American Imperialism*. Johannesburg: Wits University Press.

Corbert, J. 2020. 'Climate watchdog warns US fracking boom leading to 30% rise in greenhouse gas emissions by 2025', *Common Dreams*, 8 January. Accessed 18 January 2020, https://www.commondreams.org/news/2020/01/08/climate-watchdog-warns-us-fracking-boom-leading-30-rise-greenhouse-gas-emissions.

Crawford, N.C. 2019. 'Pentagon fuel use, climate change and the costs of war', Watson Institute for International and Public Affairs. Accessed 20 January 2020, https://watson.brown.edu/costsofwar/files/cow/imce/papers/Pentagon%20Fuel%20Use%2C%20Climate%20Change%20and%20the%20Costs%20of%20War%20Revised%20November%202019%20Crawford.pdf.

Dodd, V. and Grierson, J. 2020a. 'Terrorism police list Extinction Rebellion as extremist ideology', *The Guardian*, 10 January. Accessed 18 January 2020, https://www.theguardian.com/uk-news/2020/jan/10/xr-extinction-rebellion-listed-extremist-ideology-police-prevent-scheme-guidance.

Dodd, V. and Grierson, J. 2020b. 'Greenpeace included with neo-Nazis on UK counter-terror list', *The Guardian*, 17 January. Accessed 18 January 2020, https://www.theguardian.com/uk-news/2020/jan/17/greenpeace-included-with-neo-nazis-on-uk-counter-terror-list.

Ehrlich, P. 1968. *The Population Bomb*. New York: Ballantine Books.

Feder, J.L. 2020. 'Australia's leader called for a crackdown on environmentalists before fires broke out', *BuzzFeed News*, 17 January. Accessed 18 January 2020, https://www.buzzfeed-news.com/article/lesterfeder/environmental-protests-terrorism-australia-bushfires.

Foster, J.B. 1999. 'Marx's theory of metabolic rift: Classical foundations for environmental sociology', *American Journal of Sociology* 105 (2): 366–405.

Foster, J.B., Clark, B. and York, R. 2010. *The Ecological Rift: Capitalism's War on the Earth*. New York: Monthly Review Press.

Funes, Y. 2020. 'Bushfires are "obliterating the cultural memory" of Australia's Aboriginal people', *Earther*, 14 January. Accessed 18 January 2020, https://earther.gizmodo.com/bushfires-are-obliterating-the-cultural-memory-of-austr-1840933953?utm_medium=sharefromsite&utm_source=_facebook&fbclid=IwAR12wDEGSdx2tel-LxFs9sCq_4NiavMHmRgYnstl7CBomiw506B0mFDNK58.

Georgi, F. 2019. 'Toward fortress capitalism: The restrictive transformation of migration and border regimes as a reaction to the capitalist multicrisis', *Canadian Review of Sociology* 56 (4): 556–579.

Hansman, H. 2019. 'The environment is being weaponized for hate', Outside Online, 10 September. Accessed 18 January 2020, https://www.outsideonline.com/2401805/weaponizing-enivronment-hate?fbclid=IwAR3ypUOQP9DwQKyMOY24ct8MobeN-zI6EVen-9VdUdH_ayL16GShhAKKBehM#close.

Hausfather, Z. 2019. 'UNEP: 1.5 climate target "slipping out of reach"', *Carbon Brief*, 26 November. Accessed 18 January 2020, https://www.carbonbrief.org/unep-1-5c-climate-target-slipping-out-of-reach?utm_source=Twitter&utm_medium=Social&utm_campaign=GapReportTwitterVid112019.

Hayes, B. 2016. 'Colonising the future: Climate change and international security strategies'. In N. Buxton and B. Hayes (eds), *The Secure and Dispossessed*. London: Pluto Press, pp. 39–62.

Hill, A. 2018. 'Migration: How many people are on the move around the world?' *The Guardian*, 10 September. Accessed 18 January 2020, https://www.theguardian.com/news/2018/sep/10/migration-how-many-people-are-on-the-move-around-the-world.

Klare, M.T. 2019. *All Hell Breaking Loose: The Pentagon's Perspective on Climate Change*. New York: Henry Holt and Company.

Klein, N. 2019. *On the (Burning) Case for a Green New Deal*. New York: Simon and Schuster.

Kovensky, J. 2019. 'Latch on to climate change for mass migration hysteria', *TPM*, 16 September. Accessed 18 January 2020, https://talkingpointsmemo.com/muckraker/white-nationalists-latch-on-to-climate-change-for-mass-migration-hysteria?fbclid=I-wAR0KHJHvI_kGeipTViYsnmRNDhUl4s6ltQfNxpjK-r8DzUcyHKtPElUdqU8.

Mann, M.E. 2015. 'The Serengeti strategy: How special interests try to intimidate scientists, and how best to fight back', *Bulletin of the Atomic Scientists* 71 (1): 33–45.

McCarthy, D. 2020. 'Oil companies like Shell could destroy humanity as we know it – but not if we make fossil-fuel investments illegal', *Independent*, 8 January. Accessed 18 January 2020, https://www.independent.co.uk/voices/climate-crisis-australia-fires-shell-bp-exxon-fossil-a9274776.html.

McKibben, B. 2019. *Falter: Has the Human Game Begun to Play Itself Out?* New York: Henry Holt and Company.

Pandy, K. 2019. '195% more Africans affected due to extreme weather events in 2019', *Down To Earth*, 26 December. Accessed 18 January 2020, https://www.downtoearth.org.in/news/climate-change/195-more-africans-affected-due-to-extreme-weather-events-in-2019-68573.

Philips, T. 2019. 'Latest migrant caravan marches on as Trump again demands border wall', *The Guardian*, 17 January. Accessed 18 January 2020, https://www.theguardian.com/world/2019/jan/16/migrant-caravan-honduras-march-trump-wall.

Phillips, A. 2017. '"They're rapists." President Trump's campaign launch speech two years later, annotated', *The Washington Post*, 16 June. Accessed 18 January 2020, https://www.washingtonpost.com/news/the-fix/wp/2017/06/16/theyre-rapists-presidents-trump-campaign-launch-speech-two-years-later-annotated/.

Polanyi, K. 1944. *The Great Transformation: The Political and Economic Origins of Our Time*. Boston: Beacon Press.

Revkin, A. 2019. 'Most Americans now worry about climate change – and want to fix it', *National Geographic*, 23 January. Accessed 8 January 2019, https://www.

nationalgeographic.com/environment/2019/01/climate-change-awareness-polls-show-rising-concern-for-global-warming/.

Rich, N. 2019. *The Decade We Could Have Stopped Climate Change: Losing Earth.* New York and London: Picador.

Satgar, V. 2019. 'Black neo-fascism? The Economic Freedom Fighters in South Africa', *Canadian Review of Sociology* 56 (4): 580–605.

Satgar, V. and Cherry, J. 2019. 'Climate and food inequality: The South African Food Sovereignty Campaign response', *Globalizations* 17 (2): 317–337.

UNEP. 2019. *Emissions Gap Report 2019: Executive Summary.* Nairobi: United Nations Environment Programme. Accessed 18 January 2020, https://wedocs.unep.org/bit-stream/handle/20.500.11822/30798/EGR19ESEN.pdf?sequence=13.

Wetter, K.J., Ribeiro, S. and ETC Group. 2016. 'The fix is in: (Geo)engineering our way out of the climate crisis?' In N. Buxton and B. Hayes (eds), *The Secure and Dispossessed.* London: Pluto Press, pp. 133–151.

Ziady, H. 2020. 'Fires, storms and floods cost $150 billion in 2019. More disasters are on the way', *CNN*, 8 January. Accessed 18 January 2020, https://edition.cnn.com/2020/01/08/business/munich-re-climate-change-natural-disasters/index.html.

NEOLIBERAL CAPITALISM AGAINST DEMOCRACY GLOBALLY

3

POPULISM AND FASCISM: LESSONS FROM THE 1920s KU KLUX KLAN

Linda Gordon

When I was a young New Left socialist feminist, some activists who considered themselves revolutionary – the 'Weathermen' – liked to spell America as 'Amerika', with a swastika substituted for the K; or as 'AmeriKKKa'. I scoffed at these textual gestures, less because I thought them offensive than because I thought them naïve. The notion that the US was fascist reflected an unrealistic assessment of the American government and of the conditions and strategies that could produce progressive change. I also thought it an expression of a destructively macho approach to politics – a sign of what we feminists liked to call 'testosterone poisoning'. It is now a half-century later and the label 'fascist' is once again busy in the USA. There are good reasons for this. Numerous groups in the US, most of them thankfully rather small, are claiming a fascist or Nazi identity and honouring fascist and Nazi leaders; other groups that do not identify in that way are evoking that label from observers. All are gaining confidence from President Trump. Those of us committed to democracy, liberalism, socialism or any variety of Left social ethics have good reason for anxiety.

Now the label 'populist' has joined 'fascist' as a pejorative, albeit a weaker one. It is a condemnation rather than an analytic or even descriptive category. It obscures more than it illuminates, and its lack of precision contributes to political illiteracy. In what follows I hope to put more specificity into the concept. Many commentators have tried to do that by distinguishing between left and right populism, but those labels only muddy the concept further. Defining populist primarily by the demagogic performances of leaders – Alfredo Saad-Filho (this volume) calls them 'spectacular' politicians – is superficial at best, serving to draw the eye away from the policies such leaders promote. Focusing exclusively on rousing speeches would require including Fidel Castro, Lula and Evo Morales as populists. When pundits speak of right- and left-wing 'extremists' – typically, Trump on the Right, Bernie Sanders on the Left – this is an absurdity; Sanders is not at all extreme but rather a social democrat. In fact, the populism that worries so many today describes a right-wing version, but since the noun is typically used without a modifier, I use populism in this chapter to refer only to its right-wing forms.

My concern with the labels 'populism' and 'fascism' arose from studying the 1920s Ku Klux Klan (KKK) in the northern USA (Gordon 2017). This second coming of the Klan was little known until recently, but it was the leading American exemplar of a mass populist movement on the Right. The original, well-known KKK arose in the southern states after the Civil War and the end of Reconstruction – the short-lived attempt by the federal government to ensure that newly emancipated African Americans would actually be able to access the political and economic rights to which they were theoretically entitled. When the federal government abdicated responsibility to guarantee the rights of the freed people, the KKK formed to defend white supremacy. It was a terrorist group in the precise meaning of that term: it used torture and murder, especially lynching, as well as economic and social coercion, less to punish individuals and more to terrorise the whole African American population, to prevent any black effort to gain political rights, economic opportunity, educational achievement or social respect. Though many southern upper-class whites thought the Klan's methods distasteful, they understood that it served to protect a cheap labour supply for landowners and secured the consent of many poor whites who were made to feel lucky that they were not black. The Klan operated by constructing fear, through a chorus of scare stories about the mob rule that liberated African Americans would create. It also built a communal white hysteria about black male sexual aggression towards white women, which succeeded in drawing white women into a fearfulness that then further legitimated white terrorism.

When the KKK moved into the northern states in the 1920s, and quickly amassed somewhere between three and six million members, it was a different beast: it was not at all secret, it was a mass movement, it included women, it was strongest north of the Mason-Dixon line, and it was in the main non-violent. In the main, but not entirely. Instead, it organised a state-of-the-art electoral strategy that put into office some 16 senators, scores of congressmen, 11 state governors and thousands of state, county and municipal officials; and these were politicians who ran openly as Klan members or supporters.

The second Klan's explosive growth came from an astute strategic move: fusing anti-black racism with religious and ethnic bigotry.[1] In the north it focused on attacking Catholics and Jews. While it remained as virulently racist as the first KKK – and when it spread west extended that racism to other groups of colour, particularly Mexican, Japanese, Filipino and Chinese Americans – it built on earlier nativist anti-immigrant campaigns. The great majority of the turn-of-the-century immigrants were Catholics from southern Europe, Jews from eastern Europe, and Greek or Russian Orthodox from further east. The KKK managed to instil into millions of white Protestants who formed its constituency the fear that these outsiders represented an acute threat, not only to the essential values of the USA but even to its government.[2]

It might seem surprising that the Klan was able to create this anxiety among the WASPs (white Anglo-Saxon Protestants) who dominated politics, the economy and the culture. In fact, there are many historical examples of such unjustified anxiety.[3] The 1920s Klan was strongest in regions with few immigrants and few who were not white Protestants; in Oregon, for example, one of the strongest KKK states, Jews constituted 0.1 per cent of the population, African Americans 0.3 per cent and Catholics 8 per cent. Nevertheless, the second Klan managed to position the dominant group as victimised by subordinated groups.

In this chapter I use the 1920s Ku Klux Klan to examine what populism and fascism mean in the American context. Since much of the scholarship and popular understanding of fascism has focused on European fascism, especially the Nazi regime in Germany, I risk some comparisons with Nazism, although it is not my area of expertise. By placing the 1920s KKK and 1930s German National Socialism side by side, I attempt to put some historical substance into these two concepts, resisting the loose and imprecise use of those labels that is now so common. I am a historian and have not studied today's American white nationalism, but I suspect that those who have done so will see marked similarities to the earlier American bigotry discussed here.

*⁎⁎

As used today, populism, even without the modifier 'right-wing', refers to regimes, political parties and social movements that use demagoguery to promote bigotry and often reject the rule of law and the classic liberal guarantees of due process and civil liberties.[4] This populism is impatient, to say the least, with the rights of minorities or dissenters, even with procedural due process. It is also typically anti-intellectual and militaristic, and often angry at more traditional conservative politicians, the centrists or neoliberals today called moderate Republicans.

But like many historians, I am suspicious of attempts to develop a bounded definition of a concept like populism. I proceed empirically, instead, in an attempt to identify the specific features of movements now called populist. Doing that requires that we treat populism as a cluster concept – that is, a concept that encompasses variants that share some but not necessarily all their attributes.[5] In an attempt to do that, I have compiled a rough list of its characteristics. It is likely that no other scholar's list would be exactly the same, and mine is by no means encompassing, but it can provide a basis for greater clarity about what we mean when we talk about populism:[6]

- mobilising supporters by promoting resentment;
- claiming to speak for 'the people';
- narrowing 'the people' so as to exclude, for example, immigrants and people of the 'wrong' race, ethnicity or religion;
- cultivating fear of these 'outsiders' who threaten the dominant culture;
- condemning diversity while idolising homogeneity;
- relying on demagoguery and hyper-masculinism, through sensationalist and angry performance that uses aggressive language and gestures as opposed to the polite language of elite conservatism;
- demanding loyalty to authoritarian leadership as the ultimate form of patriotism;
- claiming that 'the people' are being victimised by alien groups, thus casting blame downward, towards less advantaged groups, rather than upward, towards those who actually have power;
- thus promoting a faulty understanding of how the system actually works;
- encouraging extreme nationalism and suspicion of foreign ideas and cultures;
- reclaiming a national 'destiny' from those who are subverting it;
- willingness to override civil liberties, the protection of minorities and, at times, the rule of law;
- promoting a 'class analysis' that defines intellectuals, experts, secular people, big-city folk, etc., as oppressive to 'the people', while creating a false nostalgia for agrarian communities or small towns;
- condemning a political establishment while remaining uncritical of corporate power;
- supporting militarised repression of dissent;
- stigmatising big cities as the home of cosmopolitanism and not the *ur* people;
- promoting anti-intellectualism;
- exhibiting a propensity for conspiracy theories;
- cultivating anti-feminism and condemning alternative family forms, LGBTQ rights and 'gender ideology' – that is, the notion that masculinity and femininity are socially constructed.

Some populist views may be uniquely American: claiming that women are victimising men; insisting on an individual's right to carry arms; isolationism; heightened, unrealistic individualism; and regular use of entirely false claims.

Many of these features reveal resemblance between the 1920s Ku Klux Klan and today's populisms. Both use demagogic rhetoric, traffic in conspiracy allegations without evidence, and seek to exclude various racial, ethnic and/or religious groups from the *echt* people, the authentic Americans. (Klan phrases such as '100% Americans' offer an uncanny prevision of the McCarthyist phrase 'unAmerican'.) Modi similarly draws a line between 'true' Indians and their enemies, as Alf Gunvald Nilsen argues in this volume. Populism typically deploys extreme nationalism. They may support tariffs and criticise free trade, but usually accept the free transnational movement of capital. But they never accept the free movement of people – especially people whose only 'capital' is their labour power. The arch-villains of right-wing populism are, accordingly, immigrants, migrants, refugees, non-dominant religious or ethnic groups, and the 'liberals' who defend them.

While some contemporary populists, occasionally including Trump, denounce corporate and financial profiteering, they do not support policies that would limit those profiteers and benefit middle-class, working-class and/or poor people. To use American language, they do not support limiting the power of the one per cent. In what might be called the populist 'class analysis', the enemy is not those who monopolise economic power but rather so-called elites, typically defined as secular professional intellectuals and/or liberal cosmopolitans (and 'cosmopolitan' has long been a code word for Jews). In the US the populists turn hierarchy upside down, arguing that government policies and liberals are indulging disadvantaged groups – people of colour, LGBTQ people, immigrants, Muslims – at the expense of the 'real' Americans. Nilsen (this volume) identifies the same pattern in India. In other words, while they may express anger towards the powerful, populists direct most of their hostility downward, towards the less privileged, a pattern described by Saad-Filho (this volume) with respect to Brazil. (In this respect anti-Semitism is a unique case, which I discuss below.) One might refer to the populist discourse about elites as a deformed class analysis.

Turning from here to fascism, one question immediately arises: is fascism a more extreme populism? First, let us note some characteristics of fascism that are not just quantitatively but also qualitatively different from populism: territorial expansionism; large-scale attempts to eliminate 'inauthentic' groups through deportation, confinement or, worse, murder; and organising supporters into military-style regiments taking orders from the top.

But fascism must also be treated as a cluster concept. Umberto Eco, in his 1995 essay 'Ur-Fascism', argued that 'fascism had no quintessence'. He called it 'a fuzzy totalitarianism, a collage . . . a beehive of contradictions . . . The fascist game can be played in many forms' (Eco 1995). Historian Robert Paxton writes that we cannot identify fascism 'by its plumage' (1998: 3). There can be no generic, universal, complete or transhistorical definition of fascism. As a result, and because the term is so weighted with historical atrocities, some scholars have suggested abandoning it altogether. I find it still useful, however, if only because it points to disturbing trajectories.

Using my research on the Ku Klux Klan as a basis, I focus in this chapter not on institutionalised fascist regimes or parties but rather on crusades or tendencies that could be labelled fascist*ic* – that is, on social and political *movements* that promote fascist*ic* values. The adjective seems to me more useful than the noun, because it can remind us of the fluidity and unpredictability of social movements.

Still, even as a movement, fascist values are often statist, and fascist movements have often promoted the state as the expression of 'the people's will'. In Mussolini's famous dictate, 'Everything inside the state. Nothing outside the state. Nothing against the state.' This was to some extent wishful thinking, and state control was never complete. Certainly, some of today's European populist leaders – Putin, Erdoğan, Orbán, for example – attempt to expand state control. Today's American populism might seem different, because much of its propaganda condemns the state for victimising 'the people'.

But populist wrath is directed only to some facets of the state. In the US it has focused more on the federal government or a loosely defined political establishment, and less on state and local governments. Constitutional electoral structures in the US under-represent large cities, which are least inclined towards populism, and over-represent smaller cities and towns, where populism is stronger. Moreover, the content of populist anti-statism is slippery. If we examine which state policies and functions populists condemn, the picture changes, and the state divides along gendered lines: favouring the warfare state as masculine and essential to patriotism, and hostile to social-democratic institutions and programmes – such as education, health and safety regulation, aid to the poor or disabled – which are presented as feminine, a 'nanny' state, a sign of national weakness. These gendered metaphors function as a discursive sleight of hand, or inconsistency, in that right-wing criticisms of 'big government' do not include the military, police or prisons as part of the objectionable state. Moreover, when populists include or ally with religious evangelicals or fundamentalists, whether Christian, Jewish, Muslim or Hindu, they often support state enforcement of repressive sexual and gendered policies such as those against abortion and birth control. Thus MAGA – Make America Great Again – the slogan of Trump supporters, embroidered on many of the baseball caps at Trump rallies, implicitly defines 'greatness' through this masculinist understanding of good state versus bad state.

The first, nineteenth-century Ku Klux Klan could be categorised as fascistic because of its violence. But it differed importantly from the Nazi movement: while the Nazis ultimately sought to eliminate whole populations of vilified groups, the first Klan sought to retain the cheap labour of its one vilified group, African Americans, by raising the cost of resistance. The 1920s Klan, by contrast, sought to exclude those who were not 'true Americans' from political and economic citizenship – a significant difference. The KKK strategy for this exclusion was mainly non-violent. Its attempts to bankrupt Jewish businesses through boycotts, exclude Jews and Catholics from political office, and teach evangelical Protestantism in the public schools were disjointed and mainly a failure, in part because the Klan imploded and its membership dropped precipitously by the late 1920s. Still, its discursive impact was great: the bigotry promoted through its 150 print publications and two radio stations was a major success in shifting public opinion. In this respect the 1920s KKK resembled early fascism more than it resembled its parent, the first Klan.

The second Klan's non-violence undercuts the view that fascism is but a more extreme populism. Although the Klan often attacked the courts – alleging, for example, that they allowed criminals to go unpunished – it remained committed to its version of democracy: a democracy of 'true' Americans, a *herrenvolk* (master race) democracy of white native-born Protestants, an illiberal democracy that would allow majorities of the enfranchised to overrule any minority rights. This vision may not deserve to be described as democracy, but it is nevertheless quite different from the Nazis' open rejection of democracy, or that of some of today's tyrants such as Orbán and Bolsonaro. As strategic projects, Nazi and Klan bigotry both worked at both ends, so to speak: persecuting one group built the loyalty of another. For the KKK, attacking Jews and Catholics served to intensify identity and pride among Protestants. Moreover, the second Klan's enemies largely matched those of Nazis: Jews, people from southern and eastern Europe (who were once often considered non-white in the US) and any people of colour.

While the Klan discourse, unlike the Nazis', did not make the problem of disability a major theme, it did support eugenics and the compulsory sterilisation of 'defectives'. Although eugenics had not always been racially or religiously discriminatory – in the 1870s and 1880s, for example, there were feminist and sex-radical eugenists who did not see particular races or social classes as inferior – by the 1920s leading eugenists were entirely devoted to bigotry, ranking racial, ethnic and religious groups along a continuum from superior to inferior (Gordon 2003). Even before the take-off of compulsory sterilisation of 'defectives', Klan politicians were contributing to state eugenics programmes – for example, through 'better babies' contests that used pretty blond babies to demonstrate WASP superiority. Although the Klan never argued for sterilisation based on religion or ethnicity, its eugenical hierarchy of the races was identical with that of the most influential eugenists. These were upper-class, highly educated men, and however much they disliked the KKK's crudeness, they did not disagree with its substance. Henry Goddard, for example, tested immigrants at Ellis Island and 'found' that 83 per cent of the Jews, 80 per cent of Hungarians and 79 per cent of Italians were either 'morons' or 'imbeciles' (Okrent 2019: 36, 237; Huntington 2004). The temperature of American eugenic bigotry reached new heights in the World War I era, through the efforts of Madison Grant, who boasted of his descent from Puritans. His 1916 book, *The Passing of the Great Race*, promoted hysteria that the 'master race' was facing extinction – this view, incidentally, is the meaning of the recent white nationalist chant 'Jews will not replace us.'

These similarities between the Klan and the Nazis were not coincidental; American eugenics exerted significant influence on Nazi 'race hygiene' policies. In fact, American eugenists influenced Nazi eugenists. The Klan's term 'Nordic' people was almost identical to and just as ideological as the Nazis' 'Aryan', and neither, of course, matched any identifiable group. Both Klan and fascists argued that these were the people who had been destined to lead the nation. As early as 1932 Walter Schultze of the Nazi euthanasia programme called on German geneticists to 'heed the example' of the US. Party ideologue Alfred Rosenberg praised Grant's book effusively. The Nazi *Handbook for Legislation* cited US immigration law as a model for Germany. Leading eugenist H. Fairfield Osborn complained that negative press about the Nazis resulted from Jewish influence. This alliance was also personal: by 1930 German and American eugenists had been meeting, sharing research, even commenting on each other's writings for several decades (Okrent 2019: chapter 12).

Neither Nazis nor Klanspeople invented their bigotry, of course. They inherited most of it, especially from the long history of European anti-Semitism. In the US, prejudice against Jews and Catholics fuelled widespread nativist sentiment in the nineteenth century, and intensified after 1880 with the massive immigration of millions from eastern and southern Europe. The nativists, however, sought immigration restriction rather than violence to rid themselves of these inferiors. Targeted restrictions, notably against Asians, had stopped or limited immigration to the west coast,[7] but there was no general immigration restriction until 1924. The

KKK literally drove this law, the Johnson-Reed Act of 1924: Congressman Albert Johnson of Washington state, a Klan enthusiast, was a co-author and sponsor of the Bill and, as chair of the Committee on Immigration, shepherded it through Congress. The law enacted a racial hierarchy of 'superior' and 'inferior' peoples, which then remained in effect until 1965.[8] But in the 1920s US – quite possibly more than in Germany – this hierarchy was entirely mainstream, a perspective widely shared among white Protestants and even among politicians who might be labelled liberal. The 1924 law passed with a small handful of dissenting votes in the House of Representatives and only nine in the Senate. In other words, the Klan's uniqueness lay in its virulence and its loudness, not in the policies it promoted; these were supported by the gentlemanly racists, such as presidents Woodrow Wilson and Calvin Coolidge, who spoke quietly but discriminated and legislated forcefully.

Ku Klux Klan cultural values could also be considered fascistic. Particularly redolent of fascism is *how* the allegedly superior population groups were represented. Both populism and fascism relied on notions of purity, of 'blood' or 'stock'. Weeding out those who were not part of the 'authentic' Germany or America was necessary to purify the nation. (These views also characterise today's white nationalism.) Both the Klan and Nazis were, of course, horrified by intermarriage, aka 'miscegenation'. To both, purity also meant homogeneity. Klan rhetoric displayed a discomfort with diversity so deep that it became for many a visceral fear. Diversity was dangerous, because it produced a 'Babel' that subverted national unity; national strength thus required homogeneity. By insisting on *religious* as well as racial homogeneity, the Klan outdid the Nazis, who tolerated Catholics as well as Protestants. Nothing represented that exaltation of uniformity more than the highly choreographed rallies and marches used by both movements, in which large groups moved in unison, forming dramatic geometric shapes.

Purity also required women's chastity. Klan propagandists, however, managed to combine their worship of chastity with a form of titillation: they told story after story, sometimes smutty, sometimes scatological, sometimes veiled, of Catholic debauchery and Jewish 'white slavers'. Nazis also found ways of indulging, through their fondness for naturism, adoration of female and especially male nude sculpture, and general eroticisation of power. (One extreme case was that of Nazi painter Adolf Ziegler, a Hitler favourite, who became known, even at the time, as 'master of the pubic hair' because of his hyperrealistic nudes [Petropoulis 2000: 255].) Female chastity flowed into the purity of motherhood, an ideal that demanded self-sacrifice, of which more below.

The content of Klan bigotry, the specifics about what was wrong with non-Protestants, illuminates the historical specificity and consistency of anti-Semitism.

For the Klan, Catholics, Jews, Russian or Greek Orthodox believers could not be patriotic Americans because they owed loyalty to foreign powers – the pope, the cabal of bankers, the patriarch. But conversion could save and cleanse the Christians: Catholics and Orthodox could convert to Protestantism, in which case they could become 'true Americans'. By contrast, a Jew could never become acceptable. Jews could not rid themselves of their uncleanness – it was embedded in the Jewish body itself. Jews were a race, not a religion.[9] The Klan's characterisation of Jews was almost identical to the Nazi version: they were dishonest merchants, avaricious bankers and international conspirators aiming to control the world economy. They were also predators intent on despoiling Aryan women.[10] Moreover, Jews were tribal; this magnified their power and made them not just an individual but a collective threat to the nation. These alleged Jewish traits derived from the age-old equivocal nature of Jewishness, as both an ethnic or 'racial' and a religious group. In this respect, as Eric K. Ward (2017) has insightfully argued, anti-Semitism is closer to racism than to religious prejudice.

Fascist ideology foregrounded the concept of a national destiny, and the KKK shared that credo. For both, destiny served to justify and build support for the movements, and to promise victory. The source of that destiny differed, however. For the 1920s Klan it was God-given, ordained by a Protestant God, of course. Klan propagandists liked to claim that if Jesus were alive, he would be a Klansman, and that the KKK had been sent by God to 'rescue' the US from those who sought to block it from achieving its destiny. This sanctification of the Klan could be considered more audacious than the claims of Nazis. For the Nazis, destiny arose not from supernatural power but from the 'will' of the German people; in a circular logic, that indomitable will would lead the master race to its destiny, while the superiority of that race was demonstrated by the strength of its will. The Nazis' version of destiny produced expansionist imperatives: Germany was destined to reclaim lands that should belong to the German people, to claim lands needed for Germany's fulfilment – e.g. *Lebensraum* (literally 'living room', meaning more space for the German people) – and to cleanse parts of the world that stood in the way of this destiny. In fascism, strength needed military aggression. In fact, strength was proved by conquest, a conception not typically found in populism and not at all in the Klan, and this constitutes a sharp difference between fascism and populism.

In contrast to the fascists, the KKK was isolationist. (Of course, the Klan had already inherited the fruits of territorial aggression, because the US had already seized lands stretching from ocean to ocean.) Isolationist policy both arose from and strengthened its hyper-nationalism. In congruence with fascist ideology, however, the Klan insisted that the nation must not be constrained by any outside power. Its strength must be supreme. This form of isolationism reflected the KKK's abhorrence for the foreign, and especially for Europe. In an ideological contradiction, Protestant Americans of western and northern European ancestry were model citizens, but Europe itself was unclean – like the *haram* (forbidden) or *treif* (not kosher) of its enemies – due to its sexual immorality, its tendencies towards secularism, its support of unconventional arts and artists, and its indulgence in alcohol. The second Klan arose simultaneously with the Prohibition amendment of 1919, and supported it passionately; most of the Klan's vigilante assaults were directed against saloons and distributors and manufacturers of liquor. (This produced a problem for the Klan, as many of its leaders were caught drinking.) Klan members had a nearly 100 per cent overlap with the evangelical Protestants who had created Prohibition, as well as with the leading organisations behind Prohibition, the Anti-Saloon League and the Women's Christian Temperance Union. Klan propaganda racialised drinking, insisting that it was a uniquely Catholic vice supported by the rapacious Jews who supplied them and exploited them.

The argument that a nation or a people has a destiny typically deploys 'tradition' as evidence. Although not all arguments from tradition rest on claims about destiny, all believers in destiny seek to restore a glorious past that, they charge, is being eroded. The concept of destiny then posits an urgent need to reclaim the imagined tradition, and thus serves as a means of arousing activism. Hallowed traditions are, of course, usually fictitious. The Klan claimed, in addition, that the US was not only ordained by God as a home and a beacon of Protestantism but had *once been* a homogeneously Protestant nation, when in fact non-Protestants had been part of the country since its origin. Klanspeople often claimed the 'founding fathers' as the heroes and progenitors of evangelical Protestantism. In fact, the 'founding fathers', some of whose political formation stemmed from Enlightenment thought, were often deists and thus heretical in relation to Protestant evangelical orthodoxy. Lack of evidence for claims about tradition could not create scepticism because tradition, like destiny, is not historical but timeless and suprahuman: it exists in the realm of the metaphysical. This is the sense in which fascism tends towards mysticism, but the Klan also indulged a bit – its secret rituals had mystical, supernatural power.

Anti-empiricism was part of populism's frequent anti-intellectual, anti-science orientation, and for Klan's passionate condemnation of evolutionary theory. In the famous 1925 trial of schoolteacher John Thomas Scopes for teaching evolution, the prosecuting attorney – William Jennings Bryan – became a KKK hero. When he died just after the trial concluded, the Klan threw him a large memorial service complete with a huge burning cross. The Ohio Grand Dragon pledged, 'We will take up the torch as it fell from [his] hand, for America cannot remain half Christian and half agnostic' (quoted in Lynd and Lynd 1965: 483; Schuyler 1985: 250; Wade 1987: 248).

What Umberto Eco (1995) wrote of the fascist view of science – 'There can be no advancement of learning. Truth has been already spelled out once and for all' – actually fit the Klan better than it fit Nazi ideology. Both Nazi and Klan animosity towards science focused particularly on scientists, who represented secular, liberal, cosmopolitan elites, particularly Jews. Obviously, regimes needed universities and scientists, while the Klan, only a social movement, did not. But the Klan loved modern technology and, like fascists, pioneered in using it. Its rallies employed state-of-the-art equipment – radio, airplanes, electric light displays, automobiles – as well as state-of-the-art publicity methods. This attraction to the spectacular fits Jeffrey Herf's (1984) phrase about Nazi Germany's 'reactionary modernism'. Both Klan and European fascists, however, were also fans of non-technological mass choreography, the Nuremberg rallies being the most well-known example.

Conspiracy theories are often fundamental to populist ideologies, and were aligned with evangelical Protestant beliefs. Conspiracy talk functions to show that the impure seek to pollute the pure and to subvert the nation; it is thus basic, even essential, to arousing fear and anger. Catholic conspiracies, both global and local, were legion in Klan discourse. The Klan contended that immigrants came to the US not because of poverty or persecution, but because they were sent by the pope, with instructions to live incognito, like moles in espionage, until the pope gave the order for the coup that would establish the United Catholic States of America. The Klan recruited 'escaped' nuns who became travelling lecturers offering salacious stories of Catholic perversions. The Jewish conspiracy was proved by the infamous 'Protocols of the Elders of Zion'.[11] That Henry Ford, a Klan supporter, funded the publication of 500 000 copies in English translation, and serialised it in his newspaper, the *Dearborn Independent*, once again points to the respectability and legitimation of KKK populism. The Klan's hostility to Hollywood was doubly grounded: the film studios were disproportionately run by Jews, and they were motivated not only by alleged Jewish greed but also because Jews conspired to subvert the morals of American women through racy images and plots.

Studying the Klan, I puzzled over why so many well-educated middle-class people – and its membership *was* mainly middle class and no less educated than the American average[12] – could believe these absurd conspiracy allegations. For evangelicals the credulousness matched a theology that emphasised the wiliness of Satan, although the fascist employment of conspiracies succeeded without theological help. Perhaps most influential in creating gullibility was the source of the conspiracy tales: they became credible when voiced by a respected authority, and the Klan's were frequently broadcast by ministers. The 1920s Klan claimed to have 40 000 ministers as members. It seduced them by exempting them from the considerable initiation fees or dues membership, by making donations to their churches and by sending them out as paid lecturers. The figure 40 000 was no doubt an exaggeration, but we know that thousands of ministers praised the Klan from the pulpit, even urged parishioners to join. Evangelical ministers were, unsurprisingly, prominent among the Klan's travelling lecturers, given their skills and long experience in writing and delivering rousing sermons. Some of these were 'big tent' celebrity evangelicals, such as the famed Aimee Semple McPherson. In the 1920s US, attending lectures remained a common leisure activity, and Klan lecturers drew large audiences and collected admission fees for themselves and their Klan sponsors. Klanspeople's gullibility also rested on something more emotional: resentment at the disdain directed at them by the Klan's critics, who regularly described it as a product of uneducated, unsophisticated hicks. This scorn was not only incorrect, but it affirmed the Klan's view that its critics were elite snobs disrespectful of ordinary, 'true' Americans.

Fascists and Klanspeople both relied on demagogic speakers to mobilise political emotion. No Klan leaders could match Hitler's or Mussolini's oratory. But the optics of the mass rallies produced by both Klan and fascists might be considered a form of demagoguery. At these large events – gargantuan in the case of Nazi Germany – the visual and aural combined to maximise their impact: the choreography and rousing rhetoric served to intensify pride in belonging to the master race as well as commitment to unity, which in the Klan's view required homogeneity.[13] The choreography amassed large numbers of people in geometric formations, or moving in unison, creating a visual symbol of unity and absence of dissonance. The Third Reich's were, of course, militaristic, unlike the Klan's. Instead, its events included family-oriented picnics featuring races, beauty contests, band concerts – in this respect quite different from Nazi rallies. But like Nazi and other fascist rallies, the Klan's mass public gatherings, typically held outdoors on America's Independence Day, also used choreographic and theatrical design to great effect: at night they erected burning crosses as high as 50 feet, an awesome display, and Klan members marched with burning torches.

These gatherings did several kinds of work. They communicated the size and power of the movement; some rallies drew people in the tens of thousands. Frequently held on American Independence Day, they symbolised the Klan's ultra-patriotism. Outsiders got entertainment and insiders got to participate in a patriotic ritual. Like many demonstrations and rallies, of the Left as well as the Right, these produced and performed a sense of belonging to a community, and of pride in that belonging. For outsiders, the rallies constituted both intimidation and invitation. Highly visible and widely reported in the press, their message to those the Klan called 'aliens' – Catholics and Jews, even native-born Catholics and Jews – was quite clear: beware, do not challenge us. These events also functioned to recruit new members by demonstrating the pleasures of being part of this movement. Above all, these events sold the organisation as legitimate, law-abiding, respectable.

The Klan was a family organisation. It organised clubs, bands and sports teams so its families could spend all their leisure time in Klan activities. So did the Nazis – for example, through organisations such as Strength Through Joy, Hitler Youth and the League of German Girls. In fascism, these tentacles of the party served to socialise future members and non-members to party values and allegiance; they were thus fundamental to its totalitarianism. The Klan did likewise, if on a much smaller scale. It operated youth groups and women's groups, and its member families participated in rituals of birth, christening, marriage and death, all choreographed according to Klan scripts. One could live a life almost entirely within the world of the KKK.

The fascist mode with which we are most familiar, the European model, glorified violence, even sacrificial death on behalf of the German *volk*. In this the Klan did not participate. The Third Reich built an aggressive mentality in part through an obsession with death, ruin and martyrdom, called a *Totenkult* (death cult) by historian George Mosse (1964). In George Orwell's words, 'Whereas Socialism, and even capitalism in a more grudging way, have said to people, "I offer you a good time", Hitler has said to them "I offer you struggle, danger and death", and as a result a whole nation flings itself at his feet' (quoted in O'Donnell 2012: 233). Paxton refers to the 'beauty of violence' in fascism (2004: 41).

The glorification of violence demonstrates the importance of gender in fascism's attraction. However mystified, fascist violence had strategic functions, attracting men – particularly young men – to the cause by equating nationalist strength with muscular manliness. In this regard, there are parallels among fascists, the 1920s Klan and white supremacists today. KKK leaders knew that they could more readily reach their goals through propaganda and electoral politics, but they also knew that offering a chance to participate in vigilantism was a powerful draw for young men. As a result, they 'dog-whistled': while publicly insisting that theirs was an entirely non-violent group, they found ways to entice young men with pugnacious, confrontational rhetoric and only slightly veiled offers of vigilante activity.

That vigilantism was an exclusively male activity did not by any means make Klanswomen uncomfortable with it, any more than Nazi militarism or death camps disturbed Nazi women (Blee 1991, 2003; Koontz 1987). Nazi women participated in violence against Jews and Jewish property, served as concentration camp guards and, according to historian of Germany Mary Nolan (pers. comm.), 'were integral to the institutionalized, legalized violence of compulsory sterilization and euthanasia'. In the US, women have cheered or even instigated male violence, a common practice in the American history of lynchings.[14] (From the history of suicide bombing, we learn how women, even mothers, could be made to accept, even endorse, the martyrdom of their children [Johnson and Kuttab 2001].) Klanswomen of the 1920s do not seem to have engaged in physical violence, but their rhetoric could be as virulent as that of Klansmen.

Nazis kept soldiers and citizens in line by glorifying sacrifice. Sacrifice as patriotic virtue infected, for example, even the *Bund Deutscher Mädel* (League of German Girls), in part because it matched the traditional socialisation of girls towards maternal self-sacrifice. Historian Claudia Koontz (2003: 143) reported the recollection of a *Jewish* girl who longed to be able to join precisely because of its call for self-sacrifice. Especially during the war, when conditions were brutal, rhetoric of maternal self-sacrifice replicated the sacrifice required to re-empower the nation. Rendering sacrifice ennobling has been a central discourse in constructing armies, but also in evoking loyalty to regimes. Here the KKK differed sharply, taking no part in the fascist emphasis on sacrifice. Neither do today's white nationalists.

Klanswomen may not have sacrificed but they performed on a large scale the labour that was their responsibility within families. They not only organised and participated in the mass public events, but also ran youth groups and the many Klan ceremonies around rites of passage, such as christenings, weddings and funerals. Nazi women performed similar jobs. In neither group, however, did all women accept the principle of female dependency and submissiveness; many seized opportunities to engage in the public sphere. This is a characteristic contradiction found often in conservative politics – even women who mouth platitudes about motherhood and declare that women belong at home are often unable to resist the satisfactions of political activism.

Commitment to sacrifice can slide into submission, which points to another key difference between fascists and Klan. Submission to a deity is a common and powerful trope in many religions, but its secular form has been prominent in fascistic movements and regimes. Fascism made the state itself a metaphysical force, fused with the destiny and will of the nation. Through submission the individual became one with the nation, and the nation was represented by the authoritarian leader. Subordination to that leader was essential for national unity. Mussolini expounded the idea that only through submission to the state could one become free. Fascist regimes thus shrank the space between leader and nation. The idea of a national destiny served to make submission to leadership imperative – anything less would become an obstacle to realising that destiny by eroding the unity of the nation or the *volk*. In fascist ideology only a single all-powerful leader can create the unity necessary to lead the nation to its destiny. These mystiques were not a part of the Klan's structure or ideology; submission to a *führer* (leader) was not a premise of Klansmanship. The Invisible Empire, the Klan's alternative name, had no emperor. The organisation was more feudal than tyrannical, with regional bosses unaccountable to and occasionally challenging the Imperial Wizard. This decentralised control was furthered by the Klan's electoral strategy, as local candidates built their own political machines. Nor did the Klan peddle a discourse of submission as duty. The proof lay in how quickly and drastically the Klan shrank in the late 1920s, as members grew increasingly impatient with the hypocrisy and corruption of their leaders.

While authoritarianism enforces submission, so submission permits and builds authoritarianism, and although Klanspeople did not defer to a national leader, they mostly followed the rituals set forth in its rule book, the Kloran.[15] Church-like, Klan rituals had to follow prescribed scripts to the letter, not only for every meeting but for every rite of passage – births, christenings, marriages, funerals. The Kloran took on greater power because it was never to be seen by 'aliens'. Part of the Klan's strategic cunning was that it managed to benefit both from secrecy and lack of secrecy. The organisation was entirely public, its large-scale gatherings open to everyone. It advertised and announced its events in newspapers, ran Klansmen as political candidates, even marched without hoods when necessary. But its arcane rituals, codes, oaths and choreography, stipulated down to the physical postures and movements during meetings, were entirely secret. Members were made to swear terrifying oaths never to reveal any of these practices, and threatened with dire punishments should they violate it. The secrecy was in itself a draw to membership, making it an honour to be party to this exclusive insider knowledge. The Klan made its members feel doubly privileged: because they were white Protestants and because they were trusted to know the cryptic rites.

That millions found Klan hocus-pocus attractive fits some of the theoretical scholarship that focused on authoritarian followers as well as leaders. Émigré Frankfurt-school scholar Adorno, struggling to explain the appeal of fascism, postulated an authoritarian personality that inclined a person to submission. This hypothesis gains strength if we do not assume a uni-causal direction in which personality structure gives rise to authoritarianism, an analysis in which personality structure is the independent variable. Adorno is suggesting that authoritarian leaders can *produce* authoritarian personalities – the causality goes both ways. The same is true of the Frankfurt-school hypothesis that fascism drew on an irrationality which in turn resulted from repression, an analysis that was reduced to a single-variable explanation by Wilhelm Reich. Influenced by these European theories, American scholars such as historian Richard Hofstadter and sociologists Joseph Gusfield, William Kornhauser and Neil Smelser characterised social movements as products of anxiety and resentment rather than rational pursuits of concrete goals. These conclusions mirrored what 1920s critics mistakenly charged: that the KKK was a movement of the uneducated, unsophisticated, unreasonable and unreasoning. These analyses equated emotion, especially fear and anger, with irrationality. Sociologist James Jasper (2014: 208) countered this argument, pointing out that anger and especially indignation, 'the morally grounded form of anger' in his definition, are by no means necessarily irrational. Mass emotion can be rational even if it rests on false beliefs.[16] Moreover, emotions can be instrumental; they can serve to justify and to create pressure for self-interested policies. Most of the time, the label 'irrational' has little explanatory value.

The irrationality label is particularly misleading about the Klan. It expertly and successfully pursued sophisticated, legal and relatively democratic electoral and economic strategies. It lobbied politicians, fielded candidates and brought its members to the polls. In 1924 it succeeded in turning its condemnation of immigration into national law. Later that year it was recognised as the major force in blocking Al Smith, Catholic governor of New York, from securing the Democratic Party presidential nomination. Even the Klan's infrequent vigilantism was calculated and instrumental. And while it rarely initiated violence, it delighted in provocation, which often produced violent resistance from its targets. For example, it incited conflicts by posting its flyers and lecture announcements on synagogues and Catholic schools.

Although rarely violent, the Klan's relations with law-enforcement officers do suggest one fascistic tendency in particular: Klan vigilantes operated with impunity through the collusion of law-enforcement officers, with the result that not a single 1920s Klansman was convicted for this vigilantism. Law-and-order officers constituted, proportionately, the single largest occupation of Klansmen. Many police departments were thoroughly 'Klanified' and some officially deputised Klansmen. There is, no doubt, a mutual causality here – men in these occupations were particularly drawn to the Klan and Klan activism then suited, or even strengthened, violent tendencies among them.

Still, as Klanspeople were marching in silence with burning crosses and publishing calls to bigotry, Nazi storm troopers were beating up Jews and destroying Jewish stores. Violence has been central to fascism not only in practice but also in culture. This difference cannot be minimised: the northern Klan's non-violence alone could well be considered enough to remove it from the fascism category.

***

How much populism and fascism overlap is open to interpretation. I tend to agree with Nilsen's formulation in this volume, that populism fuels fascism. It may be that the similarities outnumber the differences, but this quantitative conclusion is less salient than the qualitative – the violence and genocide of historical fascism distinguishes it sharply from the Klan and related populisms. Certainly, fascism's militarism, territorial aggression, romanticisation of violence and subordination to a Caesar-like leader separated it from 1920s populism. Furthermore, dwelling on the overlap may not be useful, because neither populism nor fascism can be defined in generic, abstract or ahistorical terms. Both are fuzzy and capacious labels. Moreover, seeking to define them more precisely may discourage study of specific processes and institutions, and forms of resistance.

Still, we may find it useful to conceptualise a populism/fascism continuum. The most immediately visible commonalities are discursive, particularly the identification of one racial/ethnic/religious group as the authentic essence of a nation. Most important, however, is that neither label, whether populist or fascist, is adequate to illuminate current dangers. History does not repeat itself. Labels often stand in the way of specifics, inhibiting the close observation and analysis of what is actually happening. My list of populist features, above, is not a checklist from which we can diagnose, categorise and label. New features appear. It is often the particularities of movements that are most revealing principally because the interaction of these particularities, their concurrence and their synergy can move in a fascistic direction. The journalist Dorothy Thompson, who spent years covering Nazi Germany *and* lived through the 1920s heyday of the Klan, pointed out that 'No people ever recognize their dictator in advance. He never stands for election on the platform of dictatorship. He always represents himself as the instrument [of] the Incorporated National Will . . . When our dictator turns up you can depend on it that he will be one of the boys, and he will stand for everything traditionally American' (Thompson 1935, quoted in Thomas 2006: 172).

These differences suggest that even as hateful an organisation as the Ku Klux Klan was substantially different from 1930s European fascism. We can, however, use the history of those populisms and fascisms as warnings, and as guidance in identifying fascis*tic* trends and trajectories. But it remains the case that the adjective is more helpful than the noun.

NOTES

1   I use the term 'bigotry' rather than 'racism' in order to include all the Klan's enemies, because race today refers only to those we call people of colour; in the late nineteenth and early twentieth centuries, few distinguished between 'race', ethnicity and religion.

2   It is illuminating, with respect to today's populist anti-immigrationism, to compare the massive immigration that the US experienced between 1880 and 1920 to today's. Immigrants arriving between 1900 and 1910 constituted 8.9 per cent of the population, while those arriving between 2000 and 2010 constituted 3 per cent of the US population. Today's vehement demands to stop immigrants are neither new nor proportional to their numbers.

3   Jean-Paul Sartre discussed this in his 1944 'Anti-Semite and Jew'.

4   It is now used without a modifier – populism in itself is suspect. I dislike this use of 'populism' because the historical Populist Party in the US was rarely demagogic and largely progressive. Arising in the 1890s, Populism expressed the economic grievances of small grain and cotton farmers, coal miners, railroad workers, industrial workers and small businessmen against big finance and big business. These Populists – I capitalise the name in order to distinguish them from today's populists – focused their critique on railroads in particular, because freight rates, which favoured large corporate growers, were undermining the livelihood of small farmers. But the Populist platform advanced proposals designed to benefit working people, both agricultural and industrial. It called for a progressive income tax, abolition of national banks, direct election of senators, an eight-hour working day, and government regulation of railroads, telegraphs and telephone services. The party not only spoke in the name of the common people but also mobilised common people into political activism (Postel 2007). It is true that Populism was not free of racism, especially in the south where Populists like Tom Watson realised that getting elected required using the obligatory white-supremacist appeal. But in the main this historical Populism did not prioritise racism, while bigotry is central to today's 'populism'.

5   The classic articulation of this notion was in Wittgenstein's *Philosophical Investigations* (1973: 66).

6   My list is influenced by Jan-Werner Müller's (2016) *What Is Populism?*

7   The Chinese were banned first by treaty and then by federal law in 1882, a law repealed only in 1943, and then only because of World War II alliances; a 1909 'gentlemen's agreement' limited Japanese immigration; and Filipinos were banned in 1934. Moreover, people of Asian and Latin American descent were barred from naturalisation.

8   The law did this by using census data from before the great migration that began in the 1880s, assigning quotas that reflected the proportion of ethnicities in the US population at that earlier time.

9   This fusion of 'race' and religion reverberates today, in the fact that much of the American public does not distinguish between Muslims and people from the Middle East and south Asia.

10   In 1930s Europe, of course, the Right considered Jews dangerous also because of their leftist political tendencies: they were simultaneously rapacious capitalists and revolutionary communists. Somewhat surprisingly, the 1920s Klan did not prioritise fighting communism. This may have been because the Klan had little traction in locations where most left-wing Jews could be found, such as New York City, and/or because it arose when the Bolshevik revolution was very new.

11   The 'Protocols' were a Russian forgery pretending to be the minutes of a late nineteenth-century meeting of Jewish leaders in which they discussed their plan for world domination, through control of economies and the press and through subverting the morals of Gentiles.

12 Klan members and supporters were primarily small businesspeople, white collar employees, lower professionals and especially police and other law-enforcement officers. At least one study showed that Nazi membership was similar in class terms, with 51 per cent middle class, within which 35 per cent were either self-employed or civil servants (Panayi 2007: 40), but Nazi support was far more elite than the Klan's: there was widespread support for the National Socialist German Workers Party in the universities and among the biggest and wealthiest businesses.

13 This kind of pageantry was, of course, not limited to these movements, and became particularly popular in 1930s Busby Berkeley films.

14 For a discussion of women's role in vigilante violence, see Gordon (1999).

15 That Klan leaders chose this modification of 'Koran' rather than something more American or Protestant suggests how incoherent and grab-bag was the ideology they were selling.

16 It becomes important, I would argue, to follow Weber in distinguishing formal from substantive rationality. No social or political movement could best the Nazis' meticulous, methodical, systematic and efficient pursuit of their goals – this is formal rationality. It is the goals themselves that could be considered substantively irrational. But such a judgement is never context-free, and can be made only within a set of agreed-on ethical values. Not even the fascist romanticisation of violence can be branded irrational given fascist goals, such as the weeding out of social impurity and fulfilling a national destiny.

PERSONAL COMMUNICATION

Professor Mary Nolan, New York City, 2019.

REFERENCES

Blee, K.M. 1991. *Women of the Klan: Racism and Gender in the 1920s*. Berkeley: University of California Press.

Blee, K.M. 2003. *Inside Organized Racism: Women in the Hate Movement*. Berkeley: University of California Press.

Eco, U. 1995. 'Ur-Fascism', *New York Review of Books* 42 (11): 12–15.

Gordon, L. 1999. *The Great Arizona Orphan Abduction*. Cambridge, MA: Harvard University Press.

Gordon, L. 2003. *The Moral Property of Women: The History of Birth Control Politics in America*. Champaign: University of Illinois Press.

Gordon, L. 2017. *The Second Coming of the KKK: The Ku Klux Klan and the American Political Tradition*. New York: W.W. Norton.

Grant, M. 1916. *The Passing of the Great Race: Or, the Racial Basis of European History*. New York: Charles Scribner and Sons.

Herf, J. 1984. *Reactionary Modernism: Technology, Culture and Politics in Weimar and the Third Reich*. Cambridge: Cambridge University Press.

Huntington, S.P. 2004. *Who Are We? The Challenges to America's Identity*. New York: Simon and Schuster.

Jasper, J.M. 2014. 'Constructing indignation: Anger dynamics in protest movements', *Emotion Review* 6 (3): 208–213.

Johnson, P. and Kuttab, E. 2001. 'Where have all the women (and men) gone?' *Feminist Review* 69: 21–43.

Koontz, C. 1987. *Mothers in the Fatherland: Women, the Family and Nazi Politics*. New York: St. Martin's Press.

Koontz, C. 2003. *The Nazi Conscience*. Cambridge, MA: Harvard University Press.

Lynd, R.S. and Lynd, H.M. 1965. *Middletown in Transition: A Study in Cultural Conflicts*. New York: Harcourt Brace Jovanovich.

Mosse, G.L. 1964. *The Crisis of German Ideology: Intellectual Origins of the Third Reich*. New York: Grosset and Dunlap.

Müller, J.-W. 2016. *What Is Populism?* Philadelphia: University of Pennsylvania Press.

O'Donnell, M. 2012. 'Dangerous undercurrent: Death, sacrifice and ruin in Third Reich Germany', *International Journal of Humanities and Social Science* 2 (9): 231–239.

Okrent, D. 2019. *The Guarded Gate: Bigotry, Eugenics, and the Law that Kept Two Generations of Jews, Italians and Other European Immigrants Out of America*. New York: Scribner.

Panayi, P. 2007. *Life and Death in a German Town: Osnabruck from the Weimar Republic to World War II and Beyond*. New York: Tauris Academic.

Paxton, R.O. 1998. 'The five stages of fascism', *Journal of Modern History* 70 (1): 1–23.

Paxton, R.O. 2004. *The Anatomy of Fascism*. New York: Alfred A. Knopf.

Petropoulis, J. 2000. *Faustian Bargain: The Art World in Nazi Germany*. New York: Oxford University Press.

Postel, C. 2007. *The Populist Vision*. New York: Oxford University Press.

Schuyler, M.W. 1985. 'The Ku Klux Klan in Nebraska, 1920–1930', *Nebraska History* 66(3): 234–256.

Thomas, H. 2006. *Watchdogs of Democracy? The Waning Washington Press Corps and How It Has Failed the Public*. New York: Scribner.

Wade, W.C. 1987. *The Fiery Cross: The Ku Klux Klan in America*. New York: Simon and Schuster.

Ward, E.K. 2017. 'Skin in the game: How anti-Semitism animates white nationalism', *The Public Eye*, Summer.

Wittgenstein, L. 1973. *Philosophical Investigations*. New York: Macmillan.

4

WHAT DO 'UNRULY' RIGHT-WING AUTHORITARIAN NATIONALISTS DO WHEN THEY RULE? THE US UNDER DONALD TRUMP

Ingar Solty

For Leo Panitch, in gratitude

In 2008, neoliberal financial market capitalism entered its biggest crisis since the 1930s. On 15 September of that year, the collapse of the investment bank Lehman Brothers caused a financial meltdown with global repercussions. Capitalism in its neoliberal phase had reinforced a tendency towards financial crises all across the globe: Mexico 1994–1995, South East Asia 1997–1998, Russia 1998–1999, Argentina 1998–2002. This time, however, the crisis began in the US – a core capitalist country. It was naturally the state's task to manage the crisis. The US state, however, is not just any kind of state; it developed special resources that created the political and institutional foundations of global capitalism, 'globalisation'. The country's economic recovery was up to Barack Obama, who became president at the high point of the crisis. He had initially run on the platform of a fiscal conservative, promoting pay-as-you-go, while his economic policy adviser on the campaign, Austan Goolsbee, had actually suggested a further subsumption of the working class under finance as the path to overcoming social inequality (cf. Solty 2008). Obama became the president of the crisis of capitalism. Eight years later, his successor, Donald Trump, a Republican, won the presidency. His campaign challenged 'globalisation' and liberal

internationalism and embraced, in the name of 'America First', economic protectionism in economic policy and an 'isolationist' scepticism regarding the US's traditional
interventionism in foreign policy. Trump triumphed even though the overwhelming
majority of economic, political, corporate and public media elites were against him.
His victory was a manifestation of an elite–mass rupture, particularly regarding the
assessment of globalisation and liberalism's promises of prosperity.

This chapter addresses three related questions: (i) the connection between the
Obama administration's crisis management and its globalisation policies, and
the rise of Trump's right-wing authoritarian nationalism; (ii) whether the Trump
administration caused a structural change of globalisation, emanating from the US
as the former bulwark of globalised capitalism; and (iii) how the Trump administration's policies compare to those of other right-wing 'populists'. Is it possible to
identify the limits of 'unruly' right-wing authoritarian nationalists in power?

Below, I first recapitulate historical-materialist crisis theory and state theory and
contextualise both in the contemporary debate on the periodisation of capitalism.
Then I sketch eight years of Obama rule and examine how his policies relate to the
rise of right-wing authoritarian nationalism, before analysing whether or not the
Trump administration actually pursued a nationalist politics of deglobalisation.

THEORY OF ORGANIC CRISES OF CAPITALISM AND
THE STATE'S TRANSFORMATIVE EXIT STRATEGIES

Despite their differences, the varieties of (neo-)Marxist theories are all characterised by a common assumption concerning the historical development of capitalism.
Having identified the limits of classical Marxist theories of imperialism, all start with
the premise that (i) capitalism has historically proven to be capable of significant
transformations; (ii) this indeterminate and non-linear development always neces-
sitates a historically concrete analysis as well as periodisation of capitalist social formations; and (iii) capitalism transforms itself during its *systemic* crises. In Marxist
political economy, influenced by Antonio Gramsci (Gef 7: 1561–1562), these are discussed as 'organic crises'; in French Regulation Theory, Lipietz (1985) distinguishes
between the 'small' conjunctural crises of capitalism and its 'big' crises, in which a
specific regime of accumulation and its particular mode of regulation have exhausted
their developmental potentials. The state, in which the relationship of class forces
is condensed (Poulantzas 2002: 154–191) and which operates as the central, institutional mechanism that manages the contradictions of an inherently crisis-prone
capitalism (Poulantzas 2002: 197–198), now has to seek a transformation of the

existing capitalist system – one which develops unevenly across geographic spaces (Harvey 2006) and within an international state system of unequal power resources (Hirsch 2005). Regarding the specific ways in which this process of transformation unfolds, two of Gramsci's concepts play a key role: 'trasformismo' and 'passive revolution'. According to Gramsci (cf. Gef 5: 1080, 1137–1141; Gef 6: 1242–1244), trasformismo describes a process of co-optation of the oppositional, reform-oriented anti-capitalist forces which, paradoxically, help modernise and hegemonically stabilise the existing system. The concept of passive revolution characterises a process in which pressure from below or external world order configurations enforce a modernisation from above and thus produce capitalism's transformations and the birth of a new accumulation regime and a new mode of regulation.

Within the limits of capitalist property relations and profitability, the state's crisis management is relatively contingent. In historically specific organic crises, various and even countering exit strategies are possible. In the end, the historical crisis transformations depend on the historically specific class coalitions from which they emerge. Historically, for instance, the organic crisis of the 1930s could produce both Nazi Germany's exit strategy of the elimination of organised labour plus imperialist expansion as well as Roosevelt's Keynesian 'New Deal'. In the US and the particular 1930s configuration, class struggles and rifts between various capital fractions – finance and industrial capital, internationalised and domestically oriented capital – were decisive factors for creating the space of manoeuvring for the state (Domhoff and Webber 2011; Klein 2016; Levine 1988; Roesler 2010).

Through the state's specific crisis management, the 'organic' or 'big crises' thus transform the mode of production, mode of life and the spatial arrangements of an inherently globalising capitalist system. As a result, post-crisis capitalism never looks like the status quo ante. And because of this, the periodisation of capitalism including the very specific state forms is crucial (Poulantzas 1973: 13).

Since its origins in the agrarian spaces of early seventeenth-century England (Wood 2002) capitalism has undergone four organic crises: (i) the Long Depression (1873–1896) with a transition from a liberal-internationalist ('Manchester') competitive capitalism to 'Organised Capitalism' and the age of inter-imperial rivalries (Cox 1987: 151–210); (ii) the Great Depression (1929–1939) which, by way of the Allied Forces' victory against fascism and US hegemony during the Cold War, internationalised the New Deal as Fordist welfare state capitalism under Keynesian regulation (Panitch and Gindin 2012: 67–107); (iii) the crisis of Fordism (1967–1979), from which neoliberal financial market capitalism emerged as a new developmental type (cf. Harvey 2007); and (iv) the organic crisis of this particular type of capitalism which began in 2007.

73

The onset of the global financial crisis coincided with the key question of whether or not it was, in fact, an organic crisis and, if so, which new type of capitalism would emerge from it based on which class coalitions and in the context of which international relationships of forces. Various Marxist perspectives, which assumed that we were in fact experiencing a big and even multiple crisis, now debated scenarios of 'post-neoliberalisation' (Brand 2011; Brand and Sekler 2009). Usually, varieties of three core scenarios were discussed: reforms leading to a transition towards 'green capitalism'; deepening of neoliberal financial market capitalism with an increasingly authoritarian state form; and revolutionary transition towards a kind of 'green socialism' (Bello 2009; Candeias 2014b; Jessop 2008; Rilling 2014; Solty 2011a). The process of class struggles over the shape of the new (world) order was often discussed with regards to Gramsci's concept of the 'interregnum' (Candeias 2014a; Solty 2011b, 2013) – a situation in which 'the old is dying and the new cannot be born', which, according to Gramsci (Gef 2: 354), leads to various 'morbid symptoms'.

The debate of whether or not, in the period following the global financial meltdown, we can still speak of an ongoing crisis and interregnum is itself ongoing. Decker and Sablowski (2017) maintain that the crisis consolidated neoliberal financial market capitalism; others have seen the birth of 'authoritarian capitalism' (Deppe 2013). And some have kept speaking of an interregnum pointing towards the insufficient cohesion of contemporary capitalism and the continued deep social and political symptoms of crises, including the rise of global Trumpism, and expressed scepticism about whether or not the concept of 'authoritarian capitalism' can actually and already describe the contemporary moment (Demirovic 2016: 296; Pile and Fisahn 2017: 37–41; Solty 2014).

However, everyone seems to agree that the crisis has intensified moments of authoritarian rule which threaten repercussions on globalisation (Koddenbrock 2018). Analyses focus on various aspects of authoritarianism: the rise of authoritarian leadership in the Philippines, India, Turkey, Hungary, Poland and Brazil; the increase in authoritarian measures within liberal-democratic states, such as the draconian sanctions against anti-austerity protests in Spain, the declaration of a (permanent) state of exception in France or the partially extra-legal methods and ways in which the European governments have stabilised the European monetary union (Bruff 2014; Deppe 2013; Oberndorfer 2013; Ryner 2015; Solty 2018a). Others have focused on the erosion of faith in the problem-solving capacities of liberal democracy and point towards the shrinking integrative capacities of the liberal political centre and the continental European 'catch-all' parties as well as the rise of 'right-wing populism' from below (Solty and Gill 2013) and the striking new dysfunctionality and ungovernability discourse among bourgeois intellectuals from above (Solty 2013: 67–71).

The question of internationalisation is decisive when it comes to the assessment of the state's crisis management. The increasing internationalisation of production has led to a simultaneous internationalisation of the state (Cox 1987). Forms of transnational statehood have emerged in the international arena, most notably in the European Union (Bieling 2006). International institutions were created under the conditions of empire. At the end of World War II, the US was at the peak of its power. Economically, it accounted for almost half of the world's global domestic product; financially, it was the creditor nation of Great Britain and France (which had won the war militarily but were financially bled dry), the US dollar was effectively the global currency, and the US dominated Fordist capitalism's international financial architecture through the Bretton Woods System as well as the World Bank and the International Monetary Fund (IMF); politically, the US was the most powerful state in the capitalist 'West' with the largest military and the nuclear bomb reinforcing this power; and ideologically, the three Hs – Harvard, Hollywood and Hippie bands – reinforced US hegemony in terms of ideology, culture and knowledge (Deppe et al. 2011). As the 'prototype of a global state' (Panitch 2002: 80), the US thus made global capitalism. The former international rivals Germany and Japan as well as South Korea were provided with one-sidedly advantageous trade relations in order to successfully integrate them into the empire of the capitalist West. The US's state vision was of a global system with identical rules for capital – initially in the 'Grand Area' of the West (Shoup and Minter 1977) and eventually, after the collapse of the Soviet Union and the Eastern Bloc states, also globally. This was essentially the vision of the World Trade Organization (WTO) (Panitch and Gindin 2012: 220) whose crisis during the Doha Round (2001–2006) paved the way for the projects of the Transatlantic Trade and Investment Partnership (TTIP) and the Trans-Pacific Partnership (TPP) as the next-best solutions (see Nölke 2018). 'Free trade capitalism' was always in the interest of the dominant states and globally most competitive capitals (Shaikh 2007: 50–68). As a result, this also led to resistance from semi-peripheral and peripheral states as well as from organised labour in the global North (Bieling 2018). A question to be answered is whether the challenges to the Western-dominated economic order through regional integration projects, especially in Asia, are also leading to new types of capitalism, hegemonic projects and new world order conceptions (Nölke 2018; Simon 2018).

Regarding the international dimension, 'organic crises' have always had repercussions in terms of the relation between cooperation and conflict and hence also war and peace. A key feature of the first two systemic crises – the Long Depression and the Great Depression – is that both led to increasing inter-imperialist rivalries and a fragmentation of the world market. In the interests of their politically organised, national bourgeoisies, national states pursued protectionist measures to protect national capitals from global competition and market forces. 'Hobbesian contender states' like Germany and Japan challenged the existing 'Lockean heartland' through military force (Van der Pijl 1998: 65–97). Militarisation and inter-imperialist (world) wars – World War I and World War II – were the ultimate consequence. Juxtaposed to these developments, the crisis of Fordism as well as the current crisis led to a commitment among state leaders to refrain from protectionist measures and even to deepen world market integration despite intensified competition and international rivalries resulting from overaccumulation and structural overcapacities (e.g. in the auto industry) and despite the threat of deflationary spirals associated with it (Gill and Solty 2013). The transnationalisation of capitalist production relations, which have created a transnationalised capitalist class as the dominant capital fraction within the empire (Robinson 2004: 33–84; Sklair 2001; Van der Pijl 1998), and the gradual disappearance of national bourgeoisies is suggested as an explanation for the difference between the first two and the last two organic crises (Panitch and Gindin 2012).

FAILURE OF GREEN CAPITALISM AND RISE OF RIGHT-WING AUTHORITARIAN NATIONALISM

The fact that the third and the most recent big crisis of capitalism did not lead to a disintegration of the world economy appears as evidence for the robust nature of internationalisation and the American empire. Trump's election as the 45th president of the US, however, elicits questions. He criticised 'free trade' and accused China and Germany with their respective current account surpluses vis-à-vis the US of unfair trading practices, seeking to counter them by proclaiming an 'America First' strategy. During his election campaign, he demanded renegotiations or even the termination of the 1994 North American Free Trade Agreement (Nafta) and announced an end to the negotiations concerning TPP and TTIP. He threatened China and Mexico with import tariffs of, respectively, 45 and 15 per cent. Two questions arise: What explains the rise of Trump in light of the political economy under Obama? Did Trump stick to his election campaign promises and did he actually conduct a protectionist gear change of the US economy?

The Democratic Party establishment surrounding Trump's defeated rival Hillary Clinton have sought to blame her primary election campaign rival, Bernie Sanders, and Russian interference in the election for her defeat (Clinton 2017). The rise of Trump cannot, however, be separated from Obama's crisis management, which can be divided into two main phases.

The first phase was the fiscal expansion at federal level. The core piece of this policy was the American Recovery and Reinvestment Act (ARRA) of 2009. It embodied the US variant of the stimulus programmes which nation-states across the globe initiated to prevent the effects of financial meltdown. As Obama's secretary of the treasury, Timothy Geithner (2014: 263), stated, this 'neo-Keynesian' policy was considered a lesson learned from the crisis of the 1930s, when most states cut expenditure to match the retreat of private sector investments. This politics of austerity by President Hoover in the US or Reich Chancellor Bruening in the Weimar Republic had catastrophic consequences. Economically, it led to a downward spiral which, politically, eliminated liberal democracies and replaced them with authoritarian and fascist regimes everywhere outside the islands of the US, Great Britain and the short-lived Spanish Republic of 1936 (Hobsbawm 1995: 109–141).

We now have detailed studies and investigative reports on the genealogy of ARRA (Conlan et al. 2017; Lizza 2012; Scheiber 2012; Suskind 2012; Wolffe 2011). They reveal deep rifts and struggles over the US administration's political course with a fiscally conservative (Wall Street) wing – led by Geithner and Obama's senior economic adviser, Larry Summers – and a more state-interventionist, green-capitalist wing grouped around Obama's Council of Economic Advisers chief, Christina Romer. Romer embodied the vision of a light version of a Green New Deal, which promised a (temporary) state-interventionist redynamisation – and thus also definancialisation – of neoliberal financial market capitalism and its surplus capital flooding speculatively into the financial markets. The vision ultimately sought to utilise the inevitable fiscal expansion as a kind of jump-starting mechanism financing green technologies, which could then function as an engine of growth for a new 'long wave' of capitalist prosperity with new industries developing around these new innovations (Romer 2009; Solty 2013: 15–71). The new productive investments then ought to create conditions for what Obama called a 'post-bubble economy' in a press release shortly after a decisive meeting with former Federal Reserve chief Paul Volcker (Grunwald 2013: 315; Obama 2009: 247). At the same time, green capitalism was connected to the assumption of renewal of US hegemony in the world by means of reindustrialisation (Romer 2009).

The above-mentioned accounts provide empirical material for a revisitation and renewal of materialist state theory. However, ARRA's three main contradictions are the most important aspect for our analysis here. Taken together, they embody the failure of the vision of a green-capitalist transition.

Firstly, financially, ARRA was too small to pave the way for a green-capitalist and post-neoliberalising exit path. The stimulus programme of US$787 billion was big enough to prevent the financial meltdown and limit the increase of mass unemployment. It was insufficient, however, to safeguard the US's return to its pre-crisis levels of growth, real incomes and employment. This also had to do with the fact that the fiscal expansion at the federal level was undermined by a hidden austerity programme at the local and state levels. All 50 US states except for Vermont have implemented balanced budget amendments. As acknowledged by Geithner (2014: 440), this reinforced the mechanism of (budget) 'disciplinary neoliberalism' (Gill 1998; Gill and Cutler 2015) and what Stephen Gill calls 'new constitutionalism'. As a result, despite ARRA, the US's state quota – the share of all economic activity accounted for by the state – only rose from 19.0 to 19.4 per cent between 2007 and 2010 (Kotlikoff 2011).

Secondly, ARRA was insufficiently green. Only US$27.2 billion (3.5 per cent of the stimulus programme) was used to jump-start green technologies. The overwhelming share was issued as public expenditures in favour of private construction companies (US$105.3 billion); the inevitable expansion of unemployment insurance payments and public healthcare expenditures in Medicare and Medicaid (US$67.92 billion); and tax cuts, especially for corporate employers (US$288 billion). Even China used a bigger share of its own stimulus package to finance a new green economy, directing 5.3 per cent (US$30.8 billion) invested in research and development targeting energy efficiency and renewable energies (Solty 2013: 29).

Thirdly, ARRA's employment policy was too market-oriented. Prior to Obama's start as president, he had been frequently compared to Franklin Delano Roosevelt. The contrast between Obama and Roosevelt was nowhere as striking as here. Roosevelt's New Deal shifted the relationship between state and market significantly to the public sector. Roosevelt absorbed unproductive capital by means of a marginal tax rate of 94 per cent on all incomes over US$200 000. His administration reinvested this new revenue in new forms of statecraft such as the Civilian Conservation Corps (1933–1942) and the Works Progress Administration (1935–1943). Taken together, these two public employment programmes created a total of 5.8 million new public sector jobs (Levine 1988: 64–91). In contrast, Obama rejected any such active employment policy. Largely as a result of the hidden austerity programme at the local and state levels, more than 1.1 million public sector jobs were lost during Obama's first term. Had public sector employment continued at the same pace as it did under his predecessor, Republican president George W. Bush – that is, under neoliberal normalcy conditions – Obama's administration ought to have added 1.2 million public sector jobs (Solty 2013: 35–39).

In short, the US state intervened in a comparatively much smaller dimension than it had done during the 1930s. And where it did intervene significantly, as in the partial nationalisation of the auto industry, Obama pursued a 'hands-off approach'. This entailed the state refraining from linking the need to rescue the ailing private corporations to actively impacting their investment strategies. The Obama administration did not undertake any measure towards greening them and shifting their course towards technological conversion. It did not even intervene in the composition of the managing boards, with the exception of sacking General Motors chief Richard Wagoner. The only way the state massively intervened was to halve the wages for all new hirings – from US\$48 to US\$24 – in the name of 'global competitiveness' (Solty 2013: 53–54). In this regard too, the Obama administration did the opposite of Roosevelt's. Instead of pursuing a competitive austerity approach, Roosevelt implemented the Wagner Act of 1935 to counter the downward pressure on real wages and the Fair Labor Standards Act of 1938 to facilitate labour unionisation. His administration further introduced a minimum wage as well as a public unemployment insurance and old-age security system.

Obama's policies hence facilitated the rise of the Tea Party movement and, on its back, the unforeseeable return of Republicans during the 2010 midterm elections, which severely restricted the administration's room for manoeuvring. In 2010, around the time of the G20 summit in Toronto, the US had already shifted its economic policy towards austerity, including on the federal level. Insofar as it coincided with the troika's – EU Commission, European Central Bank, IMF – first Memorandum of Understanding with Greece in May 2010, the two biggest regions in the world economy simultaneously pursued an austerity turn. This entailed a growth, employment and competitive strategy of *internal* devaluation – through downward pressure on wages and other 'competitive austerity' measures (see Albo 1994) – as well as *external* devaluation – through monetary policy means such as the Fed's extreme low-interest policy. Especially the latter was a big competitive advantage vis-à-vis the Eurozone insofar as the common currency only makes a strategy of internal devaluation possible, given that the Eurozone member states no longer have their own currencies which they could devalue in order to increase competitiveness. This may also explain why the politics of shredding collective bargaining systems (Schulten and Mueller 2013) as well as the budget-tightening constitutionalism of the new European economic governance have been pursued so viciously in the Eurozone (Oberndorfer 2013; Ryner 2015; Solty and Werner 2016).

The fact that the two economic regions, which remain the largest in the world, simultaneously pursued a strategy for growth which sought to export its way out of the crisis created a system in which competing states seek to gain a larger piece of a world economy cake whose growth, when compared to pre-crisis levels, has been relatively slow (McNally 2012). In other words, the almost global austerity turn has created a system of a global beggar-thy-neighbour capitalism (Solty 2016e: 31–34). The consequence is increasing international competition and rivalry.

The socio-economic fallout of the US's austerity turn was significant with regards to Trump's electoral triumph. The crisis and austerity turn have had tremendous consequences for the state of the US working classes, both in terms of real incomes as well as wealth inequality. Especially because Obama, unlike Roosevelt, refrained from an institutional empowerment of labour unions as a regulatory mechanism counteracting the downward pressure on real incomes (through a legislative initiative such as the Employee Free Choice Act, for instance), the impact of the crisis on the labour market was that the so-called economic recovery came in the shape of an '(involuntary) part-time/low-wage epidemic' (Zuckerman 2012). According to a study by the Federal Reserve, only 22 per cent of all jobs lost during the crisis had belonged to the low-wage sector, compared to 59 per cent of all the jobs created during the so-called recovery (National Employment Law Project 2012). This outcome has impacted the millennials generation in particular, who are leaving higher education with an average debt burden of US$26 000 for a bachelor's degree. The labour market situation has created a heavy dequalification of the commodity labour power. For instance, according to Bureau of Labor Statistics, 750 000 college graduates were working full-time in the fast-food industry in 2013, while 42 per cent of all fast-food workers had at least attended college.

The negative development of real incomes has also worsened wealth inequality. In 2007–2008, Obama's campaign also included a critique of its growth. In 2008, wealth inequality in the US had reached its peak since the beginning of the Great Depression in 1929, and it went up under Obama's leadership. A study by economists Emmanuel Saez and Gabriel Zucman (2016) showed that the number of private households with a net wealth of between US$20.6 and US$72.8 million (the top 0.1 per cent) rose from 7 per cent at the beginning of the neoliberal era in 1978 to 19 per cent in 2009, the year that Obama took office. It increased even further to 22 per cent in 2012 (Saez and Zucman 2016). At the same time, the share of the bottom 90 per cent fell from 37 to 25 per cent between 1985 and 2009 and ended up at 23 per cent by the end of Obama's first term in 2012 (Saez and Zucman 2016).

The political fallout of this crisis management was the perpetuation and actual deepening of the US's crisis of representation. Since the austerity turn, the approval ratings for all political institutions have dropped to record lows. This is particularly the case as far as Congress is concerned. According to RealClearPolitics, 33.4 per cent of Americans held a favourable view of Congress when Obama came to office in January 2009, while 60 per cent held a negative one. This figure of dissatisfaction fell even further during his two terms, reaching 76.3 per cent unfavourability and only 15.0 per cent favourability by the final week before the presidential elections of November 2016.[1]

The consequence was a 'populist gap' (Flecker and Kirschenhofer 2007). Both Sanders's left 'populism' (cf. Solty 2016b) and Trump's right-wing authoritarianism could push into this vacuum (Solty 2016a). The US two-party system was essentially characterised by a polarisation with three poles: a neoliberal-imperial 'centre' (represented by Hillary Clinton and her 'Stay the course'/'America is already great' message) which came under attack from these two forces from the Left and Right (Brie and Candeias 2016).

WHEN RIGHT-WING AUTHORITARIAN NATIONALISM WIELDS POLITICAL POWER

Trump's election was unforeseen and unwanted by the economic, political and (media) ideological elites. Most campaign donations from the Fortune 100 corporations went to Hillary Clinton, the majority of the big private and for-profit as well as public news stations supported Clinton and, even after Trump's nomination as the Republican candidate, the Republican Party establishment largely refused to support his effort. A few weeks before election day 50 Republican foreign policy advisers came out against Trump in an open letter in the *New York Times* (8 August 2016), stating that he was 'a threat to . . . national security'. The fact that Trump was rejected by large segments of the US elites had little to do with his rabid racism or sexism. Rather, it was the consequence of Trump's rhetorical rejection of two sacred core interests of the dominant transnational-imperial fraction within the US power bloc: global capitalism ('free trade') and the American empire created to safeguard its existence by all means necessary, including military force.

Hence, during his campaign Trump often sounded like a 'left-winger' – for instance, when he criticised the 'war on terror' as a disaster: when the US began the war in 2002 it was faced by a loose network of not more than a few hundred al-Qaida terrorists, but was now faced by 30 000 to 40 000 Isis fighters with millions of sympathisers around the world. According to the 'Costs of War' research project at the US Ivy League Brown University, the US war effort in Afghanistan,

Iraq and Pakistan cost US$4.79 trillion from 2002 until 2016 (Crawford 2016) – more than sixfold what the state spent on the entire stimulus programme against the global financial crisis. Given this tremendous waste for a lost war, Trump easily won the election in the populous Midwestern states, devastated by more than two decades of free trade and the economic draft, when he publicly regretted what kind of infrastructure investments would have been possible with these kinds of funds (Carl 2016).

Trump's victory was a historical novelty. First, the US in general and the Republicans in particular have frequently seen (far-right) grassroots revolts during primary elections. In 2012, the party base also expressed an 'anything but Romney' mentality. And still, by the end of the primary election season, the party establishment had managed to push their preferred candidate through (Solty 2013: 241–248). The 2016 US presidential election thus marked a temporary loss of control of the party elite. The US symbolises a paradoxical development: the crisis of representation does not lead to the emergence of smaller third, fourth, fifth and even sixth parties. On the surface, the Democratic and Republican party institutions appear stable and robust. Support for the Libertarian Party to the Right and the Greens to the Left was minimal in 2016. Yet, this external stability is juxtaposed by internal erosion. The forces of populist revolt appear to be able to replace the neoliberal-imperial 'centre' even within their own traditional institutions (Solty 2016f). Second, the 2016 presidential elections ended with the triumph of the far-right candidate, contradicting many political science scholars who have presumed, on the basis of Duverger's law, that elections in first-past-the-post electoral systems are won in 'the centre' because, while far-right/left candidates might be able to enthuse their bases, their antagonising style of politics leads to landslide defeats in wider elections due to the logic of the 'lesser evil' (Duverger 1972: 22–32). This happened to far-right candidate Barry Goldwater in 1964 and left-wing social democrat George McGovern in 1972 (see Solty 2016c: 12–14).

Trump's triumph thus reinforces the moment of the transnational-imperial power bloc fraction's temporary loss of *political* control. The authoritarian-nationalist Right – this was proven by 2016 – is increasingly capable of seizing *political* power. The far Right has risen as a political force in Europe and elsewhere: it has triumphed in Brexit (against the entire elite class) and has already come to power in Brazil, India, the Philippines, Turkey, Poland and Hungary, while partaking in political power through coalition governments in Italy and Austria (Solty 2016d). This means that we can now study empirically what the 'unruly' right-wing authoritarian nationalists do when they rule.

The key question is whether the election of right-wing authoritarian nationalist politicians actually leads to matching policies. Did Trump in power also mean nationalist policies? Did Trump actually deliver on his campaign promises? Was his administration able to enforce a (selectively) protectionist programme? If not, how can we explain the discrepancy between his campaign promises and his realpolitik?

Analysis of the first two years of the Trump presidency initially had to operate on the basis of scenarios. Three appeared plausible: a national-social right-wing Keynesianism, with massive infrastructure investments; the containment of Trump by the transnational-imperial fraction in the US power bloc; and a 'behemoth' scenario in the sense of Franz Neumann's (1984) analysis, which might be helpful for a discussion of the tensions, rifts and struggles in the institutional arena and various levels of power of the state.

The first scenario appeared to wield some kind of explanatory power in the first two weeks into the Trump administration. Trump seemed dead set on realising his promises. He initiated a general, illiberal immigration law prohibiting visitors and migrants from many Muslim-majority countries ('Muslim ban'), with the exception of Egypt and Saudi Arabia; he went ahead with preparations for the construction of a wall at the US–Mexican border; and he terminated negotiations on TPP and TTIP by executive order. The latter was a harsh blow against the transnational-imperial fraction in the power bloc, because both treaties had entailed crucial geopolitical goals by excluding Russia from TTIP and China from TPP in order to maintain US hegemony and force China in particular into subordinating itself to US domination in the hierarchy of the international division of labour.

These initial policies antagonised dominant capitals. The 'Muslim ban' created a backlash from transnational corporations given the negative impact it had both in terms of resource and export markets as well as the feared immobility of many transnational employees. Trump's 'American wall' antagonised big agribusiness, which depends on Mexican agricultural workers with precarious immigration statuses, making them vulnerable to exploitation. The termination of TPP and TTIP evoked resistance from (neo)liberal internationalists.

TRANSNATIONAL-IMPERIAL CONTAINMENT OF TRUMP

Two years into the Trump presidency, the most plausible scenario was the containment of Trump. His administration acted quite erratically, both domestically and, especially, in foreign policy. This also had to do with the internal struggles between the economic nationalist wing and the imperial internationalists over the course of direction. The signs for the transnational-imperial containment of Donald Trump were nonetheless obvious. Symbolically, the defeat of the economic nationalist wing of the Trump administration was expressed by the gradual disempowering of Trump's campaign architect and senior adviser in the White House, Steve Bannon, the far-right media mogul and self-declared economic nationalist.

In retrospect, it seems clear that Trump's initial decisions were the result of his inevitable proximity to and gratitude towards Bannon. During the campaign, Bannon had shifted Trump towards a protectionist and 'isolationist' course that won him the populous Midwest, which had more than 20 years of experience with the effects of trade in the guise of deindustrialisation, mass unemployment, infrastructure decay, population exodus and the opioid crisis. The Midwest responded positively to Trump's right-wing critique of globalisation, his message of infrastructure investments and his anti-establishment rhetoric. In his speech on the eve of his campaign, Trump announced that this was 'our Independence Day' when 'the American working class' would 'finally strike back' (ABC News, 8 November 2016).

After the electoral triumph, Bannon's power and influence was at its peak but it dwindled gradually because of the resistance against an economically nationalist course, starting with his removal from the National Security Council and ending with his dismissal shortly after the extreme-right terrorist attack of Charlottesville.

The containment of Trump by the transnational-imperial faction can be reconstructed at two levels of analysis: his cabinet and his realpolitik.

Trump's cabinet

Measured by the aggregated private wealth of Trump's secretaries, the Trump administration was not only the richest administration since the end of World War II, but also had stronger and more direct ties to the capitalist class than its predecessors. Trump's cabinet recruited itself mostly from three interest groups which all directly represent particular capital interests or are strongly connected to them: (Wall Street) finance capital, fossil-fuel capital (oil and gas) and the old Republican foreign policy establishment with its strong ties to the arms industry.

Trump and finance capital

The strong ties between finance capital and the Trump administration were particularly evident with respect to the Wall Street investment bank Goldman Sachs (GS). Behind JP Morgan, GS is the world's second largest investment bank, accounting for a global market share of 6.9 per cent. Previous US administrations recruited their economic policy agents from GS. Bill Clinton appointed the former co-CEO Robert Rubin as his secretary of the treasury. Rubin implemented Nafta and deregulated financial markets. This included the elimination of Franklin Roosevelt's

Glass-Steagall Act of 1933 which, in light of the Wall Street crash of 1929, had sepa-rated investment banks from commercial banks. George W. Bush also recruited his treasury secretary from GS. Prior to joining the Bush administration, Hank Paulson had been GS chairman and CEO and had been responsible for the collateralised debt obligations, which were later identified as the origin of the global financial crisis (Blyth 2013: 28). As Bush's treasury secretary, Paulson then initiated the bank bailouts.

During his campaign, Trump expressed a strong rhetorical critique of Wall Street. He frequently used GS as the symbolic manifestation of the 'establishment'. In February 2016, Trump attacked his Republican primary opponent Ted Cruz by saying: 'I know the guys at Goldman Sachs. They have total control over him. Just like they have total control over Hillary Clinton' (CNN, 15 March 2017). Trump's last campaign ad featured an image of the current GS CEO, Lloyd Blankfein, associating him with what the ad called the 'global power structure' which had enriched the elites and 'plundered' the US working class (CNN, 30 November 2016). Trump also insisted that Clinton's multiple Wall Street speeches, for which she received an average com-pensation of US$225 000, were, in reality, 'secret meetings with international banks' pursuing the sinister goal of 'destroying US sovereignty' (CNN, 30 November 2016).

During the process of recruiting his administration, Trump conducted a com-plete U-turn. The administration's positions in economic policy were filled with peo-ple belonging to Wall Street. Trump appointed Gary Cohn as chief of his National Economic Council. From 2006 until 2017, Cohn had been president and chief oper-ating officer of GS – the second most powerful man behind Blankfein. In the Trump administration, Cohn's key political projects were the biggest tax cut for corpora-tions and the super-rich since the end of World War II and the elimination of the moderate healthcare programme introduced by Barack Obama ('Obamacare').

Trump appointed Steven Mnuchin as his secretary of the treasury. From 1985 until 2002, Mnuchin had been a leading GS banker but left to create a few spec-ulative hedge funds, speculating particularly in housing. His nickname became 'Foreclosure King'. As treasury secretary, Mnuchin declared deregulation of finan-cial markets his top priority. This included eliminating Obama's quite moderate Dodd-Frank financial markets regulation. As early as his second week in office, Trump signed an executive order to follow through with this initiative. Apart from financial deregulation, Mnuchin was also the architect of the most radical tax-cutting programme in US postwar history. The tax reform would be legislated by the end of December 2017. It cut the corporate tax rate from 35 to 21 per cent and the marginal income tax rate from 39.6 to 35 per cent. It also eliminated taxes on large inheritances such as the 'alternative minimum tax' and the wealth tax. Trump announced his tax cuts for the rich in the name of the US working class: 'This is a revolutionary change, and the biggest winners will be the everyday American workers as jobs start pouring into our country, as companies start competing for American labour and as wages start going up at levels that you haven't seen in many years' (*New York Times*, 27 September 2017). He replicated the neoliberal voodoo credo by saying that this tax reform would 'restore our competitive edge so we can create better jobs and higher wages for American workers' (CNN, 22 October 2017). Estimates of the costs of Trump's tax reform to the US taxpayer ranged between US$1.5 trillion and US$7.0 trillion. Republican Senator Patrick J. Toomey, member of the congressional Finance Committee, said, however, that he was 'confident that a growing economy would pay for the tax cuts. This tax plan will be deficit reducing' (*New York Times*, 27 September 2017). Shortly before the congressional vote on the tax cuts, the Treasury justified the future costs with a one-page analysis. Earlier on, the government had announced that welfare cuts of US$26.7 billion during the 2018 fiscal year and US$3.7 trillion until 2027 would help finance the tax cuts for capital and the super-rich (*New York Times*, 22 May 2017).

The Trump administration justified the tax cuts in the name of global competitiveness. In consequence, there were similar demands from capitalist classes all around the world. League of German Industrialists president Dieter Kampf called Trump's tax plan an 'absolute declaration of war', stating that the new German government 'must face the aggravated international competition right away' and also cut corporate tax rates (*Handelsblatt*, 15 December 2017). Overall, the world has entered a global corporate tax rate war. In the first three quarters of 2017 alone, nine OECD countries cut their capital taxes (see Solty 2018b). This accelerated a trend which has seen the average corporate income tax rate in OECD countries drop from 32.5 per cent in 2000 to 23.9 per cent in 2018.

The close finance capital–government ties, however, went beyond Cohn and Mnuchin. Trump's secretary of commerce, Wilbur Ross, was another investment banker. On the Forbes list of the richest persons on Earth, he was credited with a net wealth of US$2.5 billion. Ross also stems from the Wall Street financial elite and enjoyed close contacts to the Democratic Party leadership. During the 1990s he worked for the Clinton administration. Moreover, he advised the New York mayor, Rudy Giuliani, on privatisations and helped open up public property for private capital accumulation. Ross is also a vehement supporter of 'free trade' (Batt and Appelbaum 2017).

Trump and fossil fuel capital

The second societal anchor of the Trump administration was the petrol and gas industry, which has traditionally been particularly close to the Republican Party and southern 'new' capital interests. Trump's first secretary of state, Rex Tillerson, had been chief executive director of ExxonMobil, the seventh-largest corporation in the world measured by gross revenue and also the seventh largest in terms of market capitalisation. ExxonMobil's gross revenue in 2016 was US$218.6 billion and increased to US$237.2 billion in the first year of the Trump presidency, becoming the second-largest US corporation in 2018, according to the Fortune 500 list. ExxonMobil has also enforced its economic interests politically and ideologically. The corporation is accused of financing global campaigns denying human-made climate change. Tillerson himself is a self-declared supporter of 'free trade' (including TPP) and of right-wing libertarian ideas.

Trump's first secretary of energy, Rick Perry, was the former governor of Texas. Perry is closely connected to the fossil fuel industry. Until the end of 2016, he sat on the board of Energy Transfer Partners, one of the biggest capital investment firms in the US. It owns a gigantic web of pipelines, including the 1 800-kilometre-long Dakota Access Pipeline, whose construction plans invoked a resistance movement of local indigenous and environmentalist groups. On 24 January 2017, Trump pushed for its construction by executive order and enforced it with massive police violence against protestors. Perry's immediate economic interests are met with his public and political stance on climate-change insofar as he represents one of the loudest voices of climate-change denialists. This continued into his work for the Trump administration. In an interview with CNBC (10 June 2017), Perry noted that carbon emissions were 'not the main cause of climate change'.

Scott Pruitt, Trump's first administrator of the Environmental Protection Agency (EPA), from 17 February 2017 until 6 July 2018, represents the same ideological positions. Pruitt became attorney general of the oil-intensive state Oklahoma with massive funding from the fossil fuel industry and then sued the EPA, which he came to head, more than a dozen times, declaring himself to be 'a leading advocate against the EPA's activist agenda' (*New York Times*, 11 August 2017). In office, he was the main architect behind Trump's rejection of the Paris climate agreement. When Pruitt stepped down in July 2018, his position was filled by Andrew R. Wheeler, another lobbyist of the coal industry against Obama's moderate energy policy and a former employee of Republican senator James Inhofe, one of the most rabid right-wing climate-change denialists.

Trump and the Republican foreign policy establishment

Trump ran his election campaign on a platform highly critical of the US's 'war on terror' and imperial approach to foreign policy. He called the 'war on terror' a 'mistake', the situation in Iraq 'a mess' and the 2011 North Atlantic Treaty Organization

(Nato) war against Libya 'a disaster' (CNN, 25 February 2016). He emphasised that, when it came to going to war, he was going to be 'very, very cautious' and 'a lot slower' than Clinton, whom he called 'trigger-happy' (NBC, 7 September 2016). As early as the end of 2015, Trump (2015: 37) stressed that, as president, he would order a complete troop removal from Afghanistan, and during the CBS primary debate of 13 February 2016 he said: '[W]e've been in the Middle East for 15 years, and we haven't won anything. We've spent $5 trillion dollars in the Middle East … we have to rebuild our country. We have to rebuild our infrastructure. You listen to [Jeb Bush and the Republican party establishment], you're going to be there for another 15 years. You'll end up with world war three.'

In sharp contrast to this rhetoric, Trump not only deployed more troops to Afghanistan but his administration also put the top military personnel responsible for the 'war on terror' in charge of his foreign policy. Trump appointed James Mattis (later replaced by Mark Esper) as his secretary of defense. From 2002 until 2004, Mattis had been a brigadier and major general in Afghanistan and Iraq. And in 2010, he became successor to General David Petraeus as commander of the US Central Command in the Middle East, East Africa and Central Asia. Mattis is thus the leader responsible for the US war operations not only in Iraq but also in Syria, and he was the protagonist behind the Nato war against Libya in 2011.

Furthermore, Trump's longest-serving White House chief of staff and former deputy secretary of homeland security, John F. Kelly, also belongs to the Republican foreign policy establishment and has very close personal ties to the arms industry. Trump's budget plan for 2018 implemented cuts or even eliminations of all federal welfare state programmes. This included public housing, public education and subsidies for the arts. Only three of the 80 federal programmes saw budget increases. All were connected to the military and repressive state apparatuses: the Department of Homeland Security, Veterans' Affairs, and the Pentagon. US military expenditures have for a long time been the highest in the world and higher than the next seven countries combined. In Trump's first budget, military expenditures increased by US$54 billion to US$639 billion. According to the Stockholm International Peace Research Institute, US arms expenditures are three times as high as China's (US$215 billion) and almost ten times as high as Russia's (US$69.2 billion). The US continued this general trajectory with the 2019 budget. On 28 September 2018, the US Congress approved a defence spending bill of US$892.7 billion, a 53 per cent increase in just two years. At the same time, the Trump administration put Nato member states under pressure to increase their own military spending according to Nato's two per cent of GDP demand. The US under Trump is therefore chiefly responsible for the new global arms race the world has entered.

Authoritarian-imperial financial market capitalism: Trump's realpolitik

Trump's realpolitik can be characterised as a resurgence of neoliberal financial market capitalism. In fact, the Trump administration radicalised the status quo with a libertarian bend. It represented a politics of 'accumulation by dispossession' (Harvey 2003: 137–182) and of new 'Landnahme [land grab]' (Dörre 2009). In this sense, its policies were oriented towards creating new profitable investment opportunities for surplus capital which in the context of overaccumulation and increasing competitive rivalries can no longer find channels of profitability. This can be illustrated with the Apple corporation, which Obama's and also Trump's reindustrialisation strategy focused on. In April 2017, Apple surpassed the US$250 billion threshold in uninvested cash reserves (*Wall Street Journal*, 30 April 2017). By 2018, this sum had increased to US$285 billion, equalling more or less the entire GDP of nations such as Denmark, Finland, Egypt, Pakistan or the Philippines. Trump's accumulation by dispossession strategy, opening up previously decommodified aspects of societal life to private capital accumulation, stretched across various policy arenas, from extractive industries in natural reserves to the education sector. His secretary of education, Betsy DeVos, heiress of a multi-billion fortune and self-declared market fundamentalist, pursued the agenda of the systematic privatisation of public schools and their replacement with publicly subsidised, private and for-profit charter schools.

Trump's announcement of infrastructure investments of US$1.5 billion must not be seen as contradicting this general agenda. Rather, they were an integral part of it. It was not aimed at increasing public expenditures in a Keynesian manner. Instead, it amounted to a plan of private–public partnerships and the privatisation of public infrastructure, including highways, bridges and tunnels. The details of the plan were developed by Vice-President Mike Pence, who, when he was still Tea Party Republican governor of Indiana, had implemented a very similar plan in his own state.

Just as the rise of Trump's 'right-wing populism' is no American exceptionalism but a *pars pro toto* of the ascent of right-wing authoritarian nationalist forces all around the world, so his realpolitik is part of a general revival of neoliberal policies under authoritarian prerogatives in a global beggar-thy-neighbour capitalism. This revival is also represented by the election of Wall Street investment banker Emmanuel Macron as the president in France, the billionaire Babiš as the president of the Czech Republic or the election of Sebastian Kurz as the chancellor of Austria. All of these politicians have invoked global competitiveness in order to cut taxes for the wealthy and pursue anti-worker labour market reforms, such as the reintroduction of a 12-hour workday in Austria or the shift towards a hire-and-fire system in France.

The US in the trade war

Many people assume that the Trump administration pursued a politics of protectionism. It is true that global beggar-thy-neighbour capitalism has increased international competition and global rivalries. However, the perception of a new American protectionism which aims at limiting 'free trade' is misleading. In reality, the US threatens protectionist measures and occasionally also implements them, not as an end in itself but rather as a means to further deepen 'free trade' and world market integration. The goal is to enforce the strictly neoliberal rules of a market-oriented developmental path and of private property guarantees overruling democratic decision-making processes. In the Trump administration's first official trade agenda of March 2017,[2] published two months into Trump's presidency, the core trade-political objectives were defined: 'use all possible sources of leverage to encourage other countries to open their markets to U.S. exports of goods and services' with the goal to '[b]reak down unfair trade barriers in other markets that block U.S. exports'. And far from eliminating the WTO, the goal was to pursue a 'more aggressive approach' to ensure that all countries around the world fulfilled the WTO's harsh private property guarantees. The objective was to safeguard 'that more markets are truly open to American goods and services and to enhance, rather than restrict, global trade and competition', with a special focus on protecting intellectual property rights.

This general orientation in trade policy was also kept in the trade agenda of 2018.[3] A particular focus was now directed at 'improving export opportunities' as well as the enforcement of 'real market competition' vis-à-vis state-interventionist developmental models – namely, China's.

For these strategic objectives, the approach to negotiate trade agreements bilaterally is the key resource of power. Under Trump, instead of a protectionist economic foreign policy, the US pursued a neo-Reaganite one which utilises the gigantic US domestic market as leverage to enforce improved export and foreign direct investment opportunities through bilateral means.

In this effort the US benefited from the significantly increased US domestic market export dependency of Germany and China. Germany's current account surplus vis-à-vis the US grew by 43 percentage points and US$64.2 billion between 2007 and 2017, while the Chinese trade surplus grew by 46 per cent and US$369.8 billion. The EU's and China's moralising discursive focus on multilateralism, which Angela Merkel and Xi Jinping expressed at the World Economic Forums of 2016 and 2017, is thus an ideological defence strategy against the power-political approach of the US in global beggar-thy-neighbour capitalism.

EXPLAINING TRUMP'S TRADE AND FOREIGN POLICY U-TURN

The crucial state-theoretical question is how one might explain Trump's U-turn, especially in trade and foreign policy – that is, his ultimate containment by the transnational-imperial faction in the US power bloc. It appears that the ruling 'centre' is *politically* increasingly weakened. Brexit, the Trump election and the rise of right-wing authoritarian nationalism in general, as well as the rise of a third, anti-neoliberal pole of conflict-oriented left-wing social democracy and democratic socialism (like Jeremy Corbyn's Labour Party in the UK or the Bernie Sanders campaign and Sanders's Democrats in the US), obviously demarcate real or impending losses of control by the neoliberal-imperial forces inside the core capitalist countries.

However, materialist state theory has identified a crucial distinction between *political* and *societal* power. Seizing governmental power is far from seizing control over the economic and social development of society. This affects both left-wing and right-wing 'populism'. Left-wing projects oriented towards taking power, such as the project of Syriza coming to power in Greece in January 2015, are facing the tremendous challenge of the 'structural power' of capital (Gill and Law 1993: 93–101): capital's mobility, and hence capital flight capacity, and its power resource of the investment strike.

The antagonism between political and societal power impacts not only left-wing politics but also right-wing authoritarian nationalism and those elements that remained of Bannon's 'shadow government' in the Trump administration, represented by the protectionist US trade representative Robert Lighthizer or Peter Navarro, the economically nationalist director of the new Office of Trade and Manufacturing Policy, which Bannon initiated. Right-wing authoritarian nationalism hardly has a real political project. As a literally reactionary movement with underdeveloped social and political theory foundations and conceptual alternatives (cf. Honderich 1994: 320; Robin 2017), the far Right depends on the old elites' expertise. Moreover, the transnationalisation of capitalist production and value chains functions as a kind of normative power of the factual. This particular economic base is the foundation of the social power of the transnational-imperial faction which compensates for the increasing instability of its political power and its political weakening. As a result, those aspects and elements of the Trump administration's pro-capitalist agenda which were oriented against neoliberal free trade capitalism and against this particular base of the transnational-imperial faction's power proved to be unenforceable. Similarly, as in other countries where right-wing authoritarian nationalists are in power, it appears that their role is rather to implement pro-capitalist and accumulation-by-dispossession policies which under normal conditions and through the established state corridors of compromise and consent could not be enforced. This includes, for instance, Bolsonaro's direct attack on the welfare state structures established by Lula's Workers' Party and the opening up of natural reservations in the Amazon rainforest for capitalist extractivism; it includes the new 'slave' law in Hungary which enables capitalist businesses to extract up to 400 unpaid overtime hours from workers per year; and it includes the introduction of the 12-hour workday in Austria (Solty 2018c). Ultimately, right-wing populism's passivising dispositif, which distinguishes it from left-wing populism's activising dispositif, is the crucial obstacle to the political mobilisation of nationalist forces (see Solty and Werner 2016). This means that at the end of the day only the common goals of both capital fractions, transnationalised and domestically oriented capital, can be realised under right-wing authoritarian rule: in this case only radically libertarian policies, which only find some resistance in less energy-intensive high-tech capital, and the politics of corporate tax rate cuts. In the end, the Trump presidency is a kind of Brechtian learning play about the relationship between political and social power in global capitalism, as well as a learning play about what 'unruly' right-wing authoritarian nationalists do and cannot do when they rule. As unruly as they may appear during election campaigns, they end up serving, in the most ruthless ways, the economic interests of the ruling class.

NOTES

1   https://www.realclearpolitics.com/epolls/other/congressional_job_approval-903.html.
2   https://ustr.gov/sites/default/files/files/reports/2017/AnnualReport/Chapter%20I%20
     -%20The%20President%27s%20Trade%20Policy%20Agenda.pdf.
3   https://ustr.gov/sites/default/files/files/Press/Reports/2018/AR/2018%20Annual%20
     Report%20FINAL.PDF.

REFERENCES

Albo, G. 1994. 'Competitive austerity and the impasse of capitalist employment policy'. In R. Miliband and L. Panitch (eds), *Between Globalism and Nationalism*. Pontypool: Merlin Press, pp. 144–170.

Batt, R. and Appelbaum, E. 2017. 'Who is Wilbur Ross?' *American Prospect*, Summer Issue. Accesssed 13 December 2019, prospect.org/article/who-wilbur-ross.

Bello, W. 2009. 'From neoliberalism to global social democracy'. Lecture, Pace University, New York, 17 April. Accessed 13 December 2019, https://www.transform-network.net/de/blog/article/from-neoliberalism-to-global-social-democracy/.

Bieling, H.-J. 2006. 'Formen transnationaler Staatlichkeit'. In L. Bretthauer, A. Gallas, J. Kannankulam and I Stützle (eds), *Poulantzas Lesen*. Hamburg: VSA, pp. 223–239.

Bieling, H.-J. 2018. 'Jenseits der (neo-)liberal-kosmopolitischen Hegemonie? Die "Doppelkrise" der transatlantischen Globalisierungspolitik', *Zeitschrift für Internationale Beziehungen* 25 (2): 164–180.

Blyth, M. 2013. *Austerity: The History of a Dangerous Idea*. Oxford: Oxford University Press.

Brand, U. 2011. *Postneoliberalismus? Aktuelle Konflikte – gegenhegemoniale Strategien*. Hamburg: VSA.

Brand, U. and Sekler, N. 2009. 'Postneoliberalism: A beginning debate', *Development Dialogue* 51: 5–14.

Brie, M. and Candeias, M. 2016. 'Rückkehr der Hoffnung: Für eine offensive Doppelstrategie', *Luxemburg*, November. Accessed 13 December 2019, https://www.zeitschrift-luxemburg.de/rueckkehr-der-hoffnung-fuer-eine-offensive-doppelstrategie/.

Bruff, I. 2014. 'The rise of authoritarian neoliberalism', *Rethinking Marxism* 2 (1): 113–129.

Candeias, M. 2014a. 'Szenarien grüner Transformation'. In M. Brie (ed.), *Futuring: Perspektiven der Transformation im Kapitalismus über ihn hinaus*. Münster: Westfälisches Dampfboot, pp. 303–329.

Candeias, M. 2014b. 'Wenn das Alte stirbt …' In M. Brie (ed.), *Die organische Krise des Finanzmarktkapitalismus*. Berlin: Dietz, pp. 14–28.

Carl, J. 2016. 'The Red Wall', *National Review* (December). Accessed 13 December 2019, www.nationalreview.com/magazine/2016-12-05-0000/donald-trump-win-voters-midwest.

Clinton, H. 2017. *What Happened*. New York: Simon & Schuster.

Conlan, T.J., Posner, P.L. and Regan, P.M. (eds). 2017. *Governing Under Stress: The Implementation of Obama's Economic Stimulus Program*. Washington, DC: Georgetown University Press.

Cox, R.W. 1987. *Production, Power, and World Order*. New York: Columbia University Press.

Crawford, N.C. 2016. 'U.S. budgetary costs of wars through 2016', Watson Institute International and Public Affairs Study Paper. Accessed 13 December 2019, http://watson.brown.edu/costsofwar/files/cow/imce/papers/2016/Costs%20of%20War%20through%202016%20FINAL%20final%20v2.pdf.

Decker, S. and Sablowski, T. 2017. 'Die G20 und die Krise des globalen Kapitalismus'. Berlin: Rosa-Luxemburg-Stiftung.

Demirovic, A. 2016. 'Demokratie – zwischen autoritären Tendenzen und gesellschaftlicher Transformation'. In A. Demirovic (ed.), *Transformation der Demokratie – demokratische Transformation*. Münster: Westfalisches Dampfboot, pp. 278–302.

Deppe, F. 2013. *Autoritärer Kapitalismus*. Hamburg: VSA.

Deppe, F., Salomon, D. and Solty, I. 2011. *Imperialismus*. Cologne: Papy Rossa.

Domhoff, G.W. and Webber, M.J. 2011. *Class and Power in the New Deal*. Stanford: Stanford University Press.

Dörre, K. 2009. 'Die neue Landnahme: Dynamiken und Grenzen des Finanzmarktkapitalismus'. In K. Dörre, S. Lessenich and H. Rosa (eds), *Soziologie – Kapitalismus – Kritik*. Frankfurt: Suhrkamp, pp. 21–86.

Duverger, M. 1972. *Party Politics and Pressure*. New York: Thomas Y. Crowell.

Flecker, J. and Kirschenhofer, S. 2007. *Die Populistische Lücke*. Wien: Edition sigma.

Geithner, T. 2014. *Stress Test: Reflections on Financial Crises*. London: Penguin.

Gill, S. 1998. 'European governance and new constitutionalism', *New Political Economy* 3 (1): 5–26.

Gill, S. and Cutler, C. 2015. *New Constitutionalism and World Order*. Cambridge: Cambridge University Press.

Gill, S. and Law, D. 1993. 'Global hegemony and the structural power of capital'. In S. Gill (ed.), *Gramsci, Historical Materialism and International Relations*. Cambridge: Cambridge University Press, pp. 93–124.

Gill, S. and Solty, I. 2013. 'Die organischen Krisen des Kapitalismus und die Demokratiefrage', *Juridikum: Zeitschrift für Kritik/Recht/Gesellschaft* No. 1: 51–65.

Gramsci, A. 1991–1999. *Gefängnishefte*. Hamburg: Argument.

Grunwald, M. 2013. *The New New Deal*. New York: Simon & Schuster.

Harvey, D. 2003. *The New Imperialism*. Oxford: Oxford University Press.

Harvey, D. 2006. *Spaces of Global Capitalism*. London and New York: Verso.

Harvey, D. 2007. *A Brief History of Neoliberalism*. Oxford: Oxford University Press.

Hirsch, J. 2005. *Materialistische Staatstheorie*. Hamburg: VSA.

Hobsbawm, E. 1995. *The Age of Extremes*. London: Michael Joseph.

Honderich, T. 1994. *Das Elend des Konservatismus: Eine Kritik*. Hamburg: Rotbuch.

Jessop, B. 2008. 'The crises of neoliberalism, neo-neoliberalism and post-neo-liberalism'. Presentation, University of Toronto, 19 September.

Klein, D. 2016. *Gespaltene Machteliten*. Hamburg: VSA.

Koddenbrock, K. 2018. 'Strukturwandel der Globalisierung? Brexit, Trump(ismus), Strategien Chinas und die politische Ökonomie der internationalen Beziehungen', *Zeitschrift für Internationale Beziehungen* 25 (2): 126–143.

Kotlikoff, L. 2011. 'Stimulus has been too small and poorly defined to judge', *The Economist*, 7 July.

Levine, R.F. 1988. *Class Struggle and the New Deal*. Lawrence: University Press of Kansas.

Lipietz, A. 1985. 'Akkumulation, Krisen und Auswege aus der Krise. Einige methodische Überlegungen zum Begriff "Regulation"', *Prokla: Zeitschrift für kritische Sozialwissenschaft* 15 (1): 109–137.

Lizza, R. 2012. 'The Obama memos: The making of a post-partisan presidency', *New Yorker*, 30 January. Accessed 13 December 2019, https://www.newyorker.com/magazine/2012/01/30/the-obama-memos.

McNally, D. 2012. *The Global Slump*. Oakland: PM Press.

National Employment Law Project. 2012. 'The low-wage recovery and growing inequality'. Accessed 31 August 2018, www.nelp.org/content/uploads/2015/03/LowWage Recovery2012.pdf.

Neumann, F. 1984. *Behemoth: Struktur und Praxis des Nationalsozialismus, 1933–1944*. Munich: Fischer.

Nölke, A. 2018. 'Vom liberalen zum organisierten Kapitalismus', *Zeitschrift für Internationale Beziehungen* 25 (2): S. 161–178.

Obama, B. 2009. 'Remarks following a meeting with president's Economic Recovery Advisory Board chairman Paul A. Volcker and an exchange with reporters: March 13, 2009'. In B. Obama, *Public Papers of the Presidents of the United States*. Washington, DC, pp. 246–248. Accessed 19 November 2020, https://www.govinfo.gov/content/pkg/PPP-2009-book1/pdf/PPP-2009-book1-doc-pg246.pdf.

Oberndorfer, L. 2013. 'Vom neuen, über den autoritären, zum progressiven Konstitutionalismus?' *Juridikum* 1: 76–86.

Panitch, L. 2002. 'Neuer Imperialismus – neue Imperialismustheorie', *Z. Zeitschrift Marxistische Erneuerung* 13 (4): 77–87.

Panitch, L. and Gindin, S. 2012. *The Making of Global Capitalism: The Political Economy of American Empire*. London and New York: Verso.

Pile, K. and Fisahn, A. 2017. 'Sicherheitsstaat und neue Formen des Autoritären (Staates) in Europa? Ein Versuch begrifflicher Annäherung'. In J. Puschke and T. Singelnstein (eds), *Der Staat und die Sicherheitsgesellschaft*. Wiesbaden: Springer VS, pp. 33–53.

Poulantzas, N. 1973. *Faschismus und Diktatur*. München: Trikont.

Poulantzas, N. 2002. *Staatstheorie*. Hamburg: VSA.

Rilling, R. 2014. 'Transformation als futuring'. In M. Brie (ed.), *Futuring: Perspektiven der Transformation im Kapitalismus über ihn hinaus*. Münster: Westfalisches Dampfboot, pp. 12–48.

Robin, C. 2017. *The Reactionary Mind*. Oxford: Oxford University Press.

Robinson, W.I. 2004. *A Theory of Global Capitalism*. Baltimore: Johns Hopkins University Press.

Roesler, J. 2010. *Der schwierige Weg in eine solidarische Wirtschaft*. Hamburg: VSA Verlag.

Romer, C. 2009. 'The case for fiscal stimulus: The likely effects of the American Recovery and Reinvestment Act'. Lecture, University of Chicago, 27 February.

Ryner, M. 2015. 'Europe's ordoliberal iron cage: Critical political economy, the Euro area crisis and its management', *Journal of European Public Policy* 22 (2): 275–294.

Saez, E. and Zucman, G. 2016. 'Wealth inequality in the United States since 1913: Evidence from capitalized income tax data', *Quarterly Journal of Economics* 131 (2): 519–578.

Scheiber, N. 2012. *The Escape Artists*. New York: Simon & Schuster.

Schulten, T. and Müller, T. 2013. 'Ein neuer europäischer Interventionismus? Die Auswirkungen des neuen Systems der Economic Governance auf Löhne und Tarifpolitik', *Wirtschaft und Gesellschaft* 39 (3): 291–321.

Shaikh, A. 2007. *Globalization and the Myths of Free Trade*. London: Routledge.

Shoup, L.H. and Minter, W. 1977. *Imperial Brain Trust: The Council on Foreign Relations and United States Foreign Policy*. New York: Monthly Review Press.

Simon, J. 2018. 'Die Rolle Chinas in den aktuellen Auseinandersetzungen um den Operationsmodus der Globalisierung', *Zeitschrift für Internationale Beziehungen* 25 (2): 144–163.

Sklair, L. 2001. *The Transnational Capitalist Class*. Oxford: Blackwell.

Solty, I. 2008. *Das Obama-Projekt: Krise und charismatische Herrschaft*. Hamburg: VSA.

Solty, I. 2011a. 'After neoliberalism: Left versus right projects of leadership in the global crisis'. In S. Gill (ed.), *Global Crises and the Crisis of Global Leadership*. Cambridge: Cambridge University Press, pp. 199–215.

Solty, I. 2011b. 'Interregnum neuer Protestbewegungen', *LuXemburg: Gesellschaftsanalyse und linke Praxis* 3 (4): 146–153.

Solty, I. 2013. *Die USA unter Obama: Charismatische Herrschaft, soziale Bewegungen und imperiale Politik in der globalen Krise*. Hamburg: Argument.

Solty, I. 2014. 'Der Name der Zeit: Autoritärer Kapitalismus?' *LuXemburg: Gesellschaftsanalyse und linke Praxis* 7 (1): 114–115.

Solty, I. 2016a. 'Donald Trump – ein amerikanischer Faschist? Legitimationskrise, Repräsentationskrise und rechter Populismus in den USA', *Sozialismus* 43 (1): 2–7.

Solty, I. 2016b. 'Warum gibt es in den USA Sozialismus?' *Sozialismus* 43 (3): 2–6.

Solty, I. 2016c. 'Die politische Artikulation der globalen Krise heute'. *Z. Zeitschrift Marxistische Erneuerung* 107 (27/3): 8–18.

Solty, I. 2016d. 'Wie konnte der herrschende Block die Kontrolle verlieren?' *Sozialismus* 43 (12): 2–12.

Solty, I. 2016e. *Exportweltmeister in Fluchtursachen: Die neue deutsche Außenpolitik, die Krise und linke Alternativen.* Berlin: Dietz.

Solty, I. 2016f. 'Goodbye Sanders? Warum die politische Revolution noch nicht am Ende ist', *LuXemburg: Gesellschaftsanalyse und linke Praxis* 8 (2): 34–42.

Solty, I. 2018a. 'Der 18. Brumaire des Donald J. Trump?' In M. Beck and I. Stützle (eds), *Die Neuen Bonapartisten.* Berlin: Dietz, pp. 74–92.

Solty, I. 2018b. 'Eine Regierung des Kapitals, durch das Kapital und für das Kapital: Trumps Steuerreform im Namen der US-Arbeiterklasse und der globale Kapital- steuersenkungskrieg', *Sozialismus* 44 (2): 28–32.

Solty, I. 2018c. 'The death of the German dream'. First part of an interview in *Jacobin*, 28 December. Accessed 13 December 2019, https://www.jacobinmag.com/2018/12/merkel- cdu-austerity-far-right-migration.

Solty, I. and Gill, S. 2013. 'Krise, Legitimität und die Zukunft Europas', *Das Argument: Zeitschrift für Philosophie und Sozialwissenschaften* 55 (1–2): 82–94.

Solty, I. and Werner, A. 2016. 'Der indiskrete Charme des Linkspopulismus', *Das Argument* 58 (2): 273–285.

Suskind, R. 2012. *Confidence Men.* New York: Harper.

Trump, D. 2015. *Time to Get Tough: Make America Great Again.* New York: Regenery Publishing.

Van der Pijl, K. 1998. *Transnational Classes and International Relations.* London: Routledge.

Wolffe, R. 2011. *Revival: The Struggle for Survival Inside the Obama White House.* New York: Broadway Books.

Wood, E.M. 2002. *The Origin of Capitalism.* New York: Verso.

Zuckerman, M. 2012. 'A part-time/low-wage epidemic', *Wall Street Journal*, 5 November. Accessed 13 December 2019, https://www.wsj.com/articles/SB10001424052970203707 604578094601253124258.

5

BRAZILIAN DEMOCRACY FACING AUTHORITARIAN NEOLIBERALISM

Alfredo Saad-Filho

INTRODUCTION

The election of Jair Bolsonaro to the Brazilian presidency, in October 2018, came as a shock to most observers. He was widely seen by critics, experts and left-wingers as being unelectable because of his inexperience; lack of organised support by established political parties, big business or social organisations; overt backing of Brazil's military dictatorship (1964–1985), torture and guns; and for discrimination against black and indigenous peoples, women and LGBTQIA+ communities. Bolsonaro was also infamous for regularly having made outrageous statements against his perceived foes, especially female members of Congress.

Although Bolsonaro polled relatively low until the middle of the year, his ratings started climbing rapidly in the weeks immediately before the elections. They were boosted by a well-organised social media campaign and by a (much disputed) attempt on his life on 6 September. Paradoxically, support for his candidacy *grew* in response to the Ele Não (Not Him) women-led movement, which culminated in large demonstrations around the country on 29 September. Despite – or, perhaps, because of – the radicalising resistance against him, Bolsonaro comfortably won the first round of the elections, on 7 October, and proceeded to win convincingly, by 55 per cent against 45 per cent to the left-wing opposition candidate, in the second round, on 28 October. The final round pitted Bolsonaro against the Workers' Party

(Partido dos Trabalhadores, PT) candidate, Fernando Haddad, himself standing in for PT leader and former president Luiz Inácio Lula da Silva (2003–2006, 2007–2010), then in jail on highly questionable corruption charges.[1]

This chapter reviews Bolsonaro's election and key traits of his administration, which was inaugurated on 1 January 2019. The study draws upon three mutually reinforcing strands. First, the worldwide rise of the political Right, leading to the diffusion of an authoritarian modality of neoliberalism in several countries, including Brazil. Second, the internal dynamics of the Brazilian Left, which can be examined through its historical cycles of rise and decline, the most recent driven by the fortunes of the PT. Third, the consolidation of a broad right-wing alliance in Brazil that has become politically dominant across a spectrum of areas. The chapter concludes that the election of Jair Bolsonaro is symptomatic of broad social processes with a wide social and geographical remit and that are unlikely to be reversed easily, or merely through a sudden reversal of fortunes of Bolsonaro's flawed administration.

GLOBAL SHIFTS

At a global level, the tide of authoritarian neoliberalism currently sweeping the world is symptomatic of three processes.[2] First, the crisis, stagnation and stumbling recovery of most neoliberal economies since the great financial crisis (GFC) starting in 2007, which subsequently morphed into a 'great stagnation' that would, eventually, implode into an unprecedented depression because of the Covid-19 pandemic (Gordon 2015; Summers 2015, 2016). Second, the crisis of political systems and institutions of representation following the GFC and the closely related policies of economic 'austerity' in many countries, which have been contributing to the decomposition of neoliberal democracy (Boffo et al. 2018). Third, the hijacking of mass discontent by the far Right, fronted by a new breed of 'spectacular' politicians, committed both to the intensified reproduction of neoliberalism and to their own self-referential power.

These processes can be summarised as follows. The global transition to neoliberalism has been associated with extensive restructuring of processes of capital accumulation, including new products and technologies; new forms of production, employment and exchange; new patterns of trade; and, above all, the exponential growth of all forms of finance, debt and fictitious capital.[3] These shifts have had profound implications for social reproduction in general and, specifically, for the composition and mode of existence of the working class (Moody 1997, 2017). Consequences include profound changes in forms and patterns of employment, modes of labour, community and class cultures and solidarities, and the decline of traditional forms of class representation, including left parties, trade unions and mass organisations.

Their weakening has been closely related to the establishment of typically neoliberal institutions, ideologies, rules, policies and practices, aiming to buttress as well as promote the neoliberalisation of production and social reproduction, and to shield market processes from social accountability. Those institutions include, for example, presumably 'independent' central banks (beholden to finance), inflation targeting regimes (primed to protect financial asset values), maximum fiscal deficit rules (for the avoidance of inflation, and to limit public spending), privatisations (to curtail potential levers of public influence over resource allocation and the pattern of growth), and the 'autonomy' of a range of public bodies (not least a range of regulatory agencies invariably captured by the corporations that they nominally control) (Dardot and Laval 2014). The decline of the Left, the neoliberal reconstruction of the state, and mounting repression, especially since 9/11, have led to a marked dislocation of the political spectrum towards the Right over the past four decades.[4]

The technological, economic, institutional, ideological and political changes outlined above, and the neoliberal restructuring of social reproduction, have created a vast array of economic 'losers', centred – in the advanced economies – on the traditional (blue-collar) working class. These 'losers' tend to be politically separated, structurally disorganised, ideologically perplexed, practically disenfranchised and, consequently, unable or unwilling to express their grievances through the political system that neoliberalism itself has imposed.

Instead of being channelled through the traditional (institutional) channels of conflict resolution, mass frustration has, increasingly, tended to be captured by, and expressed through, the right-wing media and far-right political organisations, movements and governments. They have induced the 'losers' to blame 'the other' for the damages inflicted by neoliberalism – with the alleged victims (stereotypically, in the advanced economies, hard-working, morally upright and ethnically privileged male-led blue-collar families) being defined through cultural and religious hierarchies, as well as pre-existing 'racial' categories grounded in history. These hierarchies are often ancient, and they are grounded in common knowledges and widespread prejudices; they require little explanation: a code word here and a wink there can be enough. In turn, the 'other' is unambiguously defined as the poor, immigrants, dark-skinned peoples, poorer countries, minority religions, and so on.

In sum, the politics of resentment foisted upon the working class, the underprivileged and the poor under neoliberalism has divided them politically, and bolstered new forms of collectivity grounded on nationalist, racial and religious discourses defined by exclusion and discrimination. More recently, these political platforms have tended to be fronted by self-appointed 'leaders' claiming a unique ability to 'get things done' by sheer force of will, against unresponsive 'elites' (which they purportedly do not belong to, regardless of background and personal trajectory) and institutions. Their discourse tends to mobilise through the construction of grievances based on sharp oppositions drawing upon common sense. However, when in power those leaders have tended to impose strongly neoliberal policies around taxation, trade, employment, finance, social security and housing. This experience is common to several countries – including Brazil.

CYCLES OF THE LEFT

The next peculiar aspect of the rise of authoritarian neoliberalism in Brazil is the trajectory of the political Left in the country. This can be outlined through a review of the two political cycles of the Brazilian Left in the postwar era.[5]

The first cycle began in the early 1940s, during the dictatorship of Getúlio Vargas. The Left had been crushed by the Vargas regime in the late 1930s, but it reconstituted itself largely through the campaign against Nazi-fascism, and for Brazilian participation in World War II on the side of the Allies. Left activity during this period was dominated by the Communist Party of Brazil (Partido Comunista do Brasil, PCB). The PCB was closely aligned with the USSR, and it grew rapidly during that period. In the early 1940s, the PCB had only a small band of activists, and its best-known leaders were in jail. By 1945, the PCB was a large, strong and disciplined organisation with hundreds of thousands of members, and it polled almost ten per cent of the votes in the national elections.

The PCB was proscribed in 1947. Nevertheless, it continued to influence many trade unions, social organisations and student movements. A few PCB members were elected to Congress and city administrations through other political parties, and the PCB forged relatively stable alliances with important segments of the non-Marxist Left, especially the left-populist Brazilian Labour Party (PTB) and the centrist Social Democratic Party (PSD). These alliances with 'bourgeois' parties were important strategically, because the PCB argued that progressive change in Brazil required a broad alliance between the working class, the peasantry, the middle classes and the domestic (industrial) bourgeoisie, in order to lead a democratic and national development project against the ruling alliance between imperialist forces and semi-feudal landed interests.

The strategy of the PCB was comprehensively defeated in 1964. The domestic bourgeoisie and most of the middle classes shunned the left-populist administration of President João Goulart, which was supported by the PCB; instead, they aligned themselves with the far Right, local landed interests and the US government. The workers, peasants and students were left isolated, and their organisations were destroyed. The dramatic failure of the PCB and the ensuing repression contributed to the fragmentation of the party, and led to the foundation of a whole range of small radical organisations inspired by Trotskyism, *foquismo*, Maoism, and so on. Some of them sponsored or supported armed struggles against the dictatorship. These limited attempts at urban and rural guerrilla warfare were repressed brutally.

Mass resistance re-emerged gradually, in the mid-1970s. The defeat of the organised working class and the guerrilla movements removed part of the rationale for state terrorism, and the legitimacy of the regime was shaken by the results of the 1970 census, which showed that rapid economic growth had concentrated income and failed to deliver material improvements to the majority of the population. The regime's reputation was further damaged by the economic slowdown after the first oil shock, in 1973, followed by the second shock, in 1979, and the international debt crisis, in 1982. Inflation climbed relentlessly, from 20 per cent per annum towards 200 per cent, and Brazil's economy stagnated. It became increasingly difficult for the regime to justify the denial of civil liberties in the name of 'public safety' or 'competent economic management'. In 1974, the military government was comprehensively beaten in the elections for Congress. The ruling circles realised that the regime needed to respond to its political erosion, and they chose to embark on a slow, limited and tightly controlled process of political liberalisation that ultimately led to the transfer of power to 'reliable' civilians in 1985.

The second cycle of the Brazilian Left since World War II was defined by the fortunes of the PT. In the mid-1970s, several surviving left-wing organisations banded together with progressive Catholic groups, leftist intellectuals and young activists to demand the restoration of democracy, respect for human rights and political amnesty, as well as economic policy changes.[6] Petitions were followed by demonstrations, which were sometimes ignored and often repressed. At a later stage, a new trade union movement burst onto the political scene. Those unions were based on the key industries emerging in the previous period, especially the metal, mechanical and auto industries located in and around the city of São Paulo, as well as finance, the large state-owned enterprises providing infrastructure and basic goods, and the civil service, especially the postal workers, nurses, doctors, teachers and university lecturers. Over time, and in the wake of successive strikes, the metalworkers in São

Paulo moved to the forefront of the Brazilian working class, led by their charismatic union leader, Luiz Inácio da Silva (Lula).[7]

The idea of founding a political party of a new type coalesced rapidly among those groups of activists. By late 1978, they were already discussing the foundation of a 'Workers' Party' – a 'party without bosses' – in order to defeat the dictatorship and introduce a new model of development in the country (Bianchi and Braga 2003). That party should be untainted by the traditional features of the Brazilian Left: populism, corruption, clientelism and Stalinism. The PT was eventually launched in 1980, under the leadership of Lula. The strategy and the mode of organisation of the PT corresponded to the opportunities offered by the crumbling military dictatorship, and the needs and composition of the Brazilian working class. The party grew rapidly, reaching 800 000 members in less than ten years. Its trade union confederation, CUT (Central Única dos Trabalhadores), represented up to 20 million workers, and the PT made significant inroads into the students' movement. These successes were reflected in the PT's excellent performance at the ballot box, which culminated in Lula's presidential election, in 2002, after three consecutive defeats, in 1989, 1994 and 1998.[8]

The growth of the PT was based on two main drivers. First, there were political demands for a radical democracy, incorporating but not limited to formal (procedural or 'bourgeois') democratic practices and processes. The PT demanded more: it advocated a (never clearly defined) 'socialist democracy', delivering power and economic betterment to the poor majority. Second, the PT defended the corporatist interests of the workers closely associated with the party.

Unfortunately for the PT, and importantly for what was to follow, both drivers of growth collapsed between the mid-1980s and the mid-1990s. The achievement of political democracy changed radically the terrain in which the party had originally emerged. It had been relatively easy for the PT to offer a progressive alternative to a decrepit dictatorship that was increasingly powerless to discipline the populace but that remained wedded to an anachronistic right-wing discourse, while at the same time demonstrating staggering managerial incompetence, high levels of corruption, and an abysmal track record in delivering income and welfare gains for the majority.

The restoration of democracy changed everything. The institutions of the state were validated by their democratic veneer, compelling the PT to follow the electoral calendar and operate within the 'bourgeois' framework that the party had previously denounced. Political debates shifted away from lofty principles towards matters of detail embedded within parliamentary politics. Mass demonstrations were normalised. Implementation of PT policies now required a democratic mandate that, although feasible in principle, could be achieved only if the PT submitted itself to the logic of campaign finance, coalition building, piecemeal reforms, negotiations with conflicting interest groups, and the imperatives of 'efficiency' and 'delivery' in local government. Those limitations tempered the PT's enthusiasm for direct action, and increased the weight of its internal bureaucracy at the expense of ordinary militants and (radical) affiliated movements.

Matters became worse in the late 1980s with the economic transition to neoliberalism. The neoliberal 'reforms' severely weakened the groups that were the backbone of PT, provided the bulk of its votes and were affiliated to the most active trade unions: the manufacturing workers, the middle- and lower-ranking civil servants, employees of state-owned enterprises and other formal sector workers (Branford and Kucinski 2003: 32–34; Saad-Filho and Mollo 2002). The trade union movement was severely degraded. Radicals lost ground to pragmatic leaders within CUT, and the unions split between those seeking immediate economic gains and those continuing to demand radical changes in government policy. Rapid deindustrialisation and waves of privatisation weakened the manufacturing working class and the most organised sectors of the civil service. The student movement fell into irrelevance. The PT had to reconstitute its sources of support under these challenging circumstances. The party's twofold response helps to explain its later successes, as well as the limitations of the federal administrations led by Lula and Dilma Rousseff.

After Lula's successive electoral defeats, the party leadership persuaded itself that the PT must appeal to a more centrist constituency, and downplay its commitment to social change. The PT offered a discourse based on a vaguely progressive ethics and efficiency in public administration. Increasingly, the PT presented itself non-politically, as the only party untainted by corruption in Brazil. The narrowing of the PT's transformative ambitions and the party's shift towards administrative rather than radical priorities helped it to gain new constituencies, especially the moderate middle class, informal sector workers and many domestic capitalists (Medeiros 2013: 65).

Lula's election brought the possibility of pushing for change from the top. The party was fortunate enough to reach executive power during an emerging global commodity boom, in the early 2000s. It proceeded to implement economic policies along a 'path of least resistance' (Loureiro and Saad-Filho 2019). This choice of path referred, first, to the party's commitment to political stability – that is, not trying to change the constitution or to reform finance, land ownership, the media or the judicial system; not mobilising the workers and the poor; and not challenging the economic and political hegemony of the established economic, social and political elites in the country. The consequence was that, in order to govern, the PT had to rely on an unwieldy web of unprincipled political alliances and case-by-case negotiations.

This arrangement implies that political stability during the administrations led by the PT depended on the party's ability to deliver economic gains almost to everyone, while simultaneously maintaining its credibility with the strongest fractions of capital. This turned out to be possible only in times of economic prosperity.

The second feature of the PT's path of least resistance was the party's attachment to the so-called macroeconomic policy tripod imposed by the previous administration, in 1999, that included inflation targets, floating exchange rates with free international movement of capital, and contractionary fiscal and monetary policies. The tripod was meant to secure the government's credibility with capital, but it also limited drastically the scope for developmental initiatives and distributive policies.

Third was the commitment to a national development project based on the expansion of domestic demand through public expenditures and transfers and the expansion of consumer loans, as well as state support for large domestic capital both at home and abroad. Inspired by the perceived success of the South Korean *chaebol*, the Brazilian government provided regulatory, financial and diplomatic support to large domestically owned companies in the oil, shipbuilding, telecoms, construction, food processing and other sectors, in order to facilitate their expansion at home and abroad. It was hoped that the combination of demand growth at home and support for the expansion of key firms would help to set off a virtuous circle including employment creation, the development of new technologies, growing competitiveness, and improvement in the country's balance of payments.

The fourth feature was the pursuit of distribution at the margin, primarily through the expansion of low-paid employment and rising transfers and minimum wages (which rose by 72 per cent between 2005 and 2012, while real GDP per capita increased by 30 per cent). This led to a remarkable recovery of the wage share of national income, while also leaving unchanged the distribution of assets.

The limitations of the path of least resistance emerged gradually, first through the continuing deterioration of the post-crisis environment and the tightening of the balance of payments constraint. Second was an intractable productivity gap with the Organisation for Economic Co-operation and Development (OECD), the inability of the state to deliver improvements in infrastructure and living conditions in urban areas, and the persistent dysfunctionality and speculative character of private finance. Third, the distribution of income driven by low-paid jobs and welfare transfers was limited, because it depended heavily on the marginal income created by economic growth. This model of distribution also implied that the middle class would be squeezed by the preservation of the privileges of the rich, the improvement of the poorest, and the deteriorating quality and rising cost of urban services. This could be compensated only temporarily by the expansion of personal credit and the appreciation of the currency. Fourth, for all its strengths, the administration led by Lula's successor, Dilma Rousseff, suffered from severe political and administrative shortcomings. This led to the gradual loss of support of core social groups and political parties in her coalition, to the point that, by 2016, the government could count only on disorganised, conditional and minority support across the country. A large alliance of elites, including most right-wing political leaders, finance, the media, the upper middle class, business and the higher echelons of the civil service, with strong US support, moved to impeach the president on trumped-up charges of fiscal malfeasance.[9] The coup against Rousseff marks the closure of the second cycle of the Brazilian Left. Since then, the administrations led by Rousseff's former vice-president, Michel Temer, and, more recently, by Jair Bolsonaro have devoted themselves to imposing a vicious modality of economic neoliberalism by authoritarian means, with a severe attack on fiscal policy tools and the emerging Brazilian welfare state.

AUTHORITARIAN NEOLIBERALISM IN PRACTICE

The emergence of the alliance of elites that overthrew President Rousseff also marks the third key aspect of the election of Jair Bolsonaro. In contrast with previous right-wing mobilisations – most recently, in the mid-1930s, between the mid-1950s and the mid-1960s, and in 1990–1992 – the current alliance of elites did not appeal centrally to outdated anti-communist discourses inspired by the Cold War, which would have been absurd, and it was not inspired by Catholic values, due to the much greater influence of Protestant sects today. Instead, the new alliance of elites mobilised against a poorly defined danger of 'Bolivarianism', and the fictional threat of 'left-wing authoritarianism' led by the PT. The alliance also called for 'the end of corruption', which was code for 'the destruction of the PT'. It has become evident that the strategic goal of the alliance of elites was the restriction of democracy, through the imposition of an authoritarian modality of neoliberalism, in order to eliminate government autonomy from the privileged classes, reinforce the structures of exclusion, and abolish the spaces by which the majority might control any levers of public policy (Fortes 2016; Saad-Filho and Morais 2018: chapter 9; Singer 2015).

The middle class provided critically important support for the alliance of elites. Their frustration is understandable. While large capital tended to prosper, not least through the implementation of neoliberal policies by successive governments, the workers and the poor also gained under the PT, through higher minimum wages and expanded welfare provision, the creation of millions of low-wage jobs, and new avenues for social mobility – for example, through racial quotas for universities and the civil service. In the meantime, the middle class was squeezed by the erosion of its traditional careers, especially in middle management, banking and the upper layers of the civil service.[10] The scarcity of 'good jobs' has intensified with the economic slowdown since 2011.

The middle class was penalised further by rising minimum wages and the extension of employment rights to domestic workers (cleaners, nannies, cooks, drivers, gardeners and security guards, who are ubiquitous in middle-class households). They also lost out because of the diffusion of means-tested transfer programmes, which the middle class helps to fund through the tax system, but cannot claim because their incomes exceed the threshold by a large margin. Perhaps even more serious was the expansion of citizenship rights to the poor, which threatened the paternalistic relationships in middle-class homes. During the PT administrations, while both the rich and the poor prospered, the middle class found it difficult to maintain their (relative as well as absolute) economic and social status, and their children had limited scope to emulate the achievements of their parents.

Under intense economic and ideological pressure, middle-class groups became increasingly attached to a neoliberal-globalist project that secures their advantages against the poor, even though it inevitably slows down economic growth. For example, it was often claimed that the deterioration of urban infrastructure and public services was due to rising incomes and the expansion of rights under the PT; that is, the government 'allowed' too many people to own automobiles, fly, and access universities and private health facilities which, logically, should be privatised and become more expensive in order to restore a more convenient balance between demand and supply.[11] The implications of low investment and weak development policy were ignored, perhaps because they would suggest the need for higher levels of public spending (Medeiros 2013: 59). These pressures led the middle class to abandon the PT en masse and shift their support to the PT's main rival, the Brazilian Social Democratic Party (Partido da Social Democracia Brasileira, PSDB), and other right-wing parties in the mid-2000s. Gradually, the middle class became, once again, the mass base of the far Right in Brazil (Nepomuceno 2015).

The social and political realignment in the country led to the rise of a mass movement supporting an authoritarian variety of neoliberalism. The rise of authoritarian neoliberalism in Brazil had two peculiar features, in contrast with similar political processes and movements elsewhere. First, there was a relatively subdued role for overtly racist and nationalist discourses; instead, the Brazilian variety of authoritarian neoliberalism pursues close links with the US, bordering on outright submission (see, for example, the sale of aerospace giant Embraer to Boeing, and the concession of the Alcantara rocket launch base to the US). Second, while in the advanced economies the main 'losers' are typically found among the blue-collar working class (see above), the most prominent losers during the federal administrations led by the PT were in the middle class.[12]

President Jair Bolsonaro emerged from this milieu. His electoral campaign was supported by an assortment of small parties and neophyte politicians, coalescing around four themes: (i) allegations of 'corruption' against a broad swathe of politicians, drawing upon Bolsonaro's purported status as a political outsider (despite a 28-year career as federal deputy); (ii) conservative moral values and the rollback of citizenship, (the candidate attacked social movements and the Left because they are 'corrupt', 'communist' and 'godless', and advocated the restoration of 'lost' cultural values by deathly violence); (iii) public security and easier access to weapons, which has a strong appeal in a country enduring over 60 000 murders per year; and (iv) a neoliberal economic programme, drawing upon the intuitively appealing notion of reducing bureaucracy and the deadweight of a corrupt state (this is obviously different from the context underpinning the rise of Narendra Modi in India, despite the superficial similarities between the outcomes in both countries; see Nilsen, this volume).

Once in power, the Bolsonaro administration rapidly degenerated into comical chaos, at least in its political side (for a contrast with the case of the Trump-led USA, see Solty, this volume). In contrast, the implications for the environment were nothing short of disastrous, as was amply demonstrated by the accelerated devastation of the Amazon rainforest (the global context in this regard is examined by Satgar, this volume). Finally, the economic side was dominated by finance minister Paulo Guedes, a minor 'Chicago Boy' in General Pinochet's Chile, and a banker and occasional academic in Brazil. Guedes's main priority is to dismantle Brazil's progressive pensions system in order to introduce one based on individual accounts, minimal redistribution between generations or classes, and tough restrictions on drawing up pension income. His proposal is so restrictive that most low earners with unstable jobs will never achieve the contributions threshold required to claim benefits, while the rich will tend to choose private pensions offering more flexible conditions and uncapped returns. At a further remove, Guedes has announced plans to privatise 'everything', starting with the country's airports, parts of Petrobras and a whole raft of state-owned enterprises, and, finally, a tax reform introducing a less progressive system. Across all its dimensions, then, as well as personal corruption, abetment of crime, and sheer crassness and brutality, Bolsonaro's administration expresses the worst of the worst political times in living memory.

CONCLUSION

The election of Jair Bolsonaro was part of the rise of an authoritarian modality of neoliberalism in Brazil which, in turn, is one instance among many of the rise of authoritarian neoliberalism globally. These experiences are contextual, including different combinations of organised mass movements, political parties, 'spectacular' self-referential leaders, racism, nationalism, and distinct sets of economic and social 'losers' from neoliberalism. Across these experiences, in countries as diverse as Brazil, Egypt, Hungary, Italy, the Philippines, Poland, Russia, Thailand, Turkey and the US, among others, common traits are also present among the diversity of processes, institutions and outcomes. Across this diversity of cases, it remains clear that global neoliberalism has entered a distinctive phase of crisis management in the economic sphere, through specific (authoritarian, personalistic, overtly nationalist but, at the core, radically neoliberal) modalities of crisis politics.[13]

In the case of Brazil, the rise of Jair Bolsonaro, as a clear instance of authoritarian neoliberalism, can be examined from four angles. First, since 2013 Brazilian politics has been defined by a convergence of dissatisfactions. Disparate demands and conflicting expectations have buttressed an alliance of elites supporting an authoritarian neoliberal economic, social and political programme that is destructive of collectivity and citizenship. The regressiveness of this programme was veiled by a media-sponsored far-right discourse stressing the 'incompetence' of the PT administrations, their 'populism' and rampant corruption (the concept of 'populism' in this context is debunked by Gordon, this volume).

Second, the cycles of the Brazilian Right, including the most recent one, suggest that, in Brazil, the powerful tend to rise up if their wealth is directly threatened, or if economic privilege fails to secure political prominence. Nevertheless, mass support for the revolt of the elites depends heavily on the mobilisation of the middle class.

Third, in recent years the far Right has achieved ideological hegemony and a solid electoral majority in Brazil, despite the lack of stable leadership, strong movements and solid parties. This is a paradox, and the Brazilian experience stands in sharp contrast with authoritarian neoliberalism experiences elsewhere. That is, while in several countries well-organised movements led by experienced leaders succeeded in achieving power by electoral or other means, in Brazil the state was hijacked in 2016 by a squabbling band of reactionary and deeply corrupt politicians who, in turn, passed the baton to a rabble of inexperienced, inept, idiosyncratic, corrupt and ultra-reactionary mobsters and conmen, thriving despite the lack of stable structures of support, and sowing a politics of hatred that they barely control. Their greatest ambition is to impose an uncompromising neoliberal and anti-national development strategy, which cannot flourish in a democracy: their rule can be enforced only by authoritarian means, and the inevitable political impasses will tend to be resolved outside the constitution.

Fourth, despite the fractures and insufficiencies on the Right, the Brazilian Left remains hampered by internal disputes about the past (especially the role of the PT and the consequences of its political choices), and it lacks a cogent programme for the future. The absence of alternatives and the pronounced shift in the political centre of gravity of the country to the far Right, especially in the largest urban areas and the wealthiest regions, suggest that the Left may be unable to govern Brazil even in the medium term, unless it succeeds in reinventing itself.

The worst economic crisis in Brazil's recorded history and the most severe political impasse in the last century have degraded Brazilian democracy, and made it impossible for any plausible composition of political forces to govern the country within its democratic constitution. The nation is tearing itself apart, socially, economically and politically. Whether or not Brazil will slide into an overt politics of violence, as in Colombia or Mexico, drawing upon drug wars, gun trafficking and state terrorism, or, alternatively, whether or not democracy will implode because of a military coup, it is highly likely that we are witnessing the inglorious end to a democratic experiment that has marked two generations, and that achieved significant successes during this period. The best – and, possibly, the only – alternative to this unambiguously negative outcome for the majority demands the protagonism of a new wave of left movements and organisations. They would offer the best hope to lift the curse to have befallen Brazil.

NOTES

1   For an overview of the case against Lula, see Tardelli (2017). Lula was 'provisionally' released in November 2019, after 580 days in prison.

2   For a detailed analysis, see Boffo et al. (2018).

3   See Harvey (2007) for a classic account, and Fine and Saad-Filho (2017) for an alternative view.

4   For a detailed analysis, see Boffo et al. (2018), Fine and Saad-Filho (2017) and Saad-Filho (2017).

5   The review of the history of the PT in this section draws on Branford and Kucinski (2003: chapter 1).

6   Two especially important organisations were the Brazilian Movement for Amnesty (MBA), a broad front campaigning for amnesty for all political prisoners and the right of return of Brazilians exiled or banished for political reasons, and the Movement Cost of Living (MCV), which collected millions of signatures in petitions demanding inflation control and real wage increases for the low paid.

7   He later changed his name to Luís Inácio Lula da Silva.
8   For a review of the trajectory of the PT, see Branford and Kucinski (2003).
9   For detailed accounts of Dilma's impeachment, see Amaral (2016: part I), Gentili (2016) and Saad-Filho and Morais (2018: chapter 9). Nobre (2017: 139) argues that Rousseff fell because her government could no longer function according to the rules of the Brazilian political system: it was incapable of protecting allied politicians from judicial attack, and unable to secure access to public funds for the parties in her coalition.
10 For example, while 950 000 jobs paying more than five times the minimum wage were created in the 1990s, 4.3 million were lost in the 2000s; see Pochmann (2012).
11 For a review of middle-class ideologies and policy preferences, see Ricci (2012) and Tible (2013).
12 For a detailed overview of this period, see Saad-Filho and Morais (2018).
13 For an overview, see Boffo et al. (2018).

REFERENCES

Amaral, R. 2016. *A serpente sem Casca: Da 'crise' à frente Brasil popular*. São Paulo: Fundação Perseu Abramo.

Bianchi, A. and Braga, R. 2003. 'Le PT au pouvoir: la gauche Brésilienne et le social-libéralisme', *Carré Rouge* 26: 49–60.

Boffo, M., Saad-Filho, A. and Fine, B. 2018. 'Neoliberal capitalism: The authoritarian turn'. In L. Panitch and G. Albo (eds), *Socialist Register 2019*. London: Merlin Press, pp. 247–270.

Branford, S. and Kucinski, B. 2003. *Politics Transformed: Lula and the Workers' Party in Brazil*. London: Latin American Bureau.

Dardot, P. and Laval, C. 2014. *The New Way of the World: On Neoliberal Society*. London: Verso.

Fine, B. and Saad-Filho, A. 2017. 'Thirteen things you need to know about neoliberalism', *Critical Sociology* 45 (4–5): 685–706.

Fortes, A. 2016. 'Brazil's neoconservative offensive', *NACLA Report on the Americas* 48 (3): 217–220.

Gentili, P. (ed.). 2016. *Golpe en Brasil: Genealogía de Una Farsa*. Buenos Aires: CLACSO.

Gordon, R.J. 2015. 'Secular stagnation: A supply-side view', *American Economic Review* 105 (5): 54–59.

Harvey, D. 2007. *A Brief History of Neoliberalism*. Oxford: Oxford University Press.

Loureiro, P. and Saad-Filho, A. 2019. 'The limits of pragmatism: The rise and fall of the Brazilian Workers' Party (2002–2016)', *Latin American Perspectives* 46 (1): 66–84.

Medeiros, J. 2013. 'O PT e as classes sociais no Brasil: Reflexões após dez anos de "Lulismo"'. Accessed 14 June 2019, https://fpabramo.org.br/wp-content/uploads/2013/05/ed01-fpa-discute.pdf.

Moody, K. 1997. *Workers in a Lean World: Unions in the International Economy*. London: Verso.

Moody, K. 2017. *On New Terrain: How Capital Is Reshaping the Battleground of Class War*. Chicago: Haymarket Books.

Nepomuceno, E. 2015. 'Afinal, do que se trata? Simples: destituir Dilma e liquidar o PT'. Accessed 14 June 2019, http://cartamaior.com.br/?/Especial/A-direita-nas-ruas/Afinal-do-que-se-trata-Simples-destituir-Dilma-e-liquidar-o-PT-/196/33055.

Nobre, M. 2017. '1988+30', *Novos Estudos* 35 (2): 135–149.

Pochmann, M. 2012. *Nova classe média? O trabalho na base da pirâmide social Brasileira*. São Paulo: Boitempo.

Ricci, R. 2012. 'Classe Média Tradicional se Incomoda com Classe C'. Accessed 14 June 2019, http://rudaricci.blogspot.co.uk/2012/09/classe-media-tradicional-se-incomoda.html.

Saad-Filho, A. 2017 'Neoliberalism'. In D.M. Brennan, D. Kristjanson-Gural, C. Mulder and E. Olsen (eds), *The Routledge Handbook of Marxian Economics*. London: Routledge, pp. 245–254.

Saad-Filho, A. and Mollo, M.L.R. 2002. 'Inflation and stabilization in Brazil: A political economy analysis', *Review of Radical Political Economics* 34 (2): 109–135.

Saad-Filho, A. and Morais, L. 2018. *Brazil: Neoliberalism versus Democracy*. London: Pluto Press.

Singer, A. 2015. 'PT Precisa Mudar Rápido'. Accessed 14 June 2019, http://www1.folha.uol.com.br/ilustrissima/2015/03/1605819-pt-precisa-mudar-rapido-afirma-cientista-politico-andre-singer.shtml.

Summers, L.H. 2015. 'Demand side secular stagnation', *American Economic Review* 105 (5): 60–65.

Summers, L.H. 2016. 'The age of secular stagnation. What it is and what to do about it'. Accessed 14 June 2019, https://www.foreignaffairs.com/articles/united-states/2016-02-15/age-secular-stagnation.

Tardelli, B. 2017. 'Muita Convicção, Nenuma Profa: Raio-X da Sentença de Moro no "Caso Triplex"'. Accessed 14 June 2019, https://br.noticias.yahoo.com/muita-conviccao-nen huma-prova-o-raio-x-da-sentenca-de-moro-no-caso-triplex-192344519.html.

Tible, J. 2013. '¿Una nueva clase media en Brasil? El lulismo como fenómeno político-social'. Accessed 23 October 2019, http://nuso.org/articulo/una-nueva-clase-media-en-brasil-el-lulismo-como-fenomeno-politico-social/.

6

INDIA'S TRAJECTORIES OF
CHANGE, 2004–2019

Alf Gunvald Nilsen

On 23 May 2019, the results of India's seventeenth general election were announced: the right-wing Hindu nationalist Bharatiya Janata Party (BJP) with Narendra Modi at the helm had secured another five years in power, and over-whelmingly so. Indeed, the BJP's 2019 win outstripped the impressive results of 2014 as the party increased its seat share from 282 to 303 out of a total 543 seats in the lower house of India's parliament, the Lok Sabha. The BJP-led National Democratic Alliance (NDA) now controls a huge majority of 353 parliamentary seats. The BJP also made substantial inroads into parts of India where the party had previously been on the margins of electoral politics. The eastern states of West Bengal and Odisha, where the BJP is now the second-largest party, are cases in point, and so is the southern state of Karnataka, where it won 26 of 28 seats (Nilsen 2019a).

Indian capital responded very favourably to these results. Uday Kotak, one of India's leading bankers and number 12 on Forbes' list of India's richest in 2018, tweeted in celebration: 'Time for transformation of India. Time for deep reform. I dream of us as a global superpower in my lifetime. Heartiest congratulations to @narendramodi, the BJP, and the NDA.' Kotak, who saw his fortune increase by 43 per cent to US$10.1 billion in 2017, is only one of many among India's corporate elite who have done well under Modi. Others include Mukesh Ambani, who doubled his fortune from US$23 billion to US$55 billion from 2014 to 2019, and Gautam Adani, whose rise in the Indian corporate world has been coeval with Modi's ascent to power – first in Gujarat, and then nationwide (Crabtree 2018; Muralidharan

2014; Schmidt 2017; Srujana 2019). Of course, Indian capital had clearly shown its support for Modi in the lead-up to and during the 2019 election campaigns. For example, we know that the BJP received 94.5 per cent of the bonds issued under the electoral bond scheme introduced by the party's finance minister, Arun Jaitley. As observers noted, the scheme, which yielded 31.18 per cent of all party funds for the 2019 campaigns, enables unlimited anonymous corporate donations. There is no doubt that this was instrumental in furnishing Modi and his party with the means to spend somewhere between 45 and 50 per cent of the US$8.65 billion that went into funding the 2019 elections (Business Standard Web Team 2019; Tanwar 2019; Ulmer and Ahmed 2019). Of course, this kind of capitalist elite alignment behind an authoritarian populist resonates with the American and Brazilian scenarios deciphered by Solty and Saad-Filho in this volume.

Corporate support notwithstanding, the 2019 election results defy the basic laws of political gravity in some key ways. It is crucial to bear in mind that in the world's largest democracy, it is the poor – that is, India's subaltern citizens – that exercise their right to vote most eagerly (Nilsen et al. 2019). And the poor, in turn, have not fared well under Modi's regime: unemployment has reached its highest level in 45 years, rural India's agricultural crisis has deepened and inequality has increased. In late 2018, the BJP faced losses in important state elections and major protests by farmers and agricultural workers (see Nilsen 2018a, 2019b). But despite all this, Indian voters have handed Modi and the BJP a resounding new mandate. How do we explain this? And what does Modi 2.0 signify for the future of the world's largest democracy?

To answer these questions, I consider the nature of certain key trajectories of change in India over the past one-and-a-half decades. In particular, I analyse how the hegemonic project of the Congress-led United Progressive Alliance (UPA), which ruled India from 2004 to 2014, is different from that of the incumbent Modi regime. On the economic front, of course, there is little to distinguish the two regimes from each other: the BJP has mostly followed in the footsteps of the Congress by prioritising the continuing pursuit and consolidation of neoliberalism. However, whereas the UPA regime attempted to build popular consent for its rule by combining economic policies that advanced and consolidated the market logic with rights-based legislation that enshrined new civil liberties and socio-economic entitlements, the Modi regime has fused its neoliberal policy with majoritarian and coercive initiatives. This can be thought of as a transition from 'inclusive neoliberalism' (Ruckert 2010a, 2010b) to 'authoritarian populism' (Hall 1988) as the prevailing hegemonic project in the Indian polity. This is, of course, similar in many ways to the transition from the PT regime (Partido dos Trabalhadores, or

Workers' Party) to the Bolsonaro regime in Brazil, as discussed by Saad-Filho in this volume. As Zoya Hasan (2019) remarked in response to the 2019 election results, the onward march of Modi's authoritarian populism pushes India decisively in the direction of a majoritarian democracy. If this tendency is at all to be halted, it is imperative that we understand the logic that animates it.

THE UPA REGIME AS INCLUSIVE NEOLIBERALISM

The 1990s was not a good period for the Indian National Congress. Indeed, by the end of the decade, the protracted erosion of its hegemonic position in the post-colonial polity had culminated in the installation of the first BJP-led coalition government at the national level. In the lead-up to the general elections of 2004, it was evident that senior Congress leaders were keenly aware that the party had alienated much of its popular support base, especially in rural India, as a result of spearheading the neoliberal restructuring of the economy since the early 1990s. The political resurgence of the Congress was perceived by its high command to hinge in large part on the party's ability to reconcile neoliberal accumulation strategies with new forms of legitimation that could appeal to those groups who languished in the underbelly of the Indian boom (Nilsen 2019c).

Following the general elections of 2004, the UPA regime pursued such a strategy through what political scientist Sanjay Ruparelia (2013) refers to as India's new rights agenda. This agenda established civil liberties and socio-economic entitlements as legally enforceable rights. The new rights-based legislation includes the Right to Information (RTI) Act of 2005, the National Rural Employment Guarantee Act (NREGA) and the Forest Rights Act of 2006, the Right to Education Act of 2009, and, most recently, the Right to Food Act and the Land Acquisition, Rehabilitation and Resettlement (LARR) Act, both of 2013. The laws that were put in place emerged from the Common Minimum Programme on which the UPA centred its election campaign, and which emphasised the need to achieve growth with a human face (see Das 2013). Significantly, each of these laws responded – to greater or lesser extents – to social movement projects that had crystallised in India during the 1990s. The processes of policy making that yielded these laws incorporated social movement activists and civil society actors in crucial ways, and were shaped in significant ways by extra-parliamentary mobilisations and campaigns (see Chopra 2011a, 2011b; Sharma 2015; Vaidya 2014).

In his analysis of rights-based legislation, Ruparelia (2013: 570) has argued that laws such as the NREGA and the RTI Act have the potential to establish 'new standards for social citizenship' in India. Crucially, this 'new welfare paradigm' is distinctive because of the fact that 'new governance mechanisms furnish poorer citizens with an opportunity to challenge the practices of corruption and patronage that have enabled benefits to be targeted towards or captured by particular social groups in the past' (Ruparelia 2013: 571). There is undoubtedly a grain of truth in such assessments, but it is equally important to be aware of the role that rights-based legislation played in enabling the Congress to construct a new hegemonic project that remained, at its core, essentially neoliberal. First, in terms of economic policy, the UPA did not break in any significant way with the process of neoliberalisation that the party had initially set in train in the early 1990s; on the contrary, it sought in many ways to add impetus to the globalisation of the Indian economy (see Bhaduri 2008; Drèze and Sen 2013; Nayyar 2006; Walker 2008). Second, although activists were significantly involved in shaping policy making, the law gained salience as a terrain of mobilisation in a conjuncture when many of the new social movements that emerged in India during the 1970s and 1980s were declining (Harriss 2011; Nilsen and Nielsen 2016).

Consequently, rights-based legislation is most adequately conceptualised neither as an unequivocal expression of democratic accountability on the part of the Indian state during the UPA regime, nor simply as a stratagem of co-optation and deflection. Rather, inclusive neoliberalism as it was practised in the UPA decade is arguably best understood as a complex, and at times contradictory, practice aimed at the negotiation of a compromise equilibrium between dominant groups whose economic interests are intimately linked to the exploitation of the spaces of accumulation that have been opened up by neoliberalisation in India over the past two-and-a-half decades, and subaltern groups who are both vulnerable to marginalisation *and* capable of mobilisation.[1] The introduction of rights-based legislation under the UPA regime was intended to serve this purpose by mitigating the impact of poverty, inequality and dispossession. The objective of pursuing such a strategy, in turn, was to facilitate the long-term advance of neoliberalisation in a global context where India was rapidly emerging as a serious contender for the status of the world's fastest-growing economy (Nielsen and Nilsen 2015).

Generally speaking, this was done by offering limited legal concessions to some of the longstanding demands of progressive social movements in order to curtail more radical forms of mobilisation. For example, the new LARR Act of 2013 introduced seemingly generous provisions for resettlement and rehabilitation, but, on the other hand, it widened the definition of the public purpose for which the state can acquire land. The first part of the move was a clear concession to the longstanding demands of social movements that have challenged forced displacement.

In contrast, the second part of the move makes it possible for the Indian state to continue both expanding and consolidating spaces of accumulation for corporate capital in the Indian economy (Nielsen and Nilsen 2015).

In addition, the law as such arguably creates a terrain of mobilisation that constrains the actual conduct of subaltern resistance. For example, Aradhana Sharma's (2013: 310) work on RTI activism has shown how the RTI Act relies on an insistence on the use of formal rules and terminology that normalises statist technologies of rule: 'The RTI law works as a governmental mechanism . . . that forces people to engage and audit the state in its own idiom.' Not only does this exclude subaltern groups whose knowledge and command of the state's bureaucratic vocabularies and routines might not be sufficient to pursue claims under the law, but it also channels oppositional collective action in such a way as to foster 'bureaucratized activism and procedural citizenship' (Sharma 2013: 319). Finally, as Chacko (2018) has noted, it should be borne in mind that in its second term, the relationship between activists and the UPA regime cooled down quite considerably: several activists left the National Advisory Council as a result of disagreements that flowed from attempts by Prime Minister Singh and Montek Ahluwalia, the head of the Planning Commission, to ensure that market discipline prevailed over activist claims for accountability, and the government cracked down on several movements and NGOs that were perceived to be critical of its developmental agenda. In other words, whereas the introduction of rights-based legislation was far from inconsequential from the point of view of progressive social movements, for the Congress elite its purpose was clearly to serve as a vehicle that would enable the party to win popular support for a hegemonic project that ultimately attempted to deepen the neoliberalisation of the Indian economy.

The fact that this did not ultimately succeed, and that public opinion shifted massively in favour of Modi's fusion of market liberalism and Hindu nationalism, has a lot to do with the fact that the UPA regime was unable to respond to the popular aspirations that its rule engendered – precisely because the underlying trajectory of growth failed to deliver improved employment opportunities and access to the kind of social infrastructure that equalises and enhances life chances.

THE MODI REGIME AS AUTHORITARIAN POPULISM

The 2014 elections 'signified for the first time ever the replacement of the Indian National Congress by the Hindutva-motivated Bharatiya Janata Party (BJP) as the *central point of reference* of the Indian polity' (Vanaik 2017: 343, emphasis in original). What explains this scenario?

The first thing to note is that the standard right-wing argument that the UPA regime failed to bring about growth is demonstrably false: growth rates were consistently high during both UPA periods – eight per cent from 2004 to 2009 and seven per cent from 2009 to 2014. This is the fastest growth rate witnessed in India since the onset of neoliberal restructuring in the 1990s, and exceeds the economic achievements of the BJP government that ruled India from 1998 to 2004 (Ghatak et al. 2014: 34). There was, however, a slowdown in growth during the last three years of the UPA, and combined with food price inflation and major corruption scandals, this contributed to popular discontent. However, more importantly, economic growth never translated into job opportunities; on the contrary, unemployment continued to rise during the decade that Congress and the UPA ruled India. This fostered a sense of frustrated aspirations among India's subaltern citizens that made it possible for the BJP to extend its sway downward in the Indian socio-economic pyramid (Sridharan 2014). At the same time, Indian capital sided decisively with Modi. In part this was due to the fact that, in late 2013, the BJP beat Congress in a series of state elections. However, it was clearly also a shift that was propelled by dissatisfaction with the rights-based legislation that had been put in place by the UPA: 'India's capitalists regarded these welfare and social expenditures a wasteful drain on the fisc which squandered the opportunity buoyant revenues offered to control the deficit' (Desai 2014: 53).

Just as in 2019, corporate support played an absolutely crucial role in enabling the BJP to campaign on an unprecedented scale in 2014: aided by aircrafts owned by the Adani group, Modi traversed some 300 000 kilometres between September 2013 and May 2014, and held an average of four to five meetings per day during March and April 2014 (Desai 2014; Sinha 2017; Vanaik 2017). However, this only goes some way towards answering the most crucial question about Modi's first general election victory: how did a party that initially emerged at the helm of middle-class and upper-caste reaction to lower-caste and Dalit assertion in the 1980s manage to secure electoral support from the popular classes that the Congress had attempted to appeal to through its strategy of inclusive neoliberalism? This question is best answered by considering the BJP's hegemonic project as a case of what Stuart Hall (1988) has referred to as authoritarian populism – that is, a form of conservative politics that constructs a contradiction between common people and elites, and then uses this contradiction to justify the imposition of repressive measures by the state.

Authoritarian populism under Modi is constructed, first of all, around a narrative of development that seeks to address frustrated subaltern aspirations in the context of jobless growth while opposing dynastic elitism and promulgating individual entrepreneurialism. A key strategy in this regard was to foster a narrative and an image of Modi as a man of development who had demonstrated his leadership skills during his tenure as chief minister of Gujarat from 2001 to 2014, and to build a national cross-class and cross-caste consensus around the imperative of giving power to a strong man who could make headway where others had failed. This narrative, of course, elides the inconvenient fact that Gujarat's growth rates are by no means unparalleled, and, more importantly, that growth in Gujarat has failed most dismally to translate into the kind of human development that would actually amount to the *acche din* (good days) that Modi promised to bring to Indians during his campaign for the 2014 elections (see Desai 2011; Jaffrelot 2015b; Joshi and McGrath 2015; Sud 2012). Nevertheless, as Manali Desai's (2015) research on Dalit and OBC (Other Backward Classes) informal workers in Gujarat has shown, it is a narrative with considerable persuasive force among India's subaltern citizens (see also Desai and Roy 2016). The fact that the BJP won 34 per cent of the lower-caste vote, 24 per cent of the Dalit vote and 38 per cent of the Adivasi vote in the 2014 elections only reinforces this point (see Nilsen 2019a).

The developmental narrative was linked to a putative anti-elitism that pivoted on opposition to the dynastic politics of the Congress party. Modi's objective of achieving a Congress-free India was portrayed as a quest to rid India of a privileged and corrupt elite that was out of touch with the ground realities of the country's common people (see Jaffrelot 2015a; Palshikar 2015; Sridharan 2014). Anti-elitism was closely conjoined with anti-corruption: Modi, the campaign narrative went, was not only not tainted by corruption, but also not afraid to act decisively against it. And what is more, Modi celebrated individual entrepreneurialism in opposition to the rights-based welfare approach of the Congress-led UPA regime (see Chacko 2018; Jaffrelot 2015a; Nilsen 2019c).

To some commentators, this focus on growth, good governance and development amounted to a move away from the Hindu communalism that had been so central to the BJP's expansion from the mid-1980s to the early 1990s, and which culminated in the demolition of the Babri Masjid in 1992 (see Desai 2002; Hansen 1999). Such views, however, fail to grasp the ways in which the market-oriented developmental narrative is linked to a majoritarian cultural nationalism and an ever more aggressive authoritarianism. Hindu nationalism was in no way entirely absent from the BJP campaign trail in 2013/2014, and after the elections it has become more and more central to the party's agenda (Kaul 2017). A majoritarian cultural politics has crystallised around issues such as cow protection, the communal policing of interreligious love and of women's sexuality, the rewriting of school textbooks to bring them in line with Hindutva historiography, and the promotion of religious reconversion among Muslims and Christians. Hate speech has proliferated, and majoritarian rhetoric is clearly linked to communal violence against Muslims and other marginal groups, such as Dalits (Nilsen 2019c). In fact, it was recently estimated that more than 86 per cent of all vigilante attacks on Muslims and Dalits since 2009 had taken place under Modi's premiership (Abraham and Rao 2017).

In this way, through rhetoric and through violence, the Modi regime has constructed the ominous 'other' that authoritarian populism depends on in order to frame a unitary conception of the nation and national culture. These majoritarian constructions of the 'other' are closely linked to a sustained effort to draw a line between true Indians and their enemies, and rallying popular support for a crackdown on those enemies. And crucially, the 'other' is not just the Muslim or the Dalit, but also the political dissident who dares to question and challenge a government that is acting in the interest of the people (Nilsen 2018b). Accordingly, dissidents are accused of being 'anti-national' and subjected to harassment, silencing and murderous violence, as evidenced most recently by the attempt on student activist Umar Khalid's life, and before that by the assassinations of scholars, journalists and public intellectuals such as M.M. Kalburgi, Govind Pansare, Narendra Dabholkar and Gauri Lankesh. Raids, arrests and harassment of human rights activists are also commonplace under Modi's regime, and testify to the authoritarian pattern that is beginning to emerge in the Indian polity (Nilsen et al. 2019: 9–11). Between the general election in 2014 and early 2018, the BJP consolidated its position in the Indian political system through a series of victories in state elections. At one point, the BJP's dominance in electoral politics extended from the national level in Delhi to 21 of India's 29 states. But then the tide seemed to turn. In the electoral sphere, the party's performance at state level proved disappointing, with setbacks in Gujarat, losses in by-elections in north India, and eventually, in late 2018, election defeats in the states of Rajasthan, Madhya Pradesh and Chhattisgarh, where the BJP was the incumbent. These electoral setbacks were paralleled by the emergence of a new wave of farmers' protests in India in response to an agrarian crisis that has only deepened under Modi's reign. In addition, the period from 2016 to 2018 also witnessed the emergence of new and radical Dalit–Bahujan politics that fuses opposition to caste-based discrimination with demands for land rights and dignified work (Nilsen 2019a). However, none of this made any kind of dent on the general election results: the BJP strengthened its gains from 2014 and increased its vote share from 31.1 per cent to 37.4 per cent in 2019 (Kumar and Gupta 2019). In the concluding remarks, I reflect on what this consolidation tells us about the nature and trajectory of authoritarian populism under Modi and what it might entail for Indian democracy.

CONCLUDING REMARKS ON THE MEANING OF MODI 2.0

What do we know about the rise of Modi's authoritarian populism? First, we know that it is based on the BJP extending its electoral sway downward in the Indian social pyramid in a decisive manner. Indeed, the 2019 elections saw an intensification of this trend: compared to 2014, the party increased its vote share from 34 per cent to 44 per cent among lower-caste groups, from 24 per cent to 34 per cent among Dalits, and from 37 per cent to 44 per cent among Adivasis. Whereas the party increased its vote share across all classes, the largest increase happened among poor Indians – from 24 per cent in 2014 to 36 per cent in 2019. To be sure, the core BJP vote base remains the upper castes, 61 per cent of whom voted for Modi; the lower-middle and middle classes, 37 per cent of whom voted for Modi; and the upper-middle class and the rich, 44 per cent of whom voted for Modi (Kumar and Gupta 2019; Sardesai and Attri 2019; Venkataramakrishnan 2019). However, there is no doubt that 'the BJP made disproportionate gains largely among groups where it has traditionally lacked support' (Kumar and Gupta 2019). This deepening of subaltern support for authoritarian populists is, of course, part of a larger global trend, and also witnessed in countries like Brazil and the USA (see Saad-Filho and Solty, this volume).

It is of signal importance to note that these gains happened in the context of a campaign where the BJP entirely discarded its message of growth and development in favour of unbridled and unapologetic Hindu nationalism (Jaffrelot 2019). The 2014 image of Modi as *vikas purush* – a man of development – gave way to Modi as a *chowkidar* – a watchman – who would keep India safe from both foreign and domestic enemies. This enabled the BJP to sideline questions of policy and thorny issues such as jobless growth, agrarian distress and escalating inequalities, and to assert itself as 'a relentless crusader for the cause of the Hindus . . . at the pan-India level' (Kishore 2019). Coupled with clever electoral engineering – the party reached out to specific lower-caste and Dalit groups who were not represented by established lower-caste parties and enlisted their support by offering both representation and public resources – this paid rich dividends in the form of a solidification of the Hindu vote: in 2019, 44 per cent of all Hindu voters supported Modi, up from 36 per cent in 2014 (Sardesai and Attri 2019). The ramifications of this for Indian democracy are potentially dramatic.

As Linda Gordon's chapter in this volume brings out, authoritarian populist and fascist regimes are often closely linked to reactionary social movements, and India is no exception. Indeed, in order to fully understand why the ramifications of the Modi regime are so serious for India's democracy, we have to remind ourselves that the BJP is part of a wider Hindu nationalist movement. The backbone of this movement is constituted by the Rashtriya Swayamsevak Sangh (RSS) – a deeply ideological volunteer organisation formed in 1925, which today has more than 50 000 branches and somewhere between five and six million members across India. Working towards the goal of making India a Hindu nation, the RSS is the central node of a network known as the Sangh Parivar – literally, the Sangh family – that comprises organisations that operate in specific domains and work with particular groups throughout Indian society (for example, students, workers, women and youth). Over time, the Sangh Parivar has successfully embedded itself deeply in the institutional fabric of civil society, and as a result the Hindu nationalist movement wields considerable power and influence in India today (see Jaffrelot 1996; Thachil 2016). The BJP is the electoral wing of the Sangh Parivar, and after the consecutive victories of the 2014 and 2019 elections, its mandate is far stronger than during its previous period in power at the national level in India (1998–2004). This is a crucial advance for the wider Hindu nationalist movement and its majoritarian project. Indeed, it represents nothing short of what Chatterji, Hansen and Jaffrelot (2019: 1) refer to as 'the contemporary ascendance of Hindu nationalist dominance to establish a majoritarian state in India'.

We also know that this ascendance is both enabled by and profitable to Indian capital. In saying this, I am not suggesting that there is some kind of intrinsic link between Hindu nationalism as a political project and Indian capital. As much as Indian business currently supports Modi and as much as the BJP's economic policies have shown a consistent pro-business and pro-market orientation, Indian capital has also been happy to throw its weight behind Congress when this was opportune, and Congress, of course, has played a crucial role in advancing neoliberalisation – and with that, corporate interests – in India. The current embrace between the BJP and Indian business elites, then, is first and foremost a strategic alliance. Leading Indian business houses profited handsomely under Modi's first period in power, and there is already strong evidence that this will continue under Modi 2.0. At the time of writing, Modi's new government has already introduced corporate tax cuts, and further substantial economic reforms are expected to follow, such as changes in labour laws, new rounds of privatisation and the establishment of land banks for industrial development (Sengupta 2019). What this indicates, of course, is that the next five years are sure to witness the further intensification of both the structural and instrumental power of capital in India's political economy (see Murali 2019; Sinha 2019). This will push redistributive reform even further to the margins of politics in a society where the richest one per cent of the population controls 73 per cent of all wealth, and consequently deepen the already entrenched social deficits of Indian democracy (Nilsen et al. 2019).

In 2021, the rise of Hindu nationalism as a deeply entrenched hegemonic project and the strengthening of the power of capital in India's political economy might receive a further boost if the BJP achieves a majority in the Rajya Sabha – the upper house of India's parliament. With majorities in both houses, the BJP will be in a position to push through major legal reforms without significant opposition. The fact that the party has already populated public institutions with its henchmen and will continue to do so – specifically in the judiciary – only adds to the momentum of this process. On the ground, violence and coercion has continued unabated since 23 May 2019. For example, within four days of Modi's election victory, Indian media reported six incidents of violence against people from vulnerable and marginalised communities – among them a Muslim man who was severely beaten for wearing a skullcap. And in BJP-ruled Uttar Pradesh, a freelance journalist was arrested and kept in jail for close to a week for social media posts about the state's chief minister, the Hindu priest Yogi Adityanath. Given these circumstances, there are no grounds for falling back on complacent assumptions about the resilience of Indian democracy. As historian Federico Finchelstein (2019) has pointed out, we live in an age where populism fuels fascism, and India under the authoritarian populism of Modi 2.0 might very well prove to be an example of precisely this.

NOTE

1   This analysis draws on a Gramscian perspective on hegemonic processes. See Nilsen (2015) for a full discussion of the centrality of the notion of compromise equilibrium in Antonio Gramsci's theorisation of hegemony.

REFERENCES

Abraham, D. and Rao, O. 2017. '86% killed in cow-related violence since 2010 are Muslim, 97% attacks after Modi govt came to power', *Hindustan Times*, 16 July. Accessed 10 October 2019, https://www.hindustantimes.com/india-news/86-killed-in-cow-related-violence-since2010-are-muslims-97-attacks-after-modi-govt-came-to-power/storyw9CYOksvgk9joGSSaXgpLO.html.

Bhaduri, A. 2008. 'Predatory growth', *Economic and Political Weekly* 43 (16): 10–14.

Business Standard Web Team. 2019. 'Ruling BJP got 95% of funds: Why there's an uproar over electoral bonds', *Business Standard*. Accessed 10 October 2019, https://www.businessstandard.com/article/current-affairs/ruling-bjp-bags-95-of-funds-why-there-s-anuproar-over-electoral-bonds-119040500309_1.html.

Chacko, P. 2018. 'The right turn in India: Authoritarianism, populism and neoliberalisation', *Journal of Contemporary Asia* 48 (4): 541–564.

Chatterji, A., Hansen, T.B. and Jaffrelot, C. 2019. 'Introduction'. In A. Chatterji, T.B. Hansen and C. Jaffrelot (eds), *Majoritarian State: How Hindu Nationalism Is Changing India*. Delhi: Oxford University Press, pp. 1–15.

Chopra, D. 2011a. 'Policy making in India: A dynamic process of statecraft', *Pacific Affairs* 84 (1): 89–107.

Chopra, D. 2011b. 'Interactions of "power" in the making and shaping of social policy', *Contemporary South Asia* 19 (2): 153–171.

Crabtree, J. 2018. 'The symbiotic careers of Narendra Modi and Gautam Adani', *The Wire*, 17 July. Accessed 10 October 2019, https://thewire.in/books/the-symbiotic-careers-of-modi-and-adani.

Das, S.K. 2013. *India's Rights Revolution: Has It Worked for the Poor?* Delhi: Oxford University Press.

Desai, M. 2015. 'Rethinking hegemony: Caste, class, and political subjectivities among informal workers in Ahmedabad'. In A.G. Nilsen and S. Roy (eds), *New Subaltern Politics: Rethinking Hegemony and Resistance in Contemporary India*. Delhi: Oxford University Press, pp. 54–75.

Desai, M. and Roy, I. 2016. 'Development discourse and popular articulations in urban Gujarat', *Critical Asian Studies* 48 (1): 1–26.

Desai, R. 2002. *Slouching towards Ayodhya: From Congress to Hindutva in Indian Politics*. Delhi: Three Essays Collective.

Desai, R. 2011. 'Gujarat's Hindutva of capitalist development', *South Asia* 34 (11): 354–381.

Desai, R. 2014. 'A latter-day fascism', *Economic and Political Weekly* 49 (35): 48–58.

Drèze, J. and Sen, A. 2013. *An Uncertain Glory: India and Its Contradictions*. New Delhi: Penguin Books.

Finchelstein, F. 2019. 'Cuando el populismo potencia al fascism', *New York Times*, 21 May. Accessed 10 October 2019, https://www.nytimes.com/es/2019/05/21/populismo-america-latinabolsonaro/?smid=tw-espanol&smtyp=cur.

Ghatak, G., Ghosh, P. and Khoshal, A. 2014. 'Growth in the time of UPA: Myth and reality', *Economic and Political Weekly* 49 (16): 34–43.

Hall, S. 1988. *The Hard Road to Renewal: Thatcherism and the Crisis of the Left*. London: Verso Books.

Hansen, T.B. 1999. *The Saffron Wave: Democracy and Hindu Nationalism in Modern India*. Princeton: Princeton University Press.

Harriss, J. 2011. 'How far have India's economic reforms been "guided by compassion and justice"?' In S. Ruparelia, S. Reddy, J. Harriss and S. Corbridge (eds), *Understanding India's New Political Economy: A Great Transformation?* London: Routledge, pp. 127–140.

Hasan, Z. 2019. 'This is a landslide. India is now a majoritarian democracy', *The Citizen*, 23 May. Accessed 10 October 2019, https://www.thecitizen.in/index.php/en/NewsDetail/index/2/16982/This-is-aLandslide-India-is-Now-a-Majoritarian-Democracy.

Jaffrelot, C. 1996. *The Hindu Nationalist Movement and Indian Politics*. New Delhi: Viking.

Jaffrelot, C. 2015a. 'What "Gujarat model"?—Growth without development—and with socio-political polarisation', *Contemporary South Asia* 38 (4): 820–838.

Jaffrelot, C. 2015b. 'The Modi-centric BJP 2014 election campaign: New techniques and old tactics', *Contemporary South Asia* 23 (2): 151–166.

Jaffrelot, C. 2019. 'Election results invite questions for liberals. Worldwide, they lack their rivals' discipline', *Indian Express*, 24 May. Accessed 10 October 2019, https://indianexpress.com/article/opinion/columns/narendra-modi-vikas-lok-sabha-elections-5745364/.

Joshi, D.K. and McGrath, K. 2015. 'Political ideology, public policy and human development in India: Explaining the gap between Gujarat and Tamil Nadu', *Journal of Contemporary Asia* 45 (3): 465–489.

Kaul, N. 2017. 'Rise of the political Right in India: Hindutva development mix, Modi myth, and dualities', *Journal of Labour and Society* 20 (4): 523–548.

Kishore, R. 2019. 'Mandir, mandal and markets: How BJP reversed post-2014 setbacks', *Hindustan Times*, 27 May. Accessed 10 October 2019, https://www.hindustantimes.com/india-news/how-bjpreversed-post-2014-setbacks/story-ikF2ju1A4qtvBpU08X-l6JK.html.

Kumar, S. and Gupta, P. 2019. 'Where did the BJP get its votes from in 2019?' *LiveMint*, 3 June. Accessed 10 October 2019, https://www.livemint.com/politics/news/where-did-the-bjp-get-its-votesfrom-in-2019-1559547933995.html.

Murali, K. 2019. 'Economic liberalization and the structural power of business'. In C. Jaffrelot, A. Kohli, and K. Murali (eds), *Business and Politics in India*. New York: Oxford University Press, pp. 25–49.

Muralidharan, S. 2014. 'Bull run in wake of Modi mania hikes Ambani, Adani fortunes dramatically', *NewsClick*, 29 May. Accessed 10 October 2019, https://www.newsclick.in/india/bull-run-wakemodi-mania-hikes-ambani-adani-fortunes-dramatically.

Nayyar, D. 2006. 'India's unfinished journey transforming growth into development', *Modern Asian Studies* 40 (3): 797–832.

Nielsen, K.B. and Nilsen, A.G. 2015. 'Law struggles and hegemonic processes in neoliberal India: Gramscian reflections on land acquisition legislation', *Globalizations* 12 (2): 203–216.

Nilsen, A.G. 2015. 'For a historical sociology of state-society relations in the study of subaltern politics'. In A.G. Nilsen and S. Roy (eds), *New Subaltern Politics: Reconceptualizing Hegemony and Resistance in Contemporary India*. New Delhi: Oxford University Press, pp. 31–53.

Nilsen, A.G. 2018a. 'How can we understand India's agrarian struggle beyond "Modi Sarkar Murdabad"?' *EPW Engage*, 21 December. Accessed 10 October 2019, https://www.epw.in/engage/article/howcan-we-understand-indias-agrarian-struggle-beyond-modi-sarkar-murdabad.

Nilsen, A.G. 2018b. 'An authoritarian India is beginning to emerge', *The Wire*, 31 August. Accessed 10 October 2019, https://thewire.in/politics/an-authoritarian-india-is-beginning-to-emerge.

Nilsen, A.G. 2019a. 'Modi victory secures illiberal, majority rule', *Mail and Guardian*, 29 May. Accessed 10 October 2019, https://mg.co.za/article/2019-05-29-00-modi-victory-secures-illiberalmajority-rule.

Nilsen, A.G. 2019b. 'Indian democracy has failed to advance redistributive reforms for marginalised groups', *EPW Engage*, 9 April. Accessed 10 October 2019, https://www.epw.in/engage/article/indian-democracy-has-failed-advanceredistributive-reforms-marginalised-groups.

Nilsen, A.G. 2019c. 'From inclusive neoliberalism to authoritarian populism: Trajectories of change in the world's largest democracy'. In M. Ray (ed.), *State of Democracy: Essays on the Life and Politics of Contemporary India*. Delhi: Primus Books.

Nilsen, A.G. and Nielsen, K.B. 2016. 'Social movements, state formation and democracy in India: An introduction'. In K.B. Nielsen and A.G. Nilsen (eds), *Social Movements and the State in India: Deepening Democracy?* Basingstoke: Palgrave Macmillan, pp. 1–24.

Nilsen, A.G., Nielsen, K.B. and Vaidya, A. 2019. 'Trajectories and crossroads: Indian democracy at 70'. In A.G. Nilsen, K.B. Nielsen and A. Vaidya (eds), *Indian Democracy: Origins, Trajectories, Contestations*. London: Pluto Books, pp. 1–12.

Palshikar, S. 2015. 'The BJP and Hindu nationalism: Centrist politics and majoritarian impulses', *South Asia* 38 (4): 719–735.

Ruckert, A. 2010a. 'The forgotten dimension of social reproduction: The World Bank and the poverty reduction strategy paradigm', *Review of International Political Economy* 17 (5): 816–839.

Ruckert, A. 2010b. 'The poverty reduction strategy paper of Honduras and the transformations of neoliberalism', *Canadian Journal of Latin American and Caribbean Studies* 35 (70): 113–139.

Ruparelia, S. 2013. 'India's new rights agenda: Genesis, promises, risks', *Pacific Affairs* 86 (3): 569–590.

Sardesai, S. and Attri, V. 2019. 'Post-poll survey: The 2019 verdict is a manifestation of the deepening religious divide in India', *The Hindu*, 30 May. Accessed 10 October 2019, https://www.thehindu.com/elections/lok-sabha-2019/the-verdict-is-a-manifestation-of-the-deepening-religious-divide-in-india/article27297239.ece.

Schmidt, B. 2017. 'India's richest banker Uday Kotak wins big from Narendra Modi's cash ban', *LiveMint*, 28 July. Accessed 10 October 2019, https://www.livemint.com/Industry/gIQyqXahUyF4ZsIrvp2Y2H/Indias-richestbanker-Uday-Kotak-wins-big-from-Narendra-Mod.html.

Sengupta, A. 2019. '"Big bang" reform push by Modi 2.0 govt to target workers' rights', *NewsClick*, 7 June. Accessed 10 October 2019, https://www.newsclick.in/big-bang-reform-push-modi-2.0-govttarget-worker-rights.

Sharma, A. 2013. 'State transparency after the neoliberal turn: The politics, limits, and paradoxes of India's Right to Information law', *Political and Legal Anthropology Review* 36 (2): 308–325.

Sharma, P. 2015. *Democracy and Transparency in the Indian State: The Making of the Right to Information Act*. London: Routledge.

Sinha, A. 2019. 'India's porous state: Blurred boundaries and the evolving business-state relationship'. In C. Jaffrelot, A. Kohli and K. Murali (eds), *Business and Politics in India*. New York: Oxford University Press, pp. 50–93.

Sinha, S. 2017. 'Fragile hegemony: Social media and competitive electoral populism in India', *International Journal of Communication* 11: 4158–4180.

Sridharan, E. 2014. 'Behind Modi's victory', *Journal of Democracy* 25 (4): 20–33.

Srujana, B. 2019. 'The billionaire beneficiaries of BJP's schemes', *NewsClick*, 3 May. Accessed 10 October 2019, https://www.newsclick.in/BJP-Schemes-Modi-Ambani-Adani-Baba-Ramdev-IndianBillionaire.

Sud, N. 2012. *Liberalization, Hindu Nationalism, and the State: A Biography of Gujarat*. New Delhi: Oxford University Press.

Tanwar, S. 2019. 'Indian political parties spent $8 billion on this year's elections – nearly half was by the BJP', *Quartz India*, 5 June. Accessed 10 October 2019, https://qz.com/india/1635113/modis-bjpspent-way-more-than-congress-in-indian-election-2019/.

Thachil, T. 2016. *Elite Parties, Poor Voters: How Social Services Win Votes in India*. Cambridge: Cambridge University Press.

Ulmer, A. and Ahmed, A. 2019. 'Modi's war chest leaves India election rivals in the dust', *Reuters*, 1 May. Accessed 10 October 2019, https://www.reuters.com/article/us-india-election-spendinginsight/modis-war-chest-leaves-india-election-rivals-in-the-dust-id USKCN1S738Y.

Vaidya, A.P. 2014. 'The origin of the forest, private property, and the state: The political life of India's Forest Rights Act', PhD dissertation, Harvard University.

Vanaik, A. 2017. *The Rise of Hindu Authoritarianism: Secular Claims, Communal Realities*. London: Verso Books.

Venkataramakrishnan, R. 2019. '2019 results: BJP is no longer a "Hindi heartland" party (except for Tamil Nadu and Andhra)', *Scroll*, 1 May. Accessed 10 October 2019, https://scroll.in/article/924468/2019-results-bjp-is-no-longer-a-hindi-heartland-partyexcept-for-tamil-nadu-and-andhra.

Walker, K.L.M. 2008. 'Neoliberalism on the ground in rural India: Predatory growth, agrarian crisis, internal colonization, and the intensification of class struggle', *Journal of Peasant Studies* 35 (4): 557–620.

NEOLIBERAL CAPITALISM AGAINST DEMOCRACY IN SOUTH AFRICA

7

THE DIALECTIC OF DEMOCRACY: CAPITALISM, POPULISM AND WORKING-CLASS POLITICS

Devan Pillay

INTRODUCTION

The South African socio-economic, environmental and political crisis is part of a global crisis of neoliberal carbon capitalism,[1] where increasing inequality and poverty has delegitimised democratic institutions and seen the rise of right-wing populism. The entrenched power of monopoly capitalism in South Africa, only fractionally deracialised but substantially globalised, still bears the hallmarks of apartheid capitalism. However, instead of facing a left-wing Polanyian counter-movement,[2] it has been met with a counter-force of klepto-capitalism and racial populism, which uses some of the language of the Left to win support amongst those who have been denied the fruits of the post-apartheid order.

This chapter discusses threats to South Africa's constitutional order by interrogating two competing narratives – namely, that of liberalism and the nationalist-populist countermovement. It then considers two working-class responses that attempt to rise above these dominant narratives – Marxist–Leninism and the popular-democratic (democratic eco-socialist) alternative. Through this discussion, the role of the trade union movement in the struggle for democracy emerges as a key factor.

Indeed, it is the leading component of the democratic trade union movement, the Congress of South African Trade Unions (Cosatu) – which was central to the demise, of apartheid and the promotion of a participatory-democratic socialist politics – that delivered crippling blows to that very politics. Along with the South African Communist Party (SACP), it deliberately created the 'tsunami' that from 2007 to 2009 brought into power a nascent kleptocratic bourgeoisie, led by Jacob Zuma. This was couched as an attempt to dislodge the '1996 class project', which some refer to as 'white monopoly capitalism' (WMC) (Malikane 2017b). One of its key allies at the time was the African National Congress Youth League (ANCYL) and its charismatic leader Julius Malema, who later split off to form the Economic Freedom Fighters (EFF). Zuma's administration became enmeshed with the parasitic business interests of the Gupta family from India, and together they are popularly referred to as the Zupta faction of the ruling ANC. While the EFF mobilised against Zupta corruption, its own leaders have been implicated in corruption scandals.

Although post-apartheid corruption is not confined to the Zuptas or the EFF (Von Holdt 2019), today the two most destabilising fractions of the nascent kleptocratic bourgeoisie are to be found inside the ANC (the Zuptas) and outside (the EFF), with the latter taking on a more strident form of racial populism. In the meantime, in 2014/2015 Cosatu experienced a major rupture when its biggest affiliate, the National Union of Metalworkers of South Africa (Numsa), was kicked out of the federation for resolving to stop supporting the ANC, followed by the ousting of Cosatu general secretary Zwelinzima Vavi – both with the active collusion of the SACP, which continued to offer Zuma firm support. Numsa and Vavi went on to form the South African Federation of Trade Unions (Saftu) in 2017. Ironically, by that time the SACP itself began to move away from Zuma, and participated in nationwide protests for his removal, as the depth of the corruption over which he presided became more manifest. Today, the once strident voice of Cosatu against the klepto-capitalist class fraction is diminished – but so is Vavi's voice struggling to assert itself within Saftu, as its largest affiliate Numsa seems caught up within the knots of its own WMC discourse (Pillay 2017).

In other words, the morbid symptoms of an old order refusing to die, and a new struggling to be born (Gramsci 1971), have been revealed in all their grotesqueness. The wealth and splendour of the entrenched and new elites, benefiting from what some in the 1990s called the 50 per cent economy (Morris 1993), has fuelled a racialised backlash that draws its breath from the deep sense of relative and absolute deprivation experienced by the excluded majority. This poses a direct threat to the constitutional order.

The tragedy is that the organised Left, in particular the trade union movement, today stands as transfixed as a deer caught in the headlights, while right-wing nationalist-populists steal aspects of their discourse to ride the wave of discontent (not unlike what is happening elsewhere in the world). Although there is now a concerted attempt by liberal democrats within the ANC to reassert control over the state (without upsetting the economic order), the left critique of racial capitalism, and the statist solutions some have proposed, are being used by populists to try to reopen access to state coffers.

THE LIBERAL NARRATIVE: 'WE HAVE NOW BEGUN OUR DESCENT'

Justice Malala's book *We Have Now Begun Our Descent* (2015), written while Jacob Zuma was in power, suggests that we are entering a classic post-liberation scenario written all over Africa and other parts of the post-colony, where nationalist elites vie with each other to eat at the trough, putting the country to ruins. The unstated subtext, tweeted, for example, by Democratic Alliance (DA) politician Helen Zille, is that the institutions of modernity, built by the colonial regimes according to standards primarily set in western Europe,[3] and slowly transformed post-liberation, were now in danger of being dismantled, or severely compromised. Zille was responding to the new 'woke' Fallist[4] generation, whose 'decolonial' discourse seemed to deny any positive fallout from the horrors of the colonial impact, by suggesting that they were benefiting from its infrastructural legacy (piped water, roads, hospitals, education, etc.).

Defenders of Zille argue that she was merely echoing the famous Monty Python satirical sketch in the movie *Life of Brian*, where a group of anti-Roman revolutionaries ask, 'What did the Romans ever do for us?'[5] Some go further, and say what she is doing is akin to what Karl Marx did in the *Communist Manifesto*: severely criticising capitalism as an exploitative and oppressive social system – but simultaneously acknowledging capitalism as a revolutionary phenomenon, with science, technology and rational thought sweeping away the vestiges of pre-capitalist ignorance, superstition and frozen hierarchies of oppression. For Marx, the task of socialists was not to try to return to a mythical past, but to build on the positive within capitalism, in order to take society onto a higher plane of social justice and equality. In a similar vein, Zille, while not a socialist,[6] was looking to East Asian states like Singapore and Hong Kong, where locals apparently dwell not on their colonial past, but on their post-colonial present and future.[7]

The response to Zille was harsh, labelling her as an apologist of colonialism. As a prominent politician of the liberal opposition, which has its roots as a liberal white party that challenged the apartheid government from within the apartheid parliament,[8] Zille was an easy target of the 'woke' generation. Very few black people came to her defence, for fear of being labelled an appeaser of colonial attitudes. Indeed, Zille's dogged insistence on repeating this Twitter narrative earned her rebukes from within her own party, as a new generation of black DA leaders, who promote a new 'afro-liberalism' (Jolobe 2019), became increasingly afraid of the political consequences of any suggestion that colonialism had any positive impact. On the other side of the spectrum, the tilt towards aspects of the decolonial discourse, such as a critique of white privilege and support for affirmative action, alienated right-wing DA supporters who had drifted towards the party after the demise of the National Party, the apartheid-era ruling party (see Africa 2019; Jolobe 2019).

The DA, of course, primarily represents the interests of liberal capitalism (in both its mild redistributive/afro-liberal and more strident neoliberal manifestations),[9] and its voter base has its roots in white liberal suburbia. While it has attracted a sizeable number of black voters in recent years, many middle-class black voters drifted back to the ANC under Cyril Ramaphosa, who promised a return to 'normal' capitalism[10] (i.e. based on the rule of law) by cleaning up the state, and rebuilding the integrity of state institutions and public enterprises crippled by corruption under the Zuma administration. In this he attracted support from sections of white liberal opinion (such as the former editor of *Business Day*, Peter Bruce), as he is perceived to be an important bulwark against a right-wing, parasitic populism both from within the ANC, and its EFF offshoot.

Protecting the constitutional order, however, is not only the concern of liberals within the DA and the Ramaphosa faction of the ANC. Others within the ANC Alliance and the opposition[11] (including broader civil society) also argue that, whether or not capitalism as a system is supported or criticised, stark choices have to be made in the short to medium term. The decline of Zimbabwe and Venezuela as examples of 'anti-imperialist', statist alternatives has boosted arguments that *productive* capital in the private sector, as employers of vast numbers of people and contributors to the coffers of the state (in order to, amongst other things, fund social and physical infrastructure), ought to be boosted, not lambasted. In other words, monopoly capitalism, even if it has influence over the state in some ways, must be contrasted with *unproductive* parasitic capital such as that of the Zuptas (see Basson and Du Toit 2017; Bhorat et al. 2017). In this view, while state-owned enterprises (SOEs) have an important role to play, the experience of state capture under the Zuma regime has rendered them dysfunctional and a major drag on the fiscus, with bailouts to SOEs such as electricity utility Eskom, the South African Broadcasting

Corporation (SABC) and South African Airways (SAA) being the most visible. The role of SOEs, however, remains an issue of debate within the Ramaphosa administration (Bruce 2019).

Nevertheless, as Von Holdt (2019) points out, corruption has not been confined to the Zupta nexus, but forms part of an informal political-economic system that began with ANC rule, as corruption became a mechanism of class formation for black people who were excluded from networks of established (white) capital that monopolised key sectors of the economy. Indeed, the established private sector is also not immune to corruption, as the recent Steinhoff case vividly illustrates (see Rose 2018; Styan 2018). These points are stressed by those who reduce the Zupta nexus to mere 'lizards' next to the 'crocodiles' of 'white monopoly capital' (see next section).

Even if this countercharge is conceded, defenders of the constitutional order support the view that productive private capital remains a critical component of any developmental path that seeks to reduce inequality and eliminate poverty. These sentiments are embedded within the logic of the National Development Plan (NDP), which emerged through a process chaired by former finance minister Trevor Manuel and Cyril Ramaphosa during 2010/2011. The labour movement does not necessarily question the role of private capital (at least in the short to medium term). However, it has argued for much greater state (and civil society[12]) involvement in policy determination to curb its profit-maximisation tendency and redirect the social surplus towards developmental outcomes, through a capable democratic developmental state. This is consistent with the perspectives of Keynesian left critics (and Marxists who see the logic of reforms within an overall transformational trajectory).

However, 'revolutionary' Marxists (as well as anarchists) tend to see no positive role for private capital, and seek its immediate overthrow (at least in the abstract). In such a logic *all* capital is 'corrupt', because capitalism as a system is 'corrupt', so there is no need to specify and target one form of corruption over the other (see Gentle 2019).[13] This seems to be the logic behind, for example, the rhetoric of Numsa and its recently formed Socialist Revolutionary Workers Party (SRWP)[14] – and coincides in material ways with the nationalist-populist argument, by minimising the importance of the Zupta phenomenon in favour of an exclusive focus on WMC.

In other words, the liberal-democratic constitutional order, exposed to the winds of an economic order that has failed to address racialised inequality, poverty and unemployment, has ushered in a countermovement that can threaten its very foundation.

NATIONALIST-POPULIST RESPONSES

Following liberal capitalism's global crisis of legitimacy, the term 'populism' has re-emerged in recent times, in relation to figures like Trump in the US, as well as Malema and the EFF in South Africa. In the 1980s it was used by critics (mainly within the re-emerging democratic trade union movement) to specify, firstly, the *undemocratic* leadership styles of organisations in relation to their organisational practices (with top-down leadership, often based on charismatic leaders, with weak structures of accountability); and secondly, their *non-class* ideological discourses, with an emphasis on an undifferentiated 'people', or 'black people', as opposed to a specification of class (and gender) differences. This lack of specification allowed middle-class male leaders to assume leadership of organisations, whereby working-class people were used as ladders for their elite advancement. Laclau (1979) tried to make a distinction between *bourgeois* populism and *working-class* populism – in the former a populist ideology articulates with specific bourgeois interests, whereas in the latter populism articulates with working-class (or socialist) interests. Today US media (including left media such as *Jacobin* magazine – see Venizelos and Stavrakakis 2020; Solty, this volume) tend to refer to Donald Trump and democratic socialist candidate Bernie Sanders as variants of populism (right-wing and left-wing, respectively – see Gordon, this volume). By contrast, Marxists such as Hall (1980), Mouzelis (1978) and Saul (1986) preferred the term popul*ar*, or *popular-democratic*, to differentiate a popular alliance under a democratic socialist leadership from that of elite or authoritarian populism (see later).

The ANC could be seen as a hybrid movement that, within its alliance with the SACP and Cosatu, casts itself as 'popular-democratic' (see Saul 1986), but in practice contains strong liberal-populist as well as narrow nationalist/Africanist populist impulses. The latter found full expression in the Pan Africanist Congress (PAC) split-off in 1959, and more recently through the EFF (with significant remnants coalescing around the Zupta faction of the ANC). While, as previously noted, corruption is not confined to any of these factions or split-offs (Von Holdt 2019; see also Olver 2017), it reached unprecedented heights during the Zuma administration. Today we have two major populist forces, the Zuptas and the EFF, competing at times, but increasingly finding common ground against the more liberal nationalist faction currently holding power by a thin margin within the ANC (and supported by the SACP and Cosatu). Both populist forces have ties to parasitic capital and are mired in corruption scandals.[15]

Marxist writers such as Patrick Bond (2019) have applied the US media terminology to South Africa, whereby the EFF is referred to as 'left-populist', given its
'Marxist–Leninist–Fanonist' ideological stance (EFF 2013), and its usage of red
working-class overalls in parliament to denote an identification with the working
class.[16] This is in contrast to those who have labelled it neo- or proto-fascist (see
Baccus 2013; Head 2019; Lagardien 2019; SAPA 2015; Satgar 2017), given its macho
militaristic posturing, flirtations with violence, and use of race-baiting to whip up
support amongst its followers, many of whom are alienated, unemployed youth.
Despite its 'Marxist–Leninist' pretensions, the EFF has a faint presence within the
organised working class, mobilising as it does on an anti-white, narrow nationalist
basis – a populist discourse that invokes 'black people' to its cause. Its organisational
form accords very much with a populist type, with Malema occupying an undis-
puted leadership position. His enormous charismatic appeal resonates amongst his
followers and within the party, where he seems to wield unquestioned power. While
the party does have structures at various levels (see Essop 2015), it is difficult to
imagine the EFF without Malema at the helm. His 'black consciousness' discourse,
however, often slips into a narrow Africanism (betrayed by his antagonism towards
people of Indian origin).

Despite its left-wing pretensions, the EFF more clearly resembles a right-wing narrow nationalist movement that thrives on racial polarisation (the flip side of right-
wing white nationalism). However, is it 'fascist'? As Barney Mthombothi reminded
us in his *Sunday Times* column on 28 July 2019, fascism in Italy and Germany during
the 1920s and 1930s began life within the socialist movement, and used socialist discourses and appeals to the working class to sideline and attack left-wing organisations.
However, without state power, it would be difficult to pin the EFF down as unambiguously 'fascist'.[17] It seems more like a hybrid of fascistic and Stalinist authoritarianism,
and racial populism. (In this volume, see Satgar for a more fluid understanding of
'fascism' in the context of 'eco-fascism'; Gordon, for the term 'fascistic' to describe
non-institutionalised forms of right-wing populism in the USA; Saad-Filho ['neoliberal authoritarianism'], Nilsen ['authoritarian populism'] and Solty ['right-wing
authoritarian nationalism'] avoid the term altogether in their respective analyses of
right-wing governments in Brazil, India and the USA.)

The Zupta faction of the ANC does not mobilise on an overtly racial basis, but
bears all the hallmarks of parasitic populism under the guise of a left-wing 'radical
economic transformation' discourse. As revelations about Zupta corruption reached
a crescendo in 2017 (see books by Pauw [2017] and Myburgh [2017], along with
the media publication of damning emails, and a Public Protector report on state
capture), it became increasingly difficult for Zuma supporters to mount a defence

of him. Key allies in the SACP and Cosatu deserted him, and critical voices within the ANC began to speak out more openly, alongside a range of voices within civil society and opposition parties (Basson and Du Toit 2017). The defeat of the Zuma faction within the ANC at its Nasrec conference in December 2017, and the ousting of Zuma as state president in February 2018, as well as the closing down of Gupta media outlets ANN7 and *New Age* newspaper in 2018, saw a temporary decline in public support for both Zuma and the Gupta family.

However, during 2019 the Zupta fightback, using the office of the ANC general secretary Ace Magashule, who is implicated in a number of corruption scandals (see Myburgh 2019), as well as the office of the Public Protector, was given a boost (and an informal alliance was formed with the EFF, who since Zuma's departure has targeted those exposing corruption). The strategy includes giving left-wing cover to corruption, casting aspersions on those fighting corruption, labelling journalists and other opponents apartheid spies, and issuing veiled threats of violence. Many of these tricks come out of the Trump 'fake news' playbook, with the aid of computer bots on social media. The public and key opinion formers now have to rely on the courts for credible, rational dissection, to separate the wheat from the chaff.

Chris Malikane, former economics adviser to Cosatu and Numsa, who went on to become the economic adviser to Zupta appointee Malusi Gigaba in Treasury in 2017,[18] is one of the more sophisticated defenders of the WMC thesis and its predatory discontents (see Malikane 2017a[19]). He uses the Marxist critique of the minerals-energy-financial complex (see Ashman et al. 2010), which identifies the white economic oligarchy as one power elite, against the predominantly black power elite within the state. The two have an antagonistic yet symbiotic relationship, and the creation of a black capitalist class fraction is limited by its dependence on the entrenched capitalist class, and its embeddedness in the financial sector (see Mbeki 2009; Southall 2016). Malikane believes that, compared to the crocodiles of WMC, the Guptas are mere lizards (pers. comm.).

It is widely accepted amongst left critics that monopoly capital (in both its Afrikaner and English forms) has historically benefited from its access to state power. Some further allege that monopoly capital had a secret economic agreement with Mandela and the ANC to secure their vested interests in the economy. They subsequently engineered massive capital flight during the 1990s, with the meek agreement of the ANC government (see Terreblanche 2012). Big capital played a major role in ensuring that the ANC adopted neoliberal economic policies in 1996, and is believed to be influential in ensuring that critical appointments in Treasury and the Reserve Bank meet with its approval.

For Zupta-friendly critics like Malikane, this is a form of state capture that dwarfs what the Guptas did. Indeed, in this view the Guptas, notwithstanding their corruption, by entering onto the terrain of WMC, posed a major threat to them and had to be ousted. While there may be elements of truth in this, Malikane underplays or ignores the hollowing out of state institutions during the Zuma period, which created instability and undermined the ability of productive capital (public and private) to grow and thrive (and in the process, create revenue for the state for redistribution). Taken further, if big capital is to be tamed, deracialised and demonopolised (and create decent jobs), an efficient and democratic developmental state needs to be built – but precisely this was undermined by the Zupta project.

If Oppenheimer and the Anglo American Corporation were the face of WMC in the past, today it is Afrikaner capital, the 'Stellenbosch mafia' (see Du Toit 2019), that is allegedly pulling the strings. This is an accusation levelled by both the EFF and the Zupta faction, as they seek to displace WMC through nationalisation of the land without compensation, as well as nationalisation of the mining sector, amongst other statist measures. It is an emotively powerful narrative that has enormous traction amongst the EFF's supporters, as well as within the ANC. It was used to great effect by the PR firm Bell Pottinger on behalf of the Gupta family during the 2015–2017 period, before being exposed (Basson and Du Toit 2017). In recent times the narrative has been revived, with the EFF leading the charge as it tries to discredit Ramaphosa as an agent of WMC, now that its chief protagonist Jacob Zuma is no longer at the helm of the ANC.

While the Zupta faction in the ANC does not exhibit an overtly racialised populism, the EFF displays racialised, fascist-like (or fascistic) characteristics more clearly. Both parasitic fractions, however, have posed severe threats to the liberal-democratic constitutional state, and have undermined the possibility of it becoming a capable, democratic developmental state.

What has been the response of the organised working class to populism and the democratic transition?

WORKING-CLASS RESPONSES: MARXIST–LENINISM OR POPULAR-DEMOCRATIC ECO-SOCIALISM?

Historically, working-class organisations have offered a powerful counter to both economic liberalism and narrow nationalism in the fight against racial capitalism. This includes the democratic trade union movement as well as Marxist-oriented groups and parties like the SACP and the 'Cape radicals' (see Soudien 2019;

Webster and Pampallis 2017), which since the 1920s asserted a 'non-racial' class politics. The SACP, along with Cosatu, became outspoken critics of post-apartheid black economic empowerment (BEE), labelling it black economic enrichment of the few (even if in practice many of their leaders at all levels benefited from it).[20] The vanguardist politics of the SACP, and the subordination of the working class to the ANC's 'national democratic revolution', however, severely compromised the popular-democratic potential of their politics (Pillay 2011).

Unlike populism, a *popular-democratic* politics couches, within a popular discourse, an explicit class politics, whereby the working class leads an alliance of class forces in pursuit of popular democracy. Where this issue was fudged in the 1980s related to what was meant by 'working-class leadership'. The SACP in exile whispered to its cadres that it meant the leadership of the SACP, as the supposed vanguard of the working class. This is a perverted conception of popular-democratic politics, as it reduced democracy to a catechism – a ritualistic camouflage that covers the elite politics of the vanguard within the ANC–SACP. For the democratic unions, it detracted from independent but politically engaged 'social movement unionism', and took them into the realm of 'political unionism', where in extreme versions unions sacrifice their independence and internal democratic integrity in favour of the predetermined politics of the vanguard, which gives the unions instructions (Pillay 2013).

There were those within the unions and the United Democratic Front (UDF), however, who had a richer understanding of working-class leadership, and saw it lying within the power of the working-class movement, led by the unions at that time. The unions combined a powerful mass base with the presence of a notable intellectual capacity, composed of both university-trained intellectuals and worker-intellectuals who rose through the ranks, buttressed by a strong shop steward movement. Indeed, it was the trade union movement that led the internal struggle against apartheid during the latter years of the 1980s, when the UDF was effectively banned (see Pillay 2011, 2013).

After 1990, however, Cosatu's absorption into a triple alliance with the ANC and the SACP meant that, firstly, key leaders and intellectuals would leave the union movement, either to join the ANC in various capacities (local, provincial and national parliament and government) or to become wealthy businesspeople. This severely depleted the unions' intellectual and policy-making capacity, which became known as the 'brain drain'. Secondly, Cosatu's internal politics became such that any questioning of the triple alliance was viewed with suspicion. This severely constrained its internal democracy, as well as the federation's impact on the direction the transition to democracy within the country was taking. Thirdly, the upward mobility of respected leaders created an expectation amongst new layers of leaders, such that the union affiliates became targets of patronage, and corruption became endemic. Fourthly, the formation of investment companies with little scope for oversight from members severely compromised the transparency and accountability within many unions, and opened up more avenues for corruption.

In other words, since 1990, and particularly since 1994, the unions drifted closer towards political unionism and to some extent economistic or business unionism,[21] and along with the SACP gave left cover for the liberal-populist politics of the Alliance, dressed up as the 'national democratic revolution' (see Bezuidenhout and Tshoaedi 2017; Satgar and Southall 2015).

When the ANC government adopted the neoliberal Growth, Employment and Redistribution (GEAR) macroeconomic policy in 1996, Cosatu and the SACP reacted strongly against it, particularly as they were not consulted. It was also a decisive shift away from the more socially redistributive Reconstruction and Development Programme (RDP), which the unions had initially promoted (see Marais 2011). This led to increasing tensions between the working-class components of the Tripartite Alliance and the governing party, particularly after Thabo Mbeki took over as president in 1999. Cosatu and the SACP flirted with the idea of splitting off, but the symbiotic relationship between them and the ANC, which was a gateway to upward mobility for unionists and party leaders (through positions in the state and BEE tender contracts) made that a non-option in reality. In 2003 Cosatu instead adopted the policy of 'swelling the ranks' of the ANC, with the intention of influencing the future direction of the ruling party. As mentioned previously, the two leading working-class organisations proceeded to put their weight behind Jacob Zuma to become ANC president at the 2007 Polokwane conference (Pillay 2011).

Those who disagreed with Zuma as ANC president were either expelled from the SACP or marginalised. The Marikana massacre of mine workers in 2012 (Sinwell and Mbatha 2016), along with increased dissatisfaction with ANC economic policy, eventually saw the emergence of what some have called the 'Numsa moment' in December 2013, which resulted in the formation of Saftu in 2017 (Pillay 2017) and the SRWP in December 2018.

The formation of the SRWP was the culmination of a prolonged process following the momentous 2013 decision by Numsa to stop supporting the ANC and the SACP. After a promising start, whereby Numsa showed signs of reviving the participatory-democratic ethos of its origins in the 1970s and 1980s (Forrest 2011), combined with an ecological thrust that hinted at possibilities of forging an eco-socialist working-class politics (Numsa 2012), the union eventually sidelined independent thinkers, and the leadership closed ranks around a dogmatic version of 'Marxist–Leninism' (Pillay 2017). It undermined its initial efforts around forging a united front of left-wing organisations engaged in a wide cross-section of struggles, and decided to forge ahead with forming a political party (which in the 2019 national elections received a derisory 0.14 per cent of the vote – 24 439 votes, compared with Numsa's membership of around 340 000 – winning no seats in parliament).

The idea of an independent working-class party to take on the SACP first emerged with force within the trade union movement in the 1980s, but never took off. By 1993 Numsa had given up hope of forming an alternative party, and it gradually became a key recruiting ground for the SACP, which by the 1990s had a hegemonic presence within all Cosatu affiliates. While the party imposed on the unions its 'Marxist–Leninist' interpretation of the national democratic revolution, as the first phase towards socialism, this was a much more flexible version than the more rigid Stalinist–Leninist discourses that defined the pro-Soviet party since its formation in 1921. Party general secretary Joe Slovo's seminal 1990 discussion paper, 'Has Socialism Failed?', coming after the fall of east European one-party bureaucratic state socialism, opened up a debate around the relationship between socialism and democracy. This was as much informed by developments in the Soviet Union and eastern Europe, and failures of one-party regimes across Africa, as by the social movement union practices of Cosatu.

A consensus emerged from 1990 onwards that a liberal-democratic constitution was essential to ensure democratic freedoms of various kinds, with built-in checks and balances. Within the unions and the SACP, following developments in Europe, the idea of 'democratic socialism' gained some traction. However, while the SACP ditched its formal commitment to the pursuit of a 'dictatorship of the proletariat' as a necessary precondition for an advance to stateless communism – an ideological discourse that justified vanguardist 'democratic centralist' practices, which Slovo admitted was more centralist than democratic – the SACP retained its adherence to 'Marxist–Leninism'. It seemed to adopt the view, articulated by Blade Nzimande (1992), amongst others, that socialism was *inherently* democratic, and therefore 'democratic socialism' was a tautology. Nzimande went on to become party general secretary in 1998, a position he has held onto ever since (see Williams 2008).

In the pure Leninist conception, true democracy occurs *directly* between the people and the ruling vanguard party/the state, unmediated by multiple political parties and parliaments (Legassick 2007). The promise of the eventual demise of the state under communism (an 'administration of things') legitimises 'temporary' statist-authoritarian rule in favour of the people as a whole (via the 'dictatorship of the proletariat', as a counter to the 'dictatorship of the bourgeoisie'). However, as

Polan's (1984) detailed examination of Lenin's seminal *State and Revolution* argues, the promise of pure democracy under one-party or no-party rule effectively means the rule of an unaccountable 'vanguard'. In other words, Lenin's pure democracy contains the seeds of its own negation: in the absence of opposition parties to hold rulers to account, it is actually anti-democratic. Like liberal democracy, and its populist countermovements, Marxist–Leninism is implicated in the dialectical dance of democracy/anti-democracy.[22]

The narrow and dogmatic 'Marxist–Leninism' of the SACP in the past has now been revived by the SRWP[23] and Irvin Jim, Numsa general secretary and the 2019 election face of the party. It directly contradicts the popular-democratic, social movement union ideological discourse Numsa's predecessors promoted in the 1980s (Forrest 2011). This legacy, however, remains embedded within the union movement.

Today, a popular-democratic working-class politics, which sees an integral connection between democratic freedoms and social equality, also sees a need to incorporate the fight for climate justice (which includes all environmental threats caused by carbon capitalism) – in other words, to forge an eco-socialist, working-class politics (Pillay 2017). Numsa picked up this ball in 2012, but has since dropped it, wheeling out its policy on socially owned renewable energy as a fig leaf while it has forged alliances with BEE coal interests. While Numsa and Cosatu affiliate, the National Union of Mineworkers (NUM), are beginning to work with climate justice activists (Cock 2019), it remains to be seen whether NUM can rid itself of its coal addiction, and aggressively pursue a just transition to a post-carbon future.

Encouragingly, Saftu general secretary Zwelinzima Vavi, in a *Sunday Times* article penned with climate justice campaigner Alex Lenferna, added his voice to growing concerns about climate justice (Vavi and Lenferna 2019). Saftu participated in the Johannesburg climate strike on 20 September 2019 – one of the largest environmental marches ever seen in the country (alongside others around the country, and the world). Vavi, as Cosatu general secretary, played a critical role in ensuring the labour movement defended democratic rights and freedoms during Zuma's reign, and now combined these sensibilities with an explicit identification of the need for a just transition to a post-carbon future. This builds on the work done by small groups such as the now moribund Democratic Left Front (DLF 2011), the One Million Climate Jobs Campaign (2016) and the South African Food Sovereignty Campaign,[24] which have argued for the necessity of red–green alliances (see Cock 2013; Rathzel and Uzzell 2013).

The organised working class is, however, highly fragmented, with low union density of less than 25 per cent (Marrian 2019a) and a faint presence among precarious workers (Webster and Englert 2019). Indeed, many question whether trade unions in post-apartheid South Africa represent the interests of the entire working class or merely those of a relatively privileged 'insider' elite (or, as some argue, the Big Labour flip side of Big Capital – see Gentle 2019; Seekings and Nattrass 2006). Are they a lost cause, or can they be revitalised to fulfil their popular-democratic potential? Or must those interested in building a democratic eco-socialist alternative to both liberal capitalism and statism look elsewhere? This remains a fluid, open question.

CONCLUSION

Democracy is a highly contested concept, and used to legitimate different class interests. Liberal capitalist interests might promote a liberal-democratic order that enshrines critical rights and freedoms for all. However, the promotion of relatively unhindered market power dilutes the content of those rights for the majority of citizens (as well as enshrined environmental rights). Thus, the very foundation of liberal democracy sows the seeds of its own destruction, through rising inequality, poverty and environmental degradation which, in the absence of a democratic socialist alternative, can ignite countervailing authoritarian-statist alternatives. In this scenario, democracy as process (termed 'bourgeois democracy' or, in South Africa, 'white liberal democracy') is countered with the *discourse* of democracy as outcomes (i.e. social equality) – either in the form of national-populism or Marxist–Leninism, or a hybrid of the two.

In a low-grade democracy such as South Africa, where progress towards a Weberian state has been severely compromised, statist solutions can lead to a collapsed economy. In this context the liberal critique cannot be easily dismissed, even if it is constrained by the class interests of its key proponents. Caught between a compromised and inefficient state and a profit-maximising, monopolised private sector, the democratic Left (offering substantive-democratic, non-statist and ecologically informed alternatives) struggles to make its voice heard. For the SACP and Cosatu, re-establishing 'normal' capitalism on a sound democratic basis, with rebuilt institutions able to serve a hopefully job-creating capitalist economy, and more equitable and effective redistribution of the social surplus, is in keeping with the 'first stage' of the 'national democratic revolution' (notwithstanding rhetorical flushes around a 'second phase' within the first stage). This implicitly means that it is the best that can be hoped for in the short to medium term.

For others on the Left, in social movements and NGOs (and, perhaps, some unions), reining in the fossil fuel economy – dominated by what some term 'carbon capital', within a highly constrained 'carbon democracy' (Mitchell 2011) – includes protecting rural communities under siege from mining (see Mnwana and Capps 2015; Skosana 2019), as well as moving workers out of dirty jobs into a new era of green jobs with a strong socially owned (i.e. non-state and non-market) component. These objectives are critical, as part of a longer-term vision of building an alternative working-class politics that draws on the popular-democratic promises of the 1980s, and combines it with a renewed emphasis on democratic eco-socialism. This, ultimately, is the only real safeguard against the threats of both 'neoliberal' capitalism and its parasitic, narrow nationalist and racial-populist responses.

NOTES

1   'Neoliberalism' refers to the post-1980s dominance of the private market (or corporate sector) over the state and society, which takes on many forms, while 'carbon capitalism' (or, as some prefer, 'fossil capitalism') tries to capture the centrality of fossil fuels in the emergence and consolidation of capitalism.

2   See Karl Polanyi (1944). Writing during the rise of fascism, he argued that a counter-movement to the self-regulated market can assume either a left-wing (socialist/social-democratic) or fascist form. In this he is in keeping with the Marxist view that the demise of capitalism can usher in socialism or barbarism (see Angus 2014).

3   Of course, as Karatani (2014) shows, the institutions of Western modernity copied a lot from centuries-old Asian bureaucracies.

4   'Fallist' refers to the Rhodes Must Fall and Fees Must Fall student movements that emerged during 2015–2016. The 'decolonial' discourse of many student leaders often assumed a strident Black Consciousness tone, and 'woke' was a term used for those who had awakened to their condition of blackness in the face of white supremacy and privilege.

5   They then proceed to reluctantly admit that the Romans brought the aqueduct, sanitation, roads, irrigation, medicine, education, wine, public baths, public order and peace – but then conclude, apart from all that, 'What did they do for us?'

6   Zille was regarded as being on the liberal Left in the 1970s–1980s, both as a journalist (who broke the story of Black Consciousness leader Steve Biko's murder in prison) and as an active member of the anti-apartheid women's group Black Sash. She has in recent years allied herself more firmly with the 'libertarian' faction of the DA, which flirts with white nationalism in an attempt to win back conservative white voters after an underwhelming performance in the 2019 national elections. Her subsequent election as chairperson of the DA's federal executive prompted the resignation of DA leader Mmusi Maimane and Johannesburg DA mayor Herman Mashaba.

7   The author visited Hong Kong in 2018 and encountered similar views from a wide range of Hong Kong residents, who contrasted the oppressive presence of the Beijing-friendly government, with that of the British presence (which apparently left a sound institutional legacy).

8   The DA descends from the Progressive Party, whose former leader Helen Suzman is widely respected for her work in support of black political prisoners and banned leaders such as Winnie Mandela.

9 The word 'liberal' is used in its political sense here, to denote belief in a strong liberal-democratic constitutional order. Liberal economics, on the other hand, is more akin to what is often referred to as free-market 'neoliberalism' – namely, minimal state or public intervention in the operations of the self-regulating market economy (as promoted by the race relations wing of the DA, and certain fractions of capital). In practice, since the 1980s, 'neoliberalism' has mutated and some argue it does not exist except as a rhetorical device. This remains a matter of debate.

10 Albeit with a stronger redistributive tint than that of the DA, at least at the level of rhetoric. The DA's so-called social democratic wing (seemingly coterminous with 'afro-liberalism') claims to have a very similar socio-economic agenda to that of the ANC.

11 The ANC Alliance refers to the ruling party and its SACP/Cosatu allies. Under 'liberal opposition' one can also include a wide range of very small parties that seek to uphold the liberal-democratic constitution, and do not question the market economy as such but may have varying views regarding redistributive measures to address the social deficit.

12 By this is meant public participation in various decision-making forums at national, provincial and local levels, as well as within specific sectors and workplaces, as envisaged in the RDP (see Webster and Sikwebu 2009).

13 The word 'corrupt' here is misleading. Corruption refers to operating outside the rule of law, or breaking the law, as opposed to simply being oppressive or exploitative. In a Weberian sense, it means corrupting the rationality of the bureaucratic state, and operating according to the whims of pre-modern patrimonial, clientelistic behaviour.

14 See the SRWP's Red Book, which asserts a statist form of socialism/communism, along with Lenin's 'dictatorship of the proletariat' and 'democratic centralism' (www. srwp.org.za). These sentiments were articulated by Irvin Jim during their election campaign. See various posts during the election campaign on the Facebook page 'Socialist Revolutionary Workers Party', www.facebook.com, retrieved 5 October 2019.

15 Malema was implicated in corruption scandals in Limpopo province while leader of the ANCYL, and he and the EFF had strong ties to tobacco smuggler Adriano Mazzotti, who donated money to the EFF. Malema and the EFF have also been implicated in a corruption scandal involving VBS Bank and tender deals with the city councils of Johannesburg and Tshwane (in exchange for supporting the DA governments there) (see Brummer and Reddy 2019a, 2019b; Suttner 2019).

16 Bond (2019) admits that it is difficult to pin down a consistent label for the EFF, given its hybrid character (see also Nieftagodien 2015).

17 Recent utterances against xenophobia, as opportunistic as they may be, also point to hybridity, given that xenophobia is a key defining feature of fascist mobilisation.

18 Both were dismissed soon after Ramaphosa became state president in February 2018.

19 See response by the SACP's Jeremy Cronin (2017) and a critique of both Cronin and Malikane by Lehulere (2017).

20 BEE offers incentives for established white businesses to incorporate, in the main, politically connected black people into the corporate sector – as board members, shareholders and owners (often highly indebted). A few, such as President Ramaphosa, have become billionaires as a result (but many are debt-ridden).

21 Economistic unionism has also been called collective bargaining unionism (focused on narrow member interests), while business unionism is associated with unions engaging in the capitalist market sphere – for example, through investment companies (see Marrian 2019b; Pillay 2013).

22 See Gibson (2017) for a more positive interpretation of Lenin's 'libertarian moment', where he argued for the right of independent trade unions to exist (against Trotsky and others in the party). Lenin lost this argument and his warning was not heeded: 'The proletariat was conflated with the party, the party with the state. The revolution in Russia, much like many of the anti-colonial movements to come, collapsed into authoritarianism and oppression. But Lenin remained confident about prospects for human liberation,' argues Gibson (2017: 5). No mention is made of Lenin's stance against a multiparty state and a free parliament, however.

23 The SRWP's ideological stance is also influenced by the thinking of Trotskyists from the Workers International Vanguard League, who adopt a dogmatic version of Marxist–Leninism.

24 See www.safsc.org.za.

PERSONAL COMMUNICATION

Facebook discussion with Chris Malikane, 19 July 2019.

REFERENCES

Africa, C. 2019. 'The smaller parties: Who's in and who's out?' In R. Southall (ed.), *Election 2019: Change and Stability in South Africa's Democracy*. Johannesburg: Jacana, pp. 113–131.

Angus, I. 2014. 'The origin of Rosa Luxemburg's slogan "socialism or barbarism"', *Climate & Capitalism*. Accessed 3 October 2019, https://climateandcapitalism.com/2014/10/22/origin-rosa-luxemburgs-slogan-socialism-barbarism/.

Ashman, S., Fine, B. and Newman, S. 2010. 'The crisis in South Africa: Neoliberalism, financialization and uneven and combined development'. In L. Panitch, G. Albo and V. Chibber (eds), *Socialist Register 2011: The Crisis this Time*. London: Merlin Press, pp. 174–195.

Baccus, I. 2013. 'Is Malema's EFF fascist?' *City Press*, 20 August.

Basson, A. and Du Toit, P. 2017. *Enemy of the People: How Jacob Zuma Stole South Africa and How the People Fought Back*. Johannesburg and Cape Town: Jonathan Ball.

Bezuidenhout, A. and Tshoaedi, M. (eds). 2017. *Labour Beyond Cosatu: Mapping the Rupture in South Africa's Labour Landscape*. Johannesburg: Wits University Press.

Bhorat, H., Buthelezi, M., Chipkin, I., Duma, S., Mondi, L., Peter, C., Qobo, M. and Swilling, M. 2017. 'Betrayal of the promise: How South Africa is being stolen'. Report by the State Capacity Research Project (EST, PARI, DPRU).

Bond, P. 2019. 'South Africa suffers capitalist crisis déjà vu', *Monthly Review*. Accessed 3 October 2019, https://monthlyreview.org/2019/01/01/south-africa-suffers-capitalist-crisis-deja-vu.

Bruce, P. 2019. 'Cyril has a tiger in his tank, not a kitten', *Business Day*, 1 October.

Brummer, S. and Reddy, M. 2019a. 'Tender comrades part two: Tshwane tenderpreneur's R15m "EFF tithe"', *Daily Maverick*, 29 September.

Brummer, S. and Reddy, M. 2019b. 'Tender comrades part one: Trailing the Juju tractor', *Daily Maverick*, 28 September.

Cock, J. 2013. 'Ask for a camel when you expect to get a coat: Contentious politics and the climate justice movement'. In J. Daniel, P. Naidoo, D. Pillay and R. Southall (eds), *New South African Review 3: The Second Phase: Tragedy or Farce?* Johannesburg: Wits University Press, pp. 154–172.

Cock, J. 2019. *Resistance to coal and the possibilities of a just transition in South Africa*. SWOP Working Paper 13. SWOP Institute, University of the Witwatersrand, Johannesburg.

Cronin, J. 2017. 'Chris Malikane and the Gupterisation of Marxism'. Unpublished paper.

DLF (Democratic Left Front). 2011. 'Another South Africa and world is possible!' First Democratic Left Conference Report, 20–23 January, University of the Witwatersrand, South Africa.

Du Toit, P. 2019. *The Stellenbosch Mafia: Inside the Billionaires' Club*. Cape Town and Johannesburg: Jonathan Ball.

EFF (Economic Freedom Fighters). 2013. 'Founding manifesto: Radical movement towards economic freedom in our lifetime'. Adopted by the Economic Freedom Fighters National Assembly on What is to be Done, 26–27 July.

Essop, T. 2015. 'Populism and the political character of the Economic Freedom Fighters: A view from the branch', *Labour, Capital and Society* 48 (1&2): 213–238.

Forrest, K. 2011. *Metal that Will Not Bend: National Union of Metalworkers of South Africa 1980–1995*. Johannesburg: Wits University Press.

Gentle, L. 2019. 'Can we learn something from the recent past? Reflections on the Independent Socialists in CCAWUSA-SACCAWU and the current state of the labour movement'. Unpublished draft paper, 11 September.

Gibson, N. 2017. '"The libertarian Lenin" a 100 years on: A May Day reflection', *The Con*, 1 May, pp. 1–8.

Gramsci, A. 1971. *Selections from the Prison Notebooks*. London: Lawrence and Wishart.

Hall, S. 1980. 'Popular-democractic versus authoritarian populism'. In A. Hunt (ed.), *Marxism and Democracy*. London: Lawrence and Wishart, pp. 157–185.

Head, T. 2019. 'Pravin Gordhan, six SA parties condemn EFF for "fascist" behaviour', *The South African*, 17 July.

Jolobe, Z. 2019. 'The Democratic Alliance at a crossroads: The quest for Afro-liberalism'. In R. Southall (ed.), *Election 2019: Change and Stability in South Africa's Democracy*. Johannesburg: Jacana, pp. 83–96.

Karatani, K. 2014. *The Structure of World History: From Modes of Production to Modes of Exchange*. Durham and London: Duke University Press.

Laclau, E. 1979. *Politics and Ideology in Marxist Theory*. London: Verso.

Lagardien, I. 2019. 'Covering Julius Malema and the EFF: It's not an obsession, its good journalism', *Daily Maverick*, 21 August.

Legassick, M. 2007. *Towards Socialist Democracy*. Pietermaritzburg: UKZN Press.

Lehulere, O. 2017. 'Cronin and company harness Marxism to the service of white monopoly capital'. Unpublished paper, 24 May.

Malala, J. 2015. *We Have Now Begun Our Descent: How to Stop South Africa Losing Its Way*. Johannesburg: Jonathan Ball Publishers.

Malikane, C. 2017a. 'Concerning the current situation'. Unpublished paper, 7 April.

Malikane, C. 2017b. 'Some notes on white monopoly caitalism: Definition, use and denial'. Unpublished paper, 23 June.

Marais, H. 2011. *South Africa Pushed to the Limit: The Political Economy of Change*. Cape Town: UCT Press.

Marrian, N. 2019a. 'The end of unions?' *Financial Mail*, 3 October.

Marrian, N. 2019b. 'Union investment companies: Capital fallout', *BL Premium*, 3 October.

Mbeki, M. 2009. *Architects of Poverty: Why African Capitalism Needs Changing*. Johannesburg: Picador Africa.

Mitchell, T. 2011. *Carbon Democracy: Political Power in the Age of Oil*. London and New York: Verso.

Mnwana, S. and Capps, G. 2015. *No chief ever bought a piece of land*. SWOP Working Paper 3. SWOP Institute, University of the Witwatersrand, Johannesburg.

Morris, M. 1993. 'Who's in, who's out? Side-stepping the 50% solution', *Work in Progress* No. 86.

Mouzelis, N. 1978. 'Ideology and class politics: A critique of Ernesto Laclau', *New Left Review* 112: 45–61.

Mthombothi, B. 2019. 'Nationalist militants abandoning democratic liberties? That would be fascists . . . or the EFF', *Sunday Times*, 28 July.

Myburgh, P.-L. 2017. *The Republic of Gupta: A Story of State Capture*. Cape Town: Penguin.

Myburgh, P.-L. 2019. *Gangster State: Unveiling Ace Magashule's Web of State Capture*. Cape Town: Penguin.

Nieftagodien, N. 2015. Reconstituting and re-imagining the Left after Marikana'. In D. Pillay, G.M. Khadiagala, P. Naidoo and R. Southall (eds), *New South African Review 5: Beyond Marikana*. Johannesburg: Wits University Press, pp. 18–33.

Numsa (National Union of Metalworkers of South Africa). 2012. 'Building a socially-owned renewable energy sector in SA'. Resolution of the Numsa 9th National Congress, June.

Nzimande, B. 1992. 'Let us take the people with us. A reply to Joe Slovo', *African Communist* 131 (Fourth Quarter): pp. 16–23.

Olver, C. 2017. *How to Steal a City: The Battle for Nelson Mandela Bay*. Cape Town and Johannesburg: Jonathan Ball.

One Million Climate Jobs Campaign. 2016. *One Million Climate Jobs: Moving South Africa Forward on a Low-Carbon, Wage-Led, and Sustainable Path*. Cape Town: AIDC.

Pauw, J. 2017. *The President's Keepers: Those Keeping Zuma in Power and Out of Prison*. Cape Town: NB Publishers.

Pillay, D. 2011. 'The Tripartite Alliance and its discontents: Contesting the "national democratic revolution" in the Zuma era'. In J. Daniel, P. Naidoo, D. Pillay and R. Southall (eds), *New South African Review 2: New Paths, Old Compromises?* Johannesburg: Wits University Press, pp. 31–49.

Pillay, D. 2013. 'Between social movement and political unionism: COSATU and democratic politics in South Africa', *Rethinking Development and Inequality* 2 (special issue): 10–27.

Pillay, D. 2017. *Trade union revitalisation in South Africa: Green shoots or false dawns?* GLU/ILO Working Paper No. 51. Global Labour University, Berlin.

Polan, A.J. 1984. 'The end of politics: Democracy, bureaucracy, and utopia after Lenin', PhD thesis, Durham University. Accessed 23 October 2019, http://etheses.dur.ac.uk/7150/.

Polanyi, K. 1944. *The Great Transformation: The Political and Economic Origins of Our Time*. Boston: Beacon Press.

Rathzel, N. and Uzzell, D. (eds). 2013. *Trade Unions in the Green Economy*. London and New York: Earthscan/Routledge.

Rose, R. 2018. *Steinheist: Markus Jooste, Steinhoff and SA's Biggest Corporate Fraud*. Cape Town: Tafelberg.

SAPA (South African Press Association). 2015. 'SACP slates "proto-fascist" EFF', *IOL News*, 8 March.

Satgar, V. 2017. 'The EFF's wrecking ball politics is fascist rather than Left', *Mail and Guardian*, 5 April.

Satgar, V. and Southall, R. (eds). 2015. *Cosatu in Crisis: The Fragmentation of an African Trade Union Federation*. Johannesburg: FES/KMM Review Publishing.

Saul, J. 1986. 'South Africa: The question of strategy', *New Left Review* 160: 3–23.

Seekings, J. and Nattrass, N. 2006. *Class, Race and Inequality in South Africa*. Pietermaritzburg: UKZN Press.

Sinwell, L. and Mbatha, S. 2016. *The Spirit of Marikana: The Rise of Insurgent Trade Unionism in South Africa*. Johannesburg: Wits University Press.

Skosana, D. 2019. *Grave matters: Dispossession and the desecration of ancestral graves by mining corporations on Tweefontein (Ogies), South Africa*. SWOP Working Paper 11. SWOP Institute, University of the Witwatersrand, Johannesburg.

Slovo, J. 1990. 'Has socialism failed?' *SA Labour Bulletin* 14 (6): 11–28.

Soudien, C. 2019. *The Cape Radicals: Intellectual and Political Thought of the New Era Fellowship, 1930s–1960s*. Johannesburg: Wits University Press.

Southall, R. 2016. *The New Black Middle Class in South Africa*. Johannesburg: Jacana.

Styan, J.-B. 2018. *Steinhoff: Inside SA's Biggest Corporate Crash*. Cape Town: LAPA Uitgewers.

Suttner, R. 2019. 'The threat to democracy, part two: The EFF', *Daily Maverick*, 16 July.

Terreblanche, S. 2012. *Lost in Transformation*. Johannesburg: KMM.

Vavi, Z. and Lenferna, A. 2019. 'It's time to fight for climate justice', *Sunday Times*, 15 September.

Venizelos, G. and Stavrakakis, Y. 2020. 'Left-populism is down but not out', *Jacobin*, 23 March. Accessed 26 December 2020, https://jacobinmag.com/2020/03/left-populism-political-strategy-class-power.

Von Holdt, K. 2019. *The political economy of corruption: Elite-formation, factions and violence*. SWOP Working Paper 10. SWOP Institute, University of the Witwatersrand, Johannesburg.

Webster, E. and Englert, T. 2019. 'New dawn or end of labour? From South Africa's East Rand to Ekurhuleni', *Globalisations* 17 (2): 279–293. Accessed 4 October 2019, https://www.tandfonline.com/action/showCitFormats?doi=10.1080/14747731.2019.1652465.

Webster, E. and Pampallis, K. (eds). 2017. *The Unresolved National Question: Left Thought under Apartheid*. Johannesburg: Wits University Press.

Webster, E. and Sikwebu, D. 2009. 'Tripartism and economic reforms in South Africa'. In L. Fraile (ed.), *Blunting Neoliberalism: Tripartism and Economic Reforms in the Developing World*. Geneva and New York: ILO/Palgrave Macmillan, pp. 176–223.

Williams, M. 2008. *The Roots of Participatory Democracy: Democratic Communists in South Africa and Kerala, India*. New York: Palgrave Macmillan.

8

DEMOCRACY AND THE RIGHT TO KNOW IN SOUTH AFRICA'S CAPITALIST TRANSITION

Dale T. McKinley

THE FOUNDATIONAL TERRAIN

A large part of the political, social and economic edifice of the apartheid system in South Africa was built on, and sustained by, the control of information and enforced secrecy. This was at the heart of the undemocratic character of the apartheid capitalist system. It was the glue that held together the institutionalised violation of the basic human needs and rights of South Africa's majority and shielded both the state/bureaucratic and private/corporate elites from democratic transparency and accountability.

On the other side of that historical coin, a significant component of the struggle against apartheid was fundamentally a struggle for the democratic reclamation of those human rights, not simply on an individualist basis but to be realised and enjoyed collectively. An essential element of that reclamation involved the right to know, at the heart of which is access to information as a means to ensure democratic transparency and to hold all power to account.

Indeed, as soon as they came to power in 1948, the National Party architects of the apartheid state quickly set about instituting a range of laws and decrees that would not only deepen existing legalised racism but lay the foundation for complete political and administrative control of the state and society. In turn, this ideologically saturated securocratisation of the state was then used to control all social, economic and political relations across South African society and to suppress any resistance from the oppressed black majority (McKinley 2014).

At the same time, the closing down of any meaningful space for democratic involvement by the black majority, alongside the banning of liberation organisations, saw most of those forces embracing armed struggle and moving either into exile or an internal underground. In turn, this objectively demanded highly secretive organisation and practically resulted in the minimal involvement of the majority of the oppressed sectors of the population. In the case of the African National Congress (ANC), South Africa's ruling party since 1994, and its long-time political ally, the South African Communist Party (SACP), this was further combined with a creeping centralisation of power centred on a small collection of exiled, and in some cases an internally incarcerated, leadership.

This centralisation was framed by a generalised adherence to Soviet-style commandist politics and an overarching ideology and rhetoric that did not distinguish between the liberation movement and 'the people'. As former ANC leader Raymond Suttner points out, the combined result was the generalised adoption of a 'warrior culture, the militarist tradition' which 'entailed not only heroic acts but also many cases of abuse of power' (Suttner 2008: 119), leading to the emergence of a liberation movement as a prototype of a state within a state, in which it sees itself as the only legitimate source of power (Melber 2010).

There was, particularly in the early years of exiled struggle, a significant amount of space for democratic debate and dissent within the ANC/SACP-controlled liberation movement. However, this was gradually but systematically narrowed as the demands of enforced ideological and organisational unity alongside the practical exigencies of a largely secretive, underground and exiled armed struggle increasingly took hold.

Once the ANC ascended to political power that kind of thinking and behaviour did not simply disappear. Rather, the most immediate result of the political triumph over apartheid was a continuity of 'the dominant interests that determine the strategic thrust of the South African state . . . [including] ownership of the commanding heights of the economy [and] the repressive apparatus of the state' (Vally 2003: 67). In other words, the mindsets and practices that structured the responses of the apartheid state to basic democratic demands such as access to information, alongside political–social dissent, found a generally warm embrace amongst sections of the ANC leadership and especially within the post-apartheid state's security and intelligence apparatus. Such continuities are clearly evident in how the post-1994 state has approached related legislation. Although the new parliament passed the

Safety Matters Rationalisation Act of 1996, which repealed 34 apartheid-era laws dealing with informational and security legislation, many pieces of legislation from the apartheid days were maintained, and remain as law today.

Some of the most pertinent examples are the Riotous Assemblies Act of 1956, which, amongst other things, gives the state president the power to take 'special precautions to maintain public order'; the National Key Points Act of 1980, which makes accessing and/or distributing 'classified' information and 'disrupting' the operations of secretly designated key points (e.g. airports, military bases and government buildings) serious crimes; the Protection of Information Act of 1982, whose approach to the protection and dissemination of information is informed by the demands of an authoritarian and secretive apartheid state; and the Intimidation Act of 1982 (with minor amendments in 1991), which makes it a crime punishable by up to 25 years in prison for persons who through their behaviour, speech or published writings intend to 'frighten, demoralise, incite or create fear' amongst the public.[1]

Besides these laws, the executive cabinet of government unilaterally implemented the Minimum Information Security Standards (MISS) in 1996. In the name of the 'national interest', MISS set down information security standards for all government departments and agencies based on four categories of classification for handling 'sensitive information' (restricted, confidential, secret and top secret). The MISS, together with the manipulation and non-enforcement of the legislation that was supposed to usher in a new era of transparency – the Promotion of Access to Information Act of 2000 (PAIA) – have gone a long way in preventing the free flow of both state/public and private/corporate information and placed a thick veil of secrecy over whatever was left of apartheid-era state information. This veil largely remains in place today and continues to be used to hide hugely important and politically sensitive information, especially related to corruption within the state and ruling party as well as the past role and contemporary activities of corporate capital (South African History Archive 2016). (For a broader treatment of such corruption, see Devan Pillay's chapter in this volume.)

Indeed, over the last decade the ruling party has fashioned and tried to adopt as law (with varying degrees of success) new legislation to further control and cut off the flow of information. The prime example is the Protection of State Information Bill which was introduced in 2010 by former president Jacob Zuma and his securocrats. Arguably the most regressive and anti-democratic piece of legislation in post-apartheid South Africa, the Bill faced extensive, consistent and effective opposition from progressive civil society.[2]

Amongst its most egregious elements are an open-ended definition of 'national security' that includes undefined 'state security matters' and 'economic, scientific and technological secrets'; giving extremely wide powers over classification procedures and overall management of state information to the minister of state security (and to lesser degrees, other state bodies like the police service); criminalising (with extremely harsh sentences) simple possession and/or disclosure of classified information; and failing to provide a comprehensive public interest defence to protect activists, whistleblowers and journalists (Right2Know Campaign 2012). Even though the Bill was eventually passed by parliament in 2013, for years it sat on the desks of both former president Zuma and current president Ramaphosa without being signed into law. Only recently has Ramaphosa sent it back to parliament due to 'concerns' around its constitutionality.

There are other, related pieces of legislation that further undermine (or threaten to undermine) the ongoing struggle for the right to know. Passed into law in 2013, the General Intelligence Laws Amendment Act centralised all previously existing intelligence structures into the State Security Agency (SSA), itself only created by presidential proclamation in 2009. Such centralisation of power has not only catalysed state, political party and factional secrecy, but has opened the door to much wider harassment and surveillance of those who champion the transparency and accountability that lie at the centre of the right to know. (Jane Duncan's chapter in this volume details how the police and intelligence services have engaged in such harassment and surveillance, especially in respect of community protests.)

Further, in 2015 the ANC-run state introduced the Cybercrimes and Cybersecurity Bill, which still remains in parliament. If passed into law, it will massively broaden the powers of the state's intelligence services to monitor, censor and conduct surveillance of online communication and content, both of which represent one of the most crucial, practical vehicles for gathering and distributing information. Not only does it 'threaten digital rights in significant ways, especially the freedoms of expression and association, and the right to privacy', but by placing a new 'Cyber Security Committee' under the direct political control of the SSA, the Bill 'will hand indirect control of the internet over to South Africa's spies' (Duncan 2015).

It is understandable that in the post-1994 era, the central focus of both the state and the majority of South Africans – with varying degrees of legislative and 'civic' intensity and effect – has been on those rights whose potential realisation historically provided the greatest impetus to the struggle against apartheid, such as equality before the law regardless of race, ethnic or social origin, culture and belief;

freedom and security of the person, expression and association; and the right to adequate housing, healthcare and basic education.

The indirect result, however, has been that other constitutional and indeed human rights, such as the right of access to information,[3] have taken a back seat and been generally viewed as secondary human rights, artificially detached from the realisation of the more 'central' rights. This is a major elision of South Africa's post-1994 democratic character and content. Even if contained within the ideological and institutional confines of a broader bourgeois liberalism, the right of access to information connects all other rights precisely because a commoning of, and public access to, information is the lifeblood of any meaningful democratic participation.

WHAT RIGHT TO KNOW? DEMOCRACY, THE STATE AND SOCIETY UNDER CAPITALISM

The dominant theoretical and ideological construct that has informed interrogations of, and approaches to, South Africa's post-apartheid 'democratic transition' is one of classic capitalist bourgeois liberalism. At the heart of this construct are all the usual freedoms associated with the development of modern (mostly western European) capitalism, including freedom of the individual, religion, the press, assembly, speech and, crucially, also of private property and the capitalist market.

In institutional terms, all of these freedoms are theoretically 'guaranteed' through a system of representative democracy under the rule of law, with institutional 'checks and balances' and an emphasis on a substantial role for the state in both working with and regulating capitalism and in the provision of elements of social welfare. With a few specific tweaks and additions – for example, the inclusion of a range of socio-economic rights in the constitution – this represents the basic architecture of the South African post-apartheid democratic frame.

However, the fundamental problem with this frame is that it falsely separates democratic form, content and context. As I have argued extensively (McKinley 2017), the historic starting point for the ANC's conceptualisation of 'liberation', encompassing both political and socio-economic 'freedom', was and still is a deracialised, nationalist capitalism.

As a result, since the beginning of the democratic transition, the country's 'liberation' has been analytically and practically circumscribed for the majority of its inhabitants; political 'freedom' has been separated from socio-economic 'freedom'. Political control of the state has been practically achieved with very little in the way of any corresponding transformation of the economic sphere; and we only have to take one quick glance at the contemporary results both in South Africa and in most post-independence, national liberation struggles to see what kind of democracy has been delivered.

In the context of an already dominant (neoliberal) capitalist system, that separation was made possible because democratic power was and continues to be seen as being derived foundationally from the political party 'capture' of the existent institutional forms of democracy under capitalism – for example, through the state, electoral representation, corporatism and the rule of law, all of which can, accordingly, be deracialised and built upon. While such institutional forms are arguably in and of themselves not inimical to a meaningful participatory democracy, within the (neoliberal) capitalist frame they practically reflect and represent the dominant class interests.

One of the foundational pillars of neoliberalism is the prioritisation, by both state and society, of the accumulative needs of corporate capital. According to the building plan, doing so will generate the growth and wealth that can provide the practical ways and means to address the needs of the rest of 'the people'. Although the plan was already well in motion by the mid-1990s, former president Thabo Mbeki explicitly laid out the logic in 2003, as captured in his 'two-economies' argument: 'We must work hard to ensure that our centre, the first economy, grows and develops to generate the wealth we need to achieve the goal of a better life for all . . . poverty and underdevelopment act as a fetter on the further development of the first economy' (Mbeki 2003).

Transferred onto the country's transitional political terrain, the complementary message is principally the same: that the primary source of democratic legitimacy and participation is to be found in the needs of the (ruling) party and state and that dissent, oppositional voices and the practical struggles of the majority are varyingly an attack on that legitimacy and undermining of its source. The most apt description of this is an enclosed democracy, or alternatively an 'undemocratic' democracy in practice. Within this framework, institutionalised pluralism becomes the dominant ideological and practical essence of both democracy and development, regardless of the dominant social relations within which such pluralism operates.

Under capitalist social and economic relations, such an institutionalisation has always and everywhere led to an inevitable democratic sterility. Pluralism simply becomes a catchword for a range of organisational forms and individual 'voices', regardless of their respective class and social locations, that are contained and limited within the narrow institutional and political confines of capitalist (neo)liberalism. What this has produced in South Africa is a low-intensity and commodified democracy, where the mere existence and functioning of representative democratic institutions and processes increasingly mask the decline of meaningful popular democratic participation and control. (See the linked discussion and analysis of 'authoritarian neoliberalism' in Satgar's chapter in this volume.)

We can clearly see this when looking at the ruling party and state's claimed valorisation and affirmation of participatory democracy alongside democratic dissent in actual practice as opposed to doing so within the boundaries of an elite-occupied and -run (democratic) institutional architecture. The latter is enforced according to the interests and whims of those elites who occupy and control the associated spaces, the former willingly accepted and embraced as part of an ideological and organisational commitment based on shared democratic processes and practice.

What the ruling party and state have done, with the enthusiastic backing of corporate capital, is to privilege institutionalised pluralism. What this practically means is the active limitation of democratic participation to the confines of those institutional structures it has established, and has administrative and financial control over, as receptive vehicles for supposedly dialoguing with, and listening to, the citizenry. In general, official bodies have effectively served as institutions of control and authority for a minority with political and economic power, incorporating both the public and private sectors. Practically, this has ensured that people's participation takes place on largely undemocratic terms.

Indeed, institutionalised pluralism offers precious little in the way of seriously contesting the parallel character and content of a capitalist state and the policies it implements as well as the economic and social power of corporate capital. Instead, it allows the state (and the political party that is in the driver's seat) to champion a democratic 'developmentalism' which effectively corrals and deflates grassroots participation and struggle for more systemic change. The practical, political result is that transparency and accountability become highly circumscribed due to the 'ring-fencing' of participatory spaces. In turn, this makes it extremely difficult to access relevant information and hold the ruling party and the state accountable, precisely because the entire set-up is conditional on a cooperative and in many cases submissive relationship with those in and with power. In this way, corporate capital is able to largely do as it pleases and the state not only 'legitimises itself through civil society, but also shapes [and controls] the terrain upon which civil society makes demands on it' (Greenberg and Ndlovu 2004: 24–25).

What this practically translates into is the depoliticisation of democratic content and practice. Put another way, the very foundation for any meaningful democratic politics, which is the participation of the *demos* itself (and in South Africa the majority of that *demos* are workers and the poor), is effectively separated from the institutional framework of democracy, periodic elections and representational arrangements notwithstanding (Hippler 1995).

If we accept that democratic power is derived foundationally from the active and informed participation of the majority of the *demos*, then we can fully understand why the right to know is absolutely central to democracy. Indeed, the right to know is a fundamental precondition for participatory democracy. It is not reducible to (elite-led/controlled) institutionalised and representational power, but creates the spaces and possibilities not only for a people-centred democratic terrain but also for more revolutionary, systemic transformation (which is a struggle, not an event) of the existent, primary structures of political and socio-economic power under capitalism.

THE TRANSITIONAL TRACK RECORD

The post-apartheid South African state and the ruling party that has managed it from the start have, in ideological and governance terms, closely followed the corporate model – at the heart of which is a fundamental hypocrisy. On the one hand, there is the demand for 'freedom' from state 'interference' and of the market (to freely make as much profit as is possible and to do with those profits as they please), as well as associated respect for catalysing economic 'growth', creating employment and delivering commodities that people supposedly need.

On the other hand, there is a foundational need for and reliance on the public through the representational form of the state (in a democracy) to provide, underwrite and guarantee the conditions for such 'freedom' and 'respect', regardless of the practical efficiencies and effectiveness of the model or of the more specific social, economic, political and environmental consequences for the vast majority of that public.

In much the same way, the state and ruling party employ a similar model with varying degrees of intensity and application. In their case, however, the 'freedom' demanded is to govern more or less as they please and without undue interference from the public. In other words, damn participatory democracy and the right to know that is essential to it. This is coupled to the demand for a linked 'respect' (in reality, more like obsequious knee-bending) for bringing the people their 'freedom' and/or 'liberation'. Here, the foundational reliance is also on the public, through the state as the source of institutional power and deliverer of material benefit, as well as on constructed and selective support bases within the ruling party and the private (corporate) sector.

Practically, the mutually pursued model is replete with ever-widening gaps between promise, service and the 'delivery' of 'products' (most often commodified) that are invariably overpriced, of questionable quality and whose conditions of production are objectively exploitative and destructive. Whether under Mandela, Mbeki, Zuma and now Ramaphosa's leadership, the state–party nexus has consistently ignored and/or undermined the voice and participation not only of its own core constituencies but also of the larger public which it has just as consistently claimed to democratically speak for and represent. Pillay (this volume) shows how this has played itself out within the ANC-led Alliance. While the best example of this early on in the transition was the 'non-negotiable' macroeconomic programme (Growth, Employment and Redistribution, or GEAR), there are a plethora of other examples at all levels of the state.

A continued lack of public awareness and education as well as the deployment of adequate human resources within the state to implement the PAIA, alongside the poor state of public records management, has ensured that people's access to public/state information continues to remain in intensive care. A good, representative example of this transitional reality is that of over 250 requests for information submitted to all levels of the state by a collection of civil society organisations during 2012–2013 (many of which were on behalf of poor communities), only 16 per cent resulted in the full release of requested information. The private sector is even worse; the success rate during the same period was less than ten per cent (Right2Know Campaign 2014).

Throughout the transition, the ruling party has maintained, and in many cases expanded, its and the state's cosy relationship with corporate capital, both old and new (black economic empowerment), foreign and domestic. There is no better example of this than the much hyped and oft-celebrated 2010 Soccer World Cup. The wall of secrecy thrown up around the initial 2004 deal between the South African state and the Fédération Internationale de Football Association (Fifa), protected as it was by an inbuilt confidentiality clause, was so tight that it took another seven years – after the actual tournament had been completed – for the people of South Africa to find out what their 'democratic' representatives had agreed to, in their name.

When the information finally came out into the open, as a result of lengthy political and legal battles, South Africans found out that the expenditure of public funds was almost 20 times the original estimate. Instead of the estimated R2.3 billion, the state eventually coughed up just under R40 billion. Meanwhile, Fifa took home R27 billion in tax-free profit (*Business Report* 2010). No surprise then that one of the main reasons for the outrageous overexpenditure of public funds, and the accompanying super-profits of Fifa, was the state's acceptance of confidential 'host city' and 'stadium' agreements in which 'many of the terms in the contracts had been framed in an undetermined fashion' (Parliamentary Monitoring Group 2006). If the Soccer World Cup should have taught South Africans anything, it is that secrecy is not only the symbiotic twin of corruption but is inherently antithetical to democracy.

Things have not got better since then. Over the last decade, when civil society organisations and the media have attempted to access information related to the impact of industrial and mining activities on the environment, most state departments and private companies have flatly refused access and treated the hidden information as either state or commercial 'secrets'. One of the most outrageous examples of this is that, during the 2011–2012 period, the Department of Mineral Resources refused 97 per cent of over 100 PAIA requests for information on environmental health and protection, made by the Centre for Environmental Rights (Carnie 2012).

More recently, in 2015–2016, 13 civil society organisations which make up the Access to Information Network submitted 369 PAIA requests to both government and private bodies. The results reconfirm what the Network rightfully calls 'the shocking failure to uphold the right of access to information' (Bruce 2017). Amongst the key findings are that 46 per cent of requests submitted to government were refused; only 34 per cent of requests submitted to government were granted in full; 64 per cent of the appeals submitted to government were completely ignored; 67 per cent of requests submitted to private companies were refused; and only 13 per cent of requests submitted to private companies were granted in full (Access to Information Network 2016).

Indeed, one of the core hallmarks of the 25 years of South Africa's transition has been a consistent and systemic pattern of collusive blocking of the right to know across a wide swathe of sectors/issues. Some of the more egregious examples are steamrolling ahead with the physical and electronic tolling of public roads despite consistent public demands for transparency around the private consortiums involved and associated public expenditure (The Times 2012); the processing and issuing of mining licences, particularly in environmentally protected or sensitive areas, without any community involvement and consent (Pearce 2017); increasing the number of 'national key points' and 'strategic installations' (buildings and infrastructure considered vital to 'national security') which invoke a range of strict anti-disclosure provisions of 'any information' in 'any manner whatsoever' and curtail the right of assembly in or near any key point;[4] throwing a veil of secrecy around the outsourcing, through the issuing of tenders, of public functions and services to politically connected elites and corporates, both domestic and foreign; appointing key personnel in Chapter 9 agencies (state institutions set up to service and defend the public interest) in the absence of public involvement (Right2Know Campaign 2019); and considering and often passing hugely important and impactful legislation either without any meaningful opportunities for public input or while ignoring the inputs that are made (Waterhouse 2015).

The basic defence of and battle to expand the right to know in South Africa has also been made that much more difficult by the gradual but systematic rise of an intrinsically anti-democratic surveillance- and intelligence-driven state and society (see Duncan, this volume). On the one hand, there has been the hugely expanded role of the private sector/corporate world in 'delivering' outsourced or privatised public goods and services, no more so than in respect of rapidly expanding and widely used communications networks and surveillance technology. On the other, the state has readily embraced privacy-stripping measures in response to the threat of 'terrorism', to citizen concerns around individual and residential safety, and to rising levels of organised criminal activity.

As a result, the vast majority of those who live and work in South Africa have absolutely no idea what is actually happening to their personal information. This is despite the fact that the Protection of Personal Information Act of 2013, which is designed precisely to ensure that people know the what, where and how about their personal information, has been the law for almost eight years now.

Some of the key areas of concern include the ramped-up roll-out, integration and interoperability of biometric databases and smart identification systems and cards, with specific focus on the social security and population management and control systems; the massive increase in the presence and technological sophistication of closed-circuit television (CCTV) and automated license plate recognition (ALPR) hardware and software, alongside associated surveillance in both public and private owned (public) spaces; the rapid rise in the use of drones for private use and commercial application, coupled to the incipient nature of associated regulation and the almost complete lack of enforcement; and the collection, storage, 'sharing' and commodification of ever-increasing amounts of personal information and associated metadata by both public and private sector entities, specifically in relation to mandatory subscriber identity module (SIM) card registration for cellphones and the Financial Information Centre Act of 2001 (McKinley 2016).

Cumulatively, this has produced a shifting of the foundations of power. Now, along with the coercive and disciplinary power of the state and the economic and social power of capital, we have the combined political, economic and social power that comes from 'the vast amounts of permanently stored personal data about entire populations' (Cegłowski 2016). It is this power that is now regularly being used and abused by both the South African state and the private sector for, varyingly, enhanced social control, political or factional surveillance, and financial gain.

The 'emerging picture is clear: despite incumbent president Ramaphosa's more recent rhetorical commitments to the contrary, there is, in general terms, more secrecy and less transparency and accountability. While a significant number of generic democratic spaces certainly remain open and alive, the long-term impacts of the conscious and manipulative closing down of participatory space and voice have produced a contemporary terrain dominated by enclosed structures, invited spaces, securitised politics, secretive deals and unilateral decision making. In macro-level or systemic terms, this constitutes nothing less than a contra-democratic, transitional trajectory. (There are echoes here to Satgar's discussion of eco-fascism in this volume.)

IF WE DO NOT KNOW, WE CANNOT BE …

The bottom line, whether in South Africa, Africa or across the world, is that without access to information the struggle to change a country or the world, and the accompanying desire to move beyond the narrow confines of capitalist 'democracy', will be fatally undermined. Put differently, if we do not know, then we surely cannot be the kind of (anti-capitalist) activists, dissenters and democrats that we want to and can be.

Indeed, the ongoing battle for the right to know is primarily a battle against a consciously constructed lack of knowing and against the inaccessibility and unaffordability of information that is crucial not only to survival but to the ongoing struggle for equality and justice. In this respect, Radebe (this volume) surfaces the centrality of decommodified news and information to a meaningful democracy. Its absence is a sure recipe for frustration, disempowerment and conflict. And this is precisely what has been happening for most of South Africa's democratic transition.

The sustained societal conflict and the tens of thousands of community, worker and other protests that have taken place throughout the country are not simply reducible to a lack of physical 'service delivery', state repression or the exploitative activities of capitalists. They have been one of the few available responses (whether planned or spontaneous) by workers, the poor and even sometimes sections of the middle class to the almost complete lack of information and communication, to the consistent failure of institutional, democratic transparency and accountability. If one of South Africa's most basic and central human and constitutional rights can be treated with convenient disdain simply because those in positions of privilege and power do not like the implications that accompany their realisation, then those rights are not even worth the paper on which they are written.

All of this points to seriously worrying signs of a retreat from a grounded, people's democracy; of an 'undemocratic' democracy gaining the upper hand. Those in control of the ruling party and the state, as well as corporate capital, now more than ever pick and choose which aspects of even a limited bourgeois liberal democracy apply to them and what parts of accompanying democratic processes they want the rest of society to enjoy. The terrain of genuine participatory democracy has all but been laid to waste and politically manipulated. Increased control of information, a generalised lack of regulation, a thinly disguised contempt for democratic oversight and equal application of the law, as well as increased securitisation of state and society (see Duncan, this volume, on political policing) – all these have become the hallmarks of South Africa's contemporary capitalist democracy.

And yet there are also positive signs amidst the informational carnage. It has catalysed the creation of democratic alter-spaces which have enabled new organisational voices for those that are socially, economically and politically marginalised; positive ideas and actions towards collective activism and demands for social and political redress; and the shifting of the terrain of political and social engagement and debate in South African society as a whole by pushing the enforced boundaries of democratic participation beyond the status quo frame.

South Africa's apartheid past, more recent transitional past and present have a competing but intertwined history: one of repression, injustice, inequality and secrecy; another of freedom, justice, equality and openness. Twenty-seven years on from the democratic breakthrough of 1994, South Africa is at a crossroads on multiple fronts, but arguably no more so than when it comes to the struggle for the right to know.

If those who possess political, economic and social power are fearful of what the majority of people – the *demos* – think, know and do, then they are fearful of nothing less than democracy itself. It is the enduring challenge of that majority not only to practically confront and struggle against the lived reality of what those fears produce but to create the conditions for ushering in a truly democratic democracy.

NOTES

1   For all of these pieces of legislation, see https://www.gov.za/documents.
2   For a comprehensive history of the various versions and passage of the Bill through parliament, see https://pmg.org.za/bill/278/.
3   Section 32 of the constitution, which provides for the right of access to 'any information . . . required for the exercise or protection of any right'.
4   National Key Points Act 102 of 1980, updated 31 August 2007.

REFERENCES

Access to Information Network. 2016. 'Shadow Report 2016'. Accessed 18 January 2019, https://www.wits.ac.za/media/wits-university/faculties-and-schools/commerce-law-and-management/research-entities/cals/documents/programmes/rule-of-law/resources/Access%20to%20Information%20Network%20Shadow%20Report%202016.pdf.

Bruce, L.-A. 2017. 'New report reveals shocking failure to uphold right of access to information', 24 February. Accessed 12 January 2019, https://www.wits.ac.za/news/sources/cals-news/2017/new-report-reveals-shocking-failure-to-uphold-right-of-access-to-information.html.

Business Report. 2010. 'World Cup 2010: The legacy', 12 July.

Carnie, T. 2012. 'Secrecy over environment information', The Mercury, 16 April. Accessed 15 December 2018, http://www.iol.co.za/mercury/secrecy-over-environment-information-127623.

Cegłowski, M. 2016. 'The moral economy of tech'. Text version of remarks given on 26 June at a panel on the Moral Economy of Tech at the SASE conference in Berkeley, California. Accessed 14 January 2019, http://idlewords.com/talks/sase_panel.htm.

Duncan, J. 2015, 'Inside SA's cyber-security problem', Mail & Guardian, 16 October. Accessed 15 December 2018, http://mg.co.za/article/2015-10-15-inside-sas-cyber-insecurity-problem.

Greenberg, S. and Ndlovu, N. 2004. 'Civil society relationships', Development Update 5 (2): 23–48.

Hippler, J. 1995. 'Democratisation of the Third World after the end of the Cold War'. In J. Hippler (ed.), Democratisation of Disempowerment: The Problem of Democracy in the Third World. London: Pluto Press, pp. 1–31.

Mbeki, T. 2003. 'Letter from the president, towards a people-centred new world order', ANC Today 3 (43). Accessed 20 December 2018, http://www.anc. org.za/docs/anctoday/2003/at43.htm.

McKinley, D.T. 2014. 'Secrecy and power in South Africa'. In G.M. Khadiagala, P. Naidoo, D. Pillay and R. Southall (eds), New South African Review 4: A Fragile Democracy – Twenty Years On. Johannesburg: Wits University Press, pp. 150–166.

McKinley, D.T. 2016. 'New terrains of privacy in South Africa', December. Johannesburg: Media Policy and Democracy Project and the Right2Know Campaign. Accessed 20 December 2018, https://www.mediaanddemocracy.com/uploads/1/6/5/7/16577624/r2kmpdp_new_terrains_of_privacy_in_south__africa_masterset_small.pdf.

McKinley, D.T. 2017. South Africa's Corporatised Liberation: A Critical Analysis of the ANC in Power. Johannesburg: Jacana Media.

Melber, H. 2010. 'The legacy of anti-colonial struggles in Africa: Liberation movements as governments'. Paper presented to the Conference on Election Processes, Liberation Movements and Democratic Change in Africa, 8–11 April, Maputo, Mozambique.

Parliamentary Monitoring Group. 2006. 'Sport and recreation and provincial and local government portfolio committees – 2010 agreements with municipalities briefing', 6 June. Accessed 17 December 2018, http://www.pmg.org.za/node.7874.

Pearce, F. 2017. 'Murder in Pondoland: How a proposed mine brought conflict to South Africa', The Guardian, 28 March. Accessed 11 December 2018, https://www.theguardian.com/environment/2017/mar/27/murder-pondoland-how-proposed-mine-brought-conflict-south-africa-activist-sikhosiphi-rhadebe.

Right2Know Campaign. 2012. 'Why the Secrecy Bill still fails the freedom test', 28 November. Accessed 19 December 2018, http://www.r2k.org.za/2012/11/28/guide-why-secrecy-bill-fails/.

Right2Know Campaign. 2014. 'Secret: State of the Nation Report'. Accessed 12 December 2018, http://www.r2k.org.za/wp-content/uploads/R2K-secrecy-report-2014.pdf.

Right2Know Campaign. 2019. 'Open letter to the president on SARS appointment processes – R2K', 19 February. Accessed 20 February 2019, https://www.politicsweb.co.za/politics/open-letter-to-the-president-on-appointment-proces.

South African History Archive. 2016. 'SAHA takes Reserve Bank to court over refusal to grant access to records related to alleged corruption committed', 26 February. Accessed 17 December 2018, http://saha.org.za/news/2016/February/press_release_saha_takes_reserve_bank_to_court_over_refusal_to_grant_access_to_records_related_to_alleged_corruption_committed.htm.

Suttner, R. 2008. *The ANC Underground in South Africa*. Johannesburg: Jacana Media.

The Times. 2012. 'Why won't the government come clean on e-tolling?' *Times Live*, 27 November. Accessed 13 December 2018, http://www.timeslive.co.za/opinion/editorials/2012/11/27/ why-won-t-the-government-come-clean-on-e-tolling.

Vally, S. 2003. 'The political economy of state repression in South Africa'. In S. Ndung'u (ed.), *The Right to Dissent*. Johannesburg: Freedom of Expression Institute, pp. 62–72.

Waterhouse, S. 2015. 'People's Parliament? An assessment of public participation in South Africa's legislatures', MPhil in Social Studies, University of Cape Town. Accessed 20 January 2019, https://open.uct.ac.za/bitstream/handle/11427/15198/thesis_law_2015_waterhouse_samantha_jane.pdf;sequence=1.

9

SOUTH AFRICA'S POST-APARTHEID
MEDIA AND DEMOCRACY

Mandla J. Radebe

INTRODUCTION

The 1994 democratic breakthrough in South Africa signalled, among other things, the end to repressive state regulation of the media (see Wasserman and de Beer 2005). Today, media freedom and freedom of expression are among the rights enshrined in the country's constitution. The achievement of these rights is attributable to certain sections of the media that resisted apartheid, particularly alternative media such as the *Weekly Mail* and Radio Freedom, which exposed the lived experiences of the African majority under apartheid. Many journalists risked their lives and editors like Zwelakhe Sisulu, Percy Qoboza, Joe Thloloe, Mathata Tsedu and Aggrey Klaaste were imprisoned. Publications like the *World*, *Weekend World* and *Daily Dispatch* were banned. As McKinley points out in this volume, the apartheid edifice was premised on control of information and enforced secrecy.

The post-apartheid media landscape has reconfigured along a liberal 'consensus which emphasised the independence of the media from government and a free-market environment in which the media should conduct its business' (Wasserman and de Beer 2005: 37). This has led to dichotomies within social forces that hold different views on the media's role in a democracy. Ownership and editorial shifts as well as the change from legal constraints to self-regulation are some of the major developments post-apartheid (Wasserman and de Beer 2005).

I argue that this reconfiguration and the post-apartheid media landscape developments along theories of free press and assumptions 'that the market will provide appropriate institutions and processes of public communication to support a democracy polity or, in its stronger form, ... can ensure the necessary freedom from the state control coercion' (Garnham 1992, cited in Wasserman and de Beer 2005: 46) have had a dual effect for democracy. On the one hand, they have enabled the media to play its watchdog role by exposing corruption and the abuse of power, while on the other they contribute to rapid commercialisation, which is argued to have narrowed the democratic space for subalterns.

The prevailing ethos of liberalism in the media was assumed to be critical to address apartheid legacies of unequal access to information by transforming both the personnel and ownership of the media (Wasserman and de Beer 2005). However, the reality has been a slow pace of transformation and the demise of the left-leaning alternative press which serviced subalterns. This media has either closed down or morphed into commercial media, an example being the *Weekly Mail*, which became the *Mail & Guardian*. Today, the marginalised are increasingly dependent on broadcast and social media, which are also commercialised.

The assumption of the media's importance in democracy has been raised by scholars from different theoretical currents, such as Habermas (2005), Curran (2011), McChesney (1997), McNair (2017) and many others (see Abalo 2014). However, the commercialised media is interlocked with capitalist power structures and bound by structural factors like ownership and advertising. It is difficult to delink the media from the economic base and societal context in which it is produced (see Curran et al. 1982). I argue that the location of the commercial media in the capitalist power structures limits its democratising role. Duncan (this volume) characterises this as 'elite democracy' that legitimises capitalism without providing voice to exploited social groups. In this regard, the production of ideas cannot be understood autonomously from the political and economic forces that shape the media and 'ultimately constrain it' (Flew 2007: 33). The media is crucial for democracy since it shapes the public's opinion by sharing various social, political and economic developments. However, in this process the media changes thoughts, emotions, perceptions, judgements and values through its messages (see Acar and Caglar 2014), thereby producing a consciousness that is often understood as 'natural and eternal' (Nixon 2012: 444). This chapter analyses the implications of commercialisation and the demise of the alternative media in the context of growing media digitisation and the continued growth of the broadcast media. It asks whether there is an alternative to the negative impact of commercialisation. The idea of a decommodified alternative public media is also discussed.

ORIGINS OF MODERN MEDIA IN SOUTH AFRICA AND THE RISE OF COMMERCIALISATION

South Africa's media emerged and developed in the undemocratic environment of the country's colonial past. This media gave rise to the commercial media in the twentieth century, with the English press having strong ties to mining and British imperial interests and the Afrikaans press acting as an organ of propaganda and a vehicle of Afrikaner capital accumulation (Tomaselli 1997). The black press also emerged during this period, with its roots in the mission stations (Steyn 2009). Like the written press, the South African Broadcasting Corporation (SABC) was conceived along a narrow racist apartheid logic (see Sparks 2009). The fact that the colonial and apartheid regimes were undemocratic and repressive had a significant imprint on the nature of the media and its role in society. It is not surprising that protest journalism and alternative media operating on non-racial grounds and aligned to the broader democratic movement emerged in opposition to apartheid.

The formalisation of apartheid in 1948 also formalised the racist media, excluding black people from media ownership and banning content on communism and liberation movement politics. During this period, the media was captured as an instrument for racial oppression. The post-apartheid media has vestiges and structural continuities to the colonial- and apartheid-era media. Despite these continuities, the media has remodelled itself as the champion and watchdog of democracy.

Post-apartheid media transition

The media has come a long way since the days when former president Nelson Mandela described it as untransformed, with editorial staff dominated by white middle-class males (Jacobs 2004). Mandela's concern was that an untransformed media was likely to lead to binary representations of the country's historical transition. Since then, the media landscape has indeed witnessed transformation, with the SABC becoming a public broadcaster and black players buying into both broadcast and print media houses. However, social actors like the governing African National Congress (ANC) are still grappling with this matter. The ANC accuses the media of a lack of transformation (Daniels 2013). For example, former spokesperson Zizi Kodwa labelled it the 'official opposition'. This criticism is largely directed at the press rather than broadcast media, which is perceived to be more diverse due to state regulation (Duncan 2011). Former communication minister Nomvula Mokonyane recently argued that media transformation remained a concern for government, since ownership was still in 'white hands'. 'It simply cannot be acceptable that patterns of ownership across the value chain remain largely unchanged 24 years into our democracy' (Mokonyane 2018). The *Mail & Guardian* Data Desk affirmed this view when it pointed out that the South African media, just like many companies, is mostly run by whites. 'An analysis of ownership structures, demographics and funding models shows that the boards of media houses comprise 41% white, 24% African, 17% coloured, 16% Indian and 2% of the people from elsewhere' (M&G Data Desk 2019). The top management structures of influential media institutions are largely controlled by whites and have hardly transformed to reflect the demographics of the South African population: AmaBhungane (100 per cent white), Caxton (89 per cent white), Media24 (50 per cent white) and Daily Maverick (72 per cent white) (M&G Data Desk 2019).

By maintaining these structures of control in the newsroom, the media is limited in how it represents issues and the lived experiences of the marginalised. For example, the actions of the Congress of South African Trade Unions (Cosatu) in the 2002 anti-privatisation strikes were 'deemed as stumbling blocks to the desirable and inevitable neoliberal shift' (Kariithi and Kareithi 2007: 473–474). Of course, this limiting role should not blind us to excellent journalism in the commercial media that exposed abuses such as the VBS bank looting[1] and the Xolobeni Mine Sands Project.[2] However, there is a view that this type of investigation is limited to the black elite, while largely ignoring white-dominated private sector scandals such as price fixing in the construction, tyre manufacturing, pharmaceutical and bread industries (Radebe 2017). Nevertheless, it is important to note that investigations exposing serious webs of corruption have been conducted into the likes of former Steinhoff CEO Markus Jooste and his inner circle. This watchdog role by the media is crucial for democracy.

Lack of media transformation within the broader economic transformation does not bode well for democracy. According to Duncan (2009: 7), 'This reality will probably not change fundamentally for as long as South Africa's media system is premised overwhelmingly on the commercial media model.' This model perseveres with its apartheid role where it 'served the dominant interests in the system because it was – in essence – an integral part of that system in terms of ownership and control, revenue streams, staffing, content and audiences' (Berger 1999: 82). The SABC's funding model has not helped since it experienced shifts of funding from state to commercial sources post-apartheid. Even the organisational structure embraced the commercial emphasis, such as moving away from directors general to chief executive officers (Kupe 2006). Advertising and commercial sponsorship became the dominant sources of funding, at about 75 per cent, while licence revenues and government grants accounted for 20 and 5 per cent, respectively, in 2006. The outcome was the marginalisation of subalterns through unsatisfactory use of indigenous African languages, resulting in the retention of the colonial- and apartheid-era language status quo (Kupe 2006). Currently, the SABC receives 84 per cent of its revenue from advertising, sponsorships and commercial partners; 15 per cent from television licences; and the rest from government (Phakathi 2019).

Commercialisation reproduces and perpetuates apartheid's media logic and legacy, delays transformation and maintains the concentration already prevalent in the South African media (see Duncan 2014).

COMMERCIAL MEDIA'S LIMITATIONS IN DEMOCRACY

Commercial media is dominant in liberal democracies and plays a watchdog role (Chuma et al. 2017). This media system is owned and controlled by private corporations (Radebe 2017) and is distinguishable by its commodified features (Fuchs 2009) that target advertisers and consumers alike. The notion of a public sphere argues for the emergence of 'an infrastructure of protected public discussion' where 'political domination is subordinated to democratic scrutiny by virtue of the accessibility of information to the public, guaranteed by effective rights of free speech, association, and assembly' (Barnett 2004: 185; also see Habermas 1989). However, this role of enabling individual participation in public discourse and mitigating power by the institutionalised medium of 'public deliberation' overlooks the fact that these institutions must contend with both class and gender contradictions (Barnett 2004). The public sphere is littered with conflicting interests and therefore the notion of public opinion is subjected to social structures and attendant dynamics (see McCarthy 1991).

While an active media's role is central to democracies, its underlying assumptions and concepts, such as 'deliberative' and 'watchdog', remain contested in an unequal socio-economic public sphere (Chuma et al. 2017). In this 'bifurcated' public sphere 'the media could be seen to be aligned with one side of a polarised society and add to tensions rather than ameliorate them' (Chuma et al. 2017: 105). While the media is a central public sphere infrastructure (Sekloča 2018), its sustainability is bound to the laws and strategies of the capital accumulation under which it operates, which reduces citizen-audiences into products that must be sold to advertisers (Smythe 2006). This contributes to reproducing the ideas of the dominant class in society and diminishing the democratic space for subalterns. For example, the management structures in newsrooms contribute to prioritising the vantage point of the middle class (Friedman 2011). 'This is reflected in the selection of news and commentary – what is covered and who is seen as authoritative – and how events are understood and interpreted' (Friedman 2017: 55). So, while the 'less powerful actors may get drawn into the news' (Van Dalen 2012: 35, cited in Chuma et al. 2017: 105), it is the powerful societal actors that set the tone and have the power to decide what is newsworthy. 'If the asymmetries in access to the public sphere are left unaddressed, the media might therefore prevent the marginalised or powerless from having their views heard' (Chuma et al. 2017: 106).

Another limitation is the media's 'hidden' motive or the economic rationale. Marxist media scholars historically distinguish 'between the notions of media as an ideological tool and the media as an economic resource' (Heuva 2016: 4). The point is to appreciate the 'unconscious forces governing material production' and the 'conscious forces or ideology' (Boyd-Barrett and Newbold 1995: 219–220). According to Gardner (2016), the commercial media is biased towards those who fund it: 'There were many times when we were forced to cut an advertisement or cut a story or remove something from the website because an advertiser didn't want to be associated with it and, as a result, our financial livelihoods were threatened. TV is literally at the mercy of those that fund it because it's a business.' As is the case with the SABC, television is hugely dependent on advertising revenue and therefore content is designed for consumers rather than citizens. Thus, 'there is a shared belief that the media, through its content and practices, can affect democracy' (Abalo 2014: 802). How the media frames issues and provides access to social actors is crucial for democracy.

While it must be understood as part of the 'consciousness industry' that controls 'the means of mental production' (Nixon 2012: 442), the commercial media is first and foremost an 'economic resource' (see Heuva 2016) that is not produced on a philanthropical basis. Therefore, analysing structural factors in the context of the media's role in democracy must take into account both the exchange value and the use value of culture and the meaning of cultural commodities (Nixon 2012). The media does not operate in a vacuum but 'in the context of domination, asymmetrical power relations, exploitation, oppression and control' (Fuchs 2011: 97). Some of these structural factors are discussed below.

Media ownership

Because media systems are vulnerable to being used as tools to advance the values and objectives of competing political interests (Freedman 2008), ownership is a critical factor in managing content. Herman and Chomsky (2002: 3) assert that the media functions on behalf of the powerful societal interests that control and finance them: 'This is normally not accomplished by crude intervention, but by the selection of right-thinking personnel and by the editors' and working journalists' internalisation of priorities and definition of newsworthiness that conform to the institution's policies.' Those who own and control the media thus have influence over hiring, firing and the editorial direction of news organisations (Radebe 2006). 'If employees don't like it, they can quit. Others will be found to take their place, and routine can always be changed' (Shoemaker and Reese 1991: 163).

While significant strides have been made in the racial composition of ownership, class continuity is still evident in the South African media (Duncan 2009; Teer-Tomaselli and Tomaselli 2001). Historically, ownership was concentrated in the hands of four conglomerates, mostly linked to the industrial bourgeoisie, and aimed at the white apartheid middle strata preferred by advertisers (Jacobs 2004). This picture has changed post-apartheid, with the SABC no longer guaranteed a monopoly over broadcasting with the arrival of free-to-air channel e.TV, and the emergence of community television channels such as Soweto TV (Rumney 2015). Although the press is much freer now, it is still dominated by four oligopolies: Independent News and Media SA, Tiso Black Star Group (which has evolved numerous times), Caxton-CTP and Naspers' Media24. Before democracy, the press was dominated by the Nasionale Pers, Perskor, Times Media Ltd and the Independent Group (formerly the Argus) (Rumney 2015).

Some have argued that media ownership is diverse. A study by Intellidex (2016), for example, claimed to have found 'substantial black ownership of South Africa's commercial media'. However, more recent studies demonstrate a lack of content and ownership diversity. Wasserman (2017) argues that it is hard for such media to claim that they represent the broader public. Lack of transformation and diversity delegitimises the media and negatively impacts its democratic role. This is not helped by the kind of mismanagement seen at the SABC, which has experienced an increase in political interference, as revealed in the SABC parliamentary enquiry and the Judicial Commission of Inquiry into Allegations of State Capture currently under way. According to Wasserman (2017), the media is struggling to gain the trust of an audience outside of the mainstream elite and the suburban middle class it serves (Friedman 2017). Inevitably, lack of transformation and diversity leads to the media being associated with sectarian interests (Wasserman 2017).

Media owners wield huge, unaccountable political and economic power and can deploy their market power to act as influential 'cultural gatekeepers' (Freedman 2008). If left unchecked, this might have a negative impact on democracy since a media that is excessively tied to financial interests is unlikely to be able to provide adequate checks and balances against abuse by special interests (Stiglitz 2002).

Advertising and market forces

The commercialised media's survival lies in its ability to attract an audience to sell to advertisers (Croteau and Hoynes 2006). This leads to editorial pressures and political discrimination which is 'structured into advertising allocation by the stress on people with money to buy' (Herman and Chomsky 2002: 16). Indeed, the 'media depends heavily on advertising to fund their operations, ranging from perhaps 70 percent of revenue for newspapers to more than 95 percent for television' (Herman 2002: 65). Of course, with the rise of digitisation, advertising revenues are dwindling for traditional mainstream media. Nevertheless, in an environment that supports commercial messages, advertising continues to influence the media in subtle yet fundamental ways. Over-reliance on advertising makes competition for advertising a powerful force that often coerces the media to structure its activities to meet the demands of advertisers (Barnouw 1978; Herman 2002).

Studies have shown that the media, particularly in less developed economies, is under pressure to produce content that satisfies the political and economic elite (Moholi 2015). As an external force, advertisers are in a position to manage the behaviour of the media by withdrawing patronage, humiliating the media, and ruling or legislating against them (Herman 2002). For example, in 2011, former government spokesperson Jimmy Manyi threatened to 'pull the plug' on government's R1 billion advertising spend if editors refused to put a positive spin on government news (De Waal 2011, in Radebe 2017). Advertising remains a threat to free media since existing power structures prevent it from adequately serving the needs of a democratic society (Baker 1992).

Through advertising, the 'media content produces the audiences as consumers of goods and services' (Ekman 2012: 162) rather than reinforcing citizens' role in democracy.

Commercial impact on news sources

The news production process must be grounded in 'objective' and 'authoritative' statements from 'accredited' sources. News sources are primary definers that 'establish the initial definition or primary interpretation of the topic in question' (Hall et al. 1978: 58). The news production process privileges the elite, who set the tone on key discourses with others 'forced to insert themselves into its definition' (Hall et al. 1978: 58). This leads to omissions and silencing of the marginalised as sources, as well as over-reliance on the views of the elites to decipher complex issues while granting them easy access to the media (see Radebe 2017). Additionally, personnel such as reporters and editors are carefully selected to fit the objectives of the proprietors. Through the production process the media reproduces the dominant ideas of the ruling class. Reacting to criticism of John Pilger's film *Apartheid Did Not Die*,[3] aired on SABC in 1998, the editor of *Beeld* newspaper suggested that this criticism should be used to unite the country behind a programme to build a 'successful liberal democratic capitalist economy' (Jacobs 2004: 181). Since subalterns lack control and access to the media, they 'are largely subjected to the capitalist media's construction of reality' (Harper 2012: 19).

Analysts and journalists are employed to reinforce the capitalist narrative 'regardless of the wisdom of their previous commentary or of their prior actions when they occupied positions of power' (Croteau and Hoynes 2002: 170). Critiquing the floundering economy and state-owned enterprises, *Sunday Times* journalist Ron Derby argues that 'the government has a role, and quite a significant one, in at least establishing an industry and leaving it to the private players to exploit the opportunity' (Derby 2018: 2). Valorisation of capitalism is problematic since it is renowned for its undemocratic logic of unequally distributed property rights (Merkel 2014) where the means of production and distribution is owned by a wealthy minority. 'The basic logics of capitalism and democracy are fundamentally different and lead to considerable tension between the two' (Merkel 2014: 113).

Actions that disturb capitalist production processes, like the strikes by taxi and bus drivers, and airport and mine workers, are often framed negatively and portrayed as 'inconveniences'. The impact on the capitalist economy is elevated above the plight and interest of the workers. The commercialisation of alternative publications like the *Mail & Guardian* has created a vacuum in coverage of working-class issues. For example, former editor Ferial Haffajee conceded that labour news is no longer considered as important as it was pre-democracy, when the labour movement was central to politics. 'As the role of labour moved from centre stage to its normal role in society, it is reflected by our current coverage, but I think it is a mistake' (Haffajee interview).

Even the 'sporadic' and 'episodic' coverage of community protests has been shallow, reducing legitimate community protest to 'service delivery protests' (Duncan 2014). These are seldom linked to the failure of post-apartheid capitalism. This is the likely outcome when media discourses are shaped by primary definers, largely based in institutions of power, who set the tone and reproduce the dominant worldview (Duncan 2014). As experiences from Brazil demonstrate, the media can be sucked into unprincipled and undemocratic alliances, as was the case in the impeachment of President Rousseff on trumped-up charges which Saad-Filho (this volume) describes as a coup.

RISE AND FALL OF THE ALTERNATIVE PRESS

There were many sites of struggle for democracy and against apartheid, one being the donor-driven alternative press, the demise of which post-apartheid has left a vacuum for the marginalised. Although broadcast and social media are emerging as popular and accessible platforms, they largely lack the analytical rigour and ideological orientation of the alternative press. The alternative media was pivotal during apartheid with its focus on socio-economic and political issues (Tomaselli 2004). What set it apart from its mainstream commercial counterparts was the ability to go beyond the surface of political rights to issues of redistribution aimed at redressing centuries of cumulative socio-economic neglect (Radebe 2017).

The genesis of this media is linked to the radical and underground press, such as *New Age* and *Spark*, produced under the stewardship of the then banned South African Communist Party (Pinnock 2010). This press emerged around the era of the Great Depression, which led to the demise of many independent African journals but resulted in the formation of an African commercial press, such as *Bantu World* (Radebe 2006; Switzer 1997). It soon became a target of the apartheid regime, with staff harassed and publications banned. For example, in the 1950s *New Age* and its various reincarnations were continuously banned for their association with the liberation movement (MDDA 2000). This media re-emerged in the 1980s and was crucial in the final push for democracy. 'Newspapers, magazines, journals, pamphlets and newsletters sprouted up to give platform to the voices of the resistance movement, including women, workers, students, the youth, rural people and local communities. Sympathetic foreign donors financially supported many publications' (MDDA 2000: 14).

However, post-apartheid donor funding dried up with increased commercialisation. The demise of this press – as in Britain, where newspapers such as *The Poor Man's Guardian* were pushed aside in the nineteenth century by commercial newspapers' attractiveness to advertisers despite their small circulation – highlights the class character of the media (Harper 2012). The opening up of the local media to global competition also impacted this media negatively due to commercial pressures (Harber 2002). Apart from factors such as 'tabloidisation' and the 'juniorisation' of the newsroom (Harber 2002), commercialisation narrowed the space for critical media voices representing the marginalised. In the absence of this media, access and representation for subalterns is compromised.

Founding *Mail & Guardian* co-editor Anton Harber argued that 'when the political donors and other supporters of the 1980s and 1990s fell away, this radically increased the dependence on advertisers, and that has to have an impact on the newspaper'. He maintained that 'the paper is now more driven by financial matters and therefore that would tend to move it towards the centre' (cited in Radebe 2006: 106). To be financially viable, the alternative press had to abandon its historical left tradition. Previously, publications like the *Mail & Guardian* had been able to promote views antagonistic to capitalist interests by giving prominence to working-class issues (Harber interview).

In this vacuum, digital mediums inevitably play a prominent democratising role. With internet penetration of over 54 per cent, and 80 per cent of people on smartphones,[4] social media is bound to fill the void, as observed in the #FeesMustFall student campaign.[5] The broadcast media continues to grow and is also playing an important role in democracy: 'about 28-million people tuned into South African radio stations every day between 2016 and 2018', constituting an overall reach of about 90 per cent in 2018, while television prime-time news had an estimated 13 million viewers on the five free-to-air television channels from 2016 to 2018 (Finlay 2018: 13).

TOWARDS A DECOMMODIFIED ALTERNATIVE MEDIA

The concept of a commercialised media is premised on the principle of news as a commodity which is packaged and sold to citizens, who are increasingly seen as audiences willing to buy news. These audiences are in turn sold to advertisers, the lifeblood of commercial media. The media is central for democracy since it contributes to the development of informed citizens. The commodification of news is hence problematic. At the root of commercial media, which includes paywalls on digital platforms, is the commodification of news premised on the principle of willingness to buy (Naureckas 2009), effectively denying access to many subalterns.

If the media is to play a more important role in democracy than is currently the case, then the decommodification of news must be considered as an option. Platforms must be created for the re-emergence of 'decommodified' alternative media that serve the broader public rather than narrow commercial interests (Radebe 2017). As Marx argued, 'It is the duty of the press to come forward on behalf of the oppressed in its immediate neighbourhood' (in Fuchs 2009: 391). This press 'should be non-commercial and non-profit so as not to become corrupted by capitalist pressures' (in Fuchs 2009: 391). Decommodified alternative media must have a public character and be easily accessible in order to advance general education for subalterns (Radebe 2017) as part of its democratisation role.

CONCLUSION

This chapter has argued that, notwithstanding the proud history of some sections of the media in the fight for democracy, the reconfiguration of the media post-apartheid based on liberal theory led to different understandings and clashes between social actors on the media's role in democracy. This saw the development of 'an industry largely operating on free-market principles and according to neo-liberal functional logic, whilst market segmentation displayed continuities with the societal polarisation of the past' (Wasserman and de Beer 2005: 38). The changing media landscape has not yielded the expected transformation, with ownership and management structures still resembling the apartheid logic, notwithstanding the increase in black economic empowerment participation. This mirrors the country's slow economic transformation and contributes to hostilities between social actors. While the SABC has transformed from being a state-owned broadcaster, the move towards commercialisation has not assisted in entrenching its democratic role for marginalised sections of society.

The lack of transformation contributes to continuities with the colonial and apartheid media, as observed in the media's focus on the suburban middle class (Friedman 2017) and the unsatisfactory use of indigenous African languages (Kupe 2006). Although the post-apartheid media has been vital in safeguarding democracy by exposing issues such as the VBS bank looting and Steinhoff theft, this is countered by increased commercialisation and the demise of the alternative media. This has reduced the underclasses' media access. The media could play a more robust watchdog role against creeping authoritarian tendencies coupled with fascism and populism, which diminish the expansion of democracy from below for the subaltern working class (see Duncan, this volume). At the heart of commercialisation are structural factors such as ownership, advertising and sources, which influence the media to function as a tool of the powerful ruling class that finances them (Herman and Chomsky 2002).

Finally, the emergence of digitised media and the growing influence of broadcast media must be harnessed for deepening democracy. While the demise of the alternative media left a vacuum, a decommodified alternative media must be reimagined if post-apartheid media is to play a significant role in democracy.

NOTES

1   VBS Mutual Bank collapsed in 2018 after being fleeced by the elite who were supposed to look after depositors' money.

2   This mining project by Australian company Mineral Commodities Ltd, which wants to mine titanium along a 22-kilometre stretch of the Wild Coast, is fiercely opposed by some sections of the community.

3   The film details what Pilger perceived as the betrayal of the liberation struggle by the ruling ANC, asserting that the ANC has created a 'new, economic apartheid' that has kept most black people in poverty while the white 5 per cent of the population controls 88 per cent of the nation's wealth.

4   https://www.statista.com/statistics/488376/forecast-of-smartphone-users-in-south-africa/.

5   #FeesMustFall is a student-led protest movement that began in mid-October 2015 in response to an increase in fees at South African universities. The protests also called for higher wages for low-earning university staff who worked for private contractors, such as cleaning services and campus security, and for them to be employed directly by universities. Protests started at the University of the Witwatersrand and spread to the University of Cape Town and Rhodes University before rapidly spreading to other universities across the country. See https://en.wikipedia.org/wiki/FeesMustFall.

INTERVIEWS

F. Haffajee, Chief Editor, *Mail & Guardian*, 6 December 2005.

A. Harber, Professor, Journalism and Media Studies Programme, University of the Witwatersrand, and former editor, *Mail & Guardian*, 24 September 2005.

REFERENCES

Abalo, E. 2014. 'Constructing (il)legitimate democracy: Populism and power concentration in newspaper discourse on Venezuela', *tripleC: Communication, Capitalism & Critique* 12 (2): 802–821.

Acar, N.O. and Caglar, S. 2014. 'From media as the producer of false consciousness to ecological media', *Procedia – Social and Behavioral Sciences* 155: 299–303.

Baker, C.E. 1992. *Advertising and a Democratic Press*. Princeton, NJ: Princeton University Press.

Barnett, C. 2004. 'Media, democracy and representation'. In C. Barnett and M. Low (eds), *Spaces of Democracy: Geographical Perspectives on Citizenship, Participation and Representation*. London: Sage, pp. 185–206.

Barnouw, E. 1978. *The Sponsor: Notes on a Modern Potentate* (Vol. 580). London: Transaction Publishers.

Berger, G. 1999. 'Towards an analysis of the South African media and transformation, 1994–1999'. Accessed 23 October 2019, http://journ.ru.ac.za/staff/guy/Research/Racism%20in%20the%20media/transformation.htm.

Boyd-Barrett, O. and Newbold, C. 1995. *Approaches to Media: A Reader*. London: Arnold.

Chuma, W., Wasserman, H., Bosch. T. and Pointer, R. 2017. 'Questioning the media-democracy link: South African journalists' views', *African Journalism Studies* 38 (1): 104–128.

Croteau, D.R. and Hoynes, W. 2002. *Media/Society: Industries, Images and Audiences* (third edition). Thousand Oaks, CA: Pine Forge Press.

Croteau, D.R. and Hoynes, W. 2006. *The Business of Media: Corporate Media and Public Interest*. Thousand Oaks, CA: Pine Forge Press.

Curran, J. 2011. *Media and Democracy*. London: Routledge.

Curran, J., Gurevitch, M. and Woollacott, J. 1982. 'The study of the media: Theoretical approaches'. In M. Gurevitch, T. Bennett, J. Curran and J. Woollacott (eds), *Culture, Society and the Media*. North Yorkshire: Methuen & Co., pp. 11–29.

Daniels, G. 2013. 'State of the newsroom South Africa 2013: Disruptions and transitions'. Wits Journalism, University of the Witwatersrand, Johannesburg. Accessed 23 October 2019, https://journalism.co.za/new/wpcontent/uploads/2018/03/State_of_the_newroom_2013.pdf.

Derby, R. 2018. 'Stabilising Eskom is the most difficult and important job in SA', *Sunday Times*, 9 December, p. 2.

Duncan, J. 2009. 'The uses and abuses of political economy: The ANC's media policy', *Transformation* 70: 1–30.

Duncan, J. 2011. 'The print media transformation dilemma', *New South African Review* 2: 345–368.

Duncan, J. 2014. 'South African journalism and the Marikana massacre: A case study of an editorial failure', *The Political Economy of Communication* 1 (2): 65–88.

Ekman, M. 2012. 'Understanding accumulation: The relevance of Marx's theory of primitive accumulation in media and communication studies', *tripleC: Communication, Capitalism & Critique* 10 (2): 156–170.

Finlay, A. 2018. 'State of the newsroom 2018 – structured/unstructured'. Accessed 23 October 2019, https://journalism.co.za/resources/state-of-the-newsroom/.

Flew, T. 2007. *Understanding Global Media*. Basingstoke: Palgrave Macmillan.

Freedman, D. 2008. *The Politics of Media Policy*. Cambridge: Polity Press.

Friedman, S. 2011. 'Whose freedom? South Africa's press, middle-class bias and the threat of control', *Ecquid Novi* 32 (2): 106–121.

Friedman, S. 2017. 'Speaking power's truth: South African media in the service of the suburbs'. In A. Garman and H. Wasserman (eds), *Media and Citizenship: Between Marginalisation and Participation*. Cape Town: HSRC Press, pp. 55–71.

Fuchs, C. 2009. 'Some theoretical foundations of critical media studies: Reflections on Karl Marx and the media', *International Journal of Communication* 3: 369–402.

Fuchs, C. 2011. *Foundations of Critical Media and Information Studies*. London: Routledge.

Gardner, S. 2016. '5 hidden truths about mainstream news media'. Accessed 20 September 2019, https://www.collective-evolution.com/2016/02/06/5-hidden-truths-about-mainstream-news-media/.

Habermas, J. 1989. *The Structural Transformation of the Public Sphere: An Inquiry into a Category of Bourgeois Society*. Translated by T. Burger with the assistance of F. Lawrence. Cambridge, MA: MIT Press.

Habermas, J. 2005. *Democracy and the Public Sphere*. London: Pluto Press.

Hall, S., Critcher, C., Jefferson, T., Clarke, J. and Roberts, B. 1978. *Policing the Crisis: Mugging, the State and Law and Order*. London: Macmillan.

Harber, A. 2002. 'Journalism in the age of the market'. Harold Wolpe Memorial Lecture. Accessed 21 September 2019, http://ccs.ukzn.ac.za/default.asp?3,28,10,452.

Harper, S. 2012. *Beyond the Left: The Communist Critique of the Media*. Alresford, Hants: John Hunt Publishing.

Herman, E.S. 2002. 'The media and markets in the United States'. In World Bank (ed.), *The Right to Tell: The Role of Mass Media in Economic Development*. Washington, DC: World Bank, pp. 61–81.

Herman, E.S. and Chomsky, N. 2002. *Manufacturing Consent: The Political Economy of the Mass Media*. New York: Pantheon.

Heuva, W.E. 2016. 'Commodification of celebrities' crimes: The "live" broadcasting of Oscar Pistorius' murder trial', *French Journal for Media Research* [online]. Accessed 24 October 2019, http://frenchjournalformediaresearch.com/lodel-1.0/main/index.php?id =842.

Intellidex. 2016. 'Who owns the news media in SA?' Accessed 20 August 2019, https://www. intellidex.co.za/insights/who-owns-the-news-media-in-sa/.

Jacobs, S.H. 2004. 'Public sphere, power and democratic politics: Media and policy debates in post-apartheid South Africa', PhD dissertation, Birkbeck, University of London.

Kariithi, N. and Kareithi, P. 2007. 'It's off to work you go! A critical discourse analysis of media coverage of the anti-privatisation strike in South Africa in October 2002', *Journalism Studies* 8 (3): 465–480.

Kupe, T. 2006. 'The mandate of the SABC Public Service Division'. Presentation at the SABC PBS Programming Conference, 25 July, Malelane Hotel, Mpumalanga Province.

M&G Data Desk. 2019. 'Who runs SA's media is a black-and-white issue'. Accessed 26 August 2019, https://mg.co.za/article/2019-01-04-00-who-runs-sas-media-is-a-black-and-white-issue.

McCarthy, T. 1991. 'Introduction'. In J. Habermas, *The Structural Transformation of the Public Sphere: An Inquiry into a Category of Bourgeois Society*. Cambridge, MA: MIT Press, pp. xi–xiv.

McChesney, R.W. 1997. *Corporate Media and the Threat to Democracy*. New York: Seven Stories Press.

McNair, B. 2017. *An Introduction to Political Communication*. New York: Routledge.

MDDA (Media Development and Diversity Agency). 2000. *A draft position paper*. Accessed 23 October 2019, http://www.gcis.gov.za/docs/act_bill/mddapos.htm.

Merkel, W. 2014. 'Is capitalism compatible with democracy?' *Zeitschrift für Vergleichende Politikwissenschaft* 8 (2): 109–128.

Moholi, F. 2015. 'The influence of government advertising on print media content in Lesotho', unpublished dissertation, University of the Witwatersrand, Johannesburg.

Mokonyane, N. 2018. 'Transformation of SA media still a problem – Mokonyane', *The Citizen*, 19 July. Accessed 23 January 2019, https://citizen.co.za/news/south-africa/1983628/ transformation-of-sa-media-still-a-problem-mokonyane/.

Naureckas, J. 2009. 'Public media and the decommodification of news'. Accessed 25 September 2019, https://fair.org/extra/public-media-and-the-decommodification-of-news/2671/.

Nixon, B. 2012. 'Dialectical method and the critical political economy of culture', *tripleC: Communication, Capitalism & Critique* 10 (2): 439–456.

Phakathi, B. 2019. 'SABC goes ahead with plans to lift TV licence fees, despite objections', *Business Day*, 17 September. Accessed 21 September 2019, https://www.businesslive. co.za/bd/national/2019-09-17-sabc-goes-ahead-with-plans-to-lift-tv-licence-fees-despite-objections/.

Pinnock, S. 2010. 'Review of Richard Grigg, *Gods after God: An Introduction to Contemporary Radical Theologies* Albany: SUNY Press, 2006', *Sophia* 49 (2): 315–316.

Radebe, M.J. 2006. 'The coverage of industrial action by the *Mail & Guardian*, 1999–2004', unpublished MA dissertation, University of the Witwatersrand, Johannesburg.

Radebe, M.J. 2017. 'Corporate media and the nationalisation of the economy in South Africa: A critical Marxist political economy approach', PhD dissertation, University of the Witwatersrand, Johannesburg.

Rumney, R. 2015. '20 years of changes in media ownership: Journalism now', *Rhodes Journalism Review* 35: 66–69.

Sekloča, P. 2018. 'The centre and the periphery: Productivity and the global networked public sphere', *tripleC: Communication, Capitalism & Critique* 17 (1): 1–18.

Shoemaker, P.J. and Reese, S.D. 1991. *Mediating the Message: Theories of Influences on Mass Media Content*. White Plains, NY: Longman.

Smythe, D.W. 2006 [1981]. 'On the audience commodity and its work'. In M.G. Durham and D.M. Kellner (eds), *Media and Cultural Studies*. Malden, MA: Blackwell, pp. 230–256.

Sparks, C. 2009. 'South African media in transition', *Journal of African Media Studies* 1 (2): 195–220.

Steyn, E. 2009. 'Changed ownership models and trends in the post-aparthied South African media: Efforts towards effective and efficient media transformation'. Paper for the Future of Journalism Conference, 9–10 September, Cardiff University.

Stiglitz, J. 2002. 'Transparency in government'. In World Bank (ed.), *The Right to Tell: The Role of Mass Media in Economic Development*. Washington, DC: World Bank, pp. 27–44.

Switzer, L. (ed.). 1997. *South Africa's Alternative Press: Voices of Protest and Resistance, 1880–1960*. Cambridge: Cambridge University Press.

Teer-Tomaselli, R. and Tomaselli, G.K. 2001. 'Transformation, nation-building and the South African media'. In K. Tomaselli and H. Dunn (eds), *Media, Democracy and Renewal in Southern Africa*. New Brunswick, NJ: Transaction Publishers.

Tomaselli, K. 1997. 'Ownership and control in the South African print media: Black empowerment after apartheid, 1990–1997', *Ecquid Novi* 18 (1): 67–68.

Tomaselli, K. 2004. 'Transformation of the South African media', *Critical Arts* 18(1): 1–6.

Wasserman, H. 2017. 'South Africa's media is still held back by a lack of diversity and undue political influence'. Accessed 22 September 2019, https://qz.com/africa/1108617/media-freedom-in-south-africa-media-is-held-back-by-a-lack-of-diversity-and-undue-political-influence/.

Wasserman, H. and De Beer, A. 2005. 'Whose public? Whose interest? The South African media and its role during the first ten years of democracy', *Critical Arts* 19 (1&2): 36–51.

10

THE ENEMY WITHIN: SECURITISING PROTESTS AS DOMESTIC INSTABILITY IN SOUTH AFRICA

Jane Duncan

INTRODUCTION

Democracy in the public imagination has all too often been conflated with elite democracy, which gives nominal legitimacy to capitalism while failing to give a meaningful voice to exploited social groups. In South Africa, one of the most unequal countries in the world yet still largely a democracy, this tension between the democratic ideal and the reality of social exclusion, exploitation and oppression is stark. In fact, it seems fair to say that despite the trappings of formal democracy – such as the extension of franchise rights to all South Africans and reasonably independent democratic institutions – the unemployed and even sections of the working class (such as casual workers) lack a meaningful voice in the post-apartheid social order. South African society remains highly volatile and susceptible to social explosions (Alexander et al. 2018), but the ruling hegemonic bloc – with the African National Congress and its alliance partners at the apex – still remains in power, albeit with a significantly reduced majority. It has also become clear that the ruling bloc does not have answers to South Africa's systemic problems of inequality and unemployment and, in fact, these problems are worsening.

The post-apartheid state has struggled with how to respond to worker and community struggles, moving between using coercion and concessions coupled with limited incorporation into the political system. Furthermore, South Africa's constitution and reasonably robust institutions (such as the media and the judiciary) make outright coercion very difficult. However, this point must be made with the caveat that South Africa lacks a media system characterised by decommodified, alternative media, resulting in distorted representations of the socio-political and economic landscape (see Radebe, this volume, for more details). The country has experienced a sharp upturn in struggles in the past decade, as has the entire sub-Saharan African region. These struggles need to be understood – but often are not – in the context of the global wave of anti-austerity protests triggered by the 2008 capitalist crisis (Branch and Mampilly 2015: 1–13; Duncan 2016; Paret 2017: 4). This failure to locate these protests in their proper historical context impoverishes our understanding of their world-historical significance. Furthermore, a purely regional or local focus on these dynamics will miss the shifting modes of social control, and how they are transmitted as purported security 'best practices' around the world.

This chapter explores how the capitalist downturn and subsequent anti-austerity protests in South Africa have changed the forms of social control used by the security agencies of the state. To the extent that there have been changes, the chapter questions whether they have led to South Africa becoming more or less democratic in a global moment when even liberal democracy is under threat. These issues are explored through an analysis of security responses to the most recent wave of protests in South Africa following the historic strikes in the platinum belt. I am particularly interested in the period commencing in 2015, and including (but not confined to) the #FeesMustFall student protests that engulfed university campuses. This strike and protest wave led to the state identifying domestic instability as a major security threat alongside other serious crimes, and responding accordingly. I look at the police and prosecutorial responses to the protests in the post-Marikana period, and what they tell us about the extent of political space and democracy more broadly in South Africa. This chapter complements those in this volume by McKinley and Radebe, respectively, on struggles around access to information, and media transformation in South Africa. Both are important indicators of substantive democracy that allows for a genuine incorporation of the masses into the political process.

ASCENDANCE OF INTELLIGENCE-LED POLICING IN SAPS

Far from discouraging protests, at a certain point repression can, in fact, escalate protests (Della Porta 2013: 32–69). South Africa is no exception in this respect. Politically, the South African Police Service (SAPS) cannot risk many more high-profile shoot-outs with protestors, as the long-term political costs will simply be too great. In fact, popular agency often places far more enduring limits on the capacities of the state for organised violence than legislative or policy reforms (Cox 2014). The Marikana massacre contributed to important shifts in popular politics; for instance, it was a factor in independent trade union growth, culminating in the breakaway of several trade unions from the Congress of South African Trade Unions, and the formation of a new federation, as well as the establishment of the Economic Freedom Fighters. Police militarisation, which was identified by a commission of enquiry chaired by retired judge Ian Farlam as being a key factor in the massacre, has become a highly politicised issue. The commission recommended reforms to public order policing, including demilitarisation and professionalisation of the police in line with the fairly vague recommendations of the National Planning Commission, and a review of the uses of police equipment in public order situations (Farlam et al. 2015: 551–552).

In view of the public backlash against police militarisation, the police sought a policing model that allowed them to practise less visible forms of social control, and intelligence-led policing provided them with just that. This model contributed to the state's efforts to increase surveillance powers more generally across society (for a fuller discussion of these efforts, see McKinley, this volume). Intelligence-led policing was conceptualised in the United States and the United Kingdom in the 1990s, but only really gained currency after the terrorist attacks on those countries in 2001 and 2005 respectively. As its name suggests, this form of policing is based on the assessment and management of risk, and the targeting of these risks by the police. Intelligence-led policing is meant to ensure more efficient uses of policing resources, and is closely related to predictive policing, which uses data analytics to predict likely occurrences of crime based on historic patterns (Bezuidenhout 2008).

Intelligence-led policing relies on paid informants and surveillance techniques, including physical surveillance; surveillance of electronic signals, including communication signals (a form of intelligence that is known as SIGINT, or signals intelligence); and other forms of data-driven surveillance. The intelligence gathered from these sources becomes integral to policing operations. It has a proactive element in that the police use intelligence sources and surveillance methods to profile actual or potential criminal suspects, rather than responding only when criminal incidents take place (Bezuidenhout 2008).

However, intelligence-led policing blurs the line between domestic policing and civilian intelligence, which can lead to a securitisation of policing where social problems are treated increasingly as security threats. As a policing model, intelligence-led policing is particularly predisposed to abuse given the high levels of secrecy attached to intelligence work. The police have also been known to disrupt social movements they consider to be security threats, including by employing agents provocateurs in public order situations to delegitimise and criminalise the movements (Savage 2011). The 'spycops' scandal in the UK – where police officers infiltrated social movements and formed abusive relationships with women ostensibly as part of their undercover work – points to some of the dangers (Choudry 2019). For SAPS, intelligence-led policing is key to enabling them to 'disturb, disrupt and erupt on crime' (South African Police Service 2014, 2018). The Crime Intelligence Division of SAPS has become central to this new policing strategy, which has put it in a very powerful position.

EARLY POLICE RESPONSES TO PROTESTS

If police and prosecutorial responses to unlawful protests were proportionate to the levels of threat to public safety and national security, then it could be expected that the number of convictions relative to the number of arrests and prosecutions would be high, as the evidence of crimes having been committed would have been tested in open court and found to be credible. Conversely, high levels of arrest and prosecution, coupled with low levels of conviction, would suggest more securitised responses as flimsy cases that may even have been designed to crush protests are thrown out. Therefore, it is instructive to look at patterns of arrests and convictions, especially in view of the 'talk-tough' approach the state adopted towards violent protests over the period commencing in 2015. This approach was informed by the Medium Term Strategic Framework of 2014–2019, which included ensuring domestic stability as an objective. This objective included the sub-objective of 'contributing to domestic stability through the successful prosecution of criminal and violent conduct in public protests' (National Prosecuting Authority 2016: 18).

Building on this objective, the Justice, Crime Prevention and Security (JCPS) cluster applied a four-pillar approach to addressing domestic stability, and these four pillars guided the police responses to the protests: community and stakeholder engagement; legal and regulatory interventions; safety and security interventions; and mass communication (South African Police Service 2017a: 14). In relation to the #FeesMustFall protests, SAPS sought to have the protestors prosecuted in normal courts, but in a prioritised manner. As a general rule, they also opposed the granting of bail while investigations were under way, and sought prosecution-guided investigations to increase their chances of securing successful prosecutions by the

National Prosecuting Authority (NPA). SAPS advocated for civil remedies to be followed, including claims against organisers and those who caused damage (South African Police Service 2017a). SAPS also activated an intelligence-gathering network and dedicated investigation teams, conducted analyses and risk assessments, prepared and distributed early warnings, coordinated safety and security inside the universities, and appointed liaison officers at institution level to engage with relevant stakeholders. The civilian intelligence agency, the State Security Agency (SSA), also became interested in the protests, suggesting that they had been escalated from being framed as a public safety threat to a national security threat.

By 2015, when the #FeesMustFall protests started, SAPS was concentrating on '[improving] the detection rate and trial ready case dockets towards successful prosecutions of criminal and violent conduct in public protests' (South African Police Service 2015: 26). Despite being a priority area, they did not achieve their target for convictions (74 per cent), as only 68.2 per cent of the cases finalised resulted in convictions. However, the conviction rate increased towards the end of the financial year as a result of a more strategic focus and improved technology. Consequently, the conviction rate during the last five months of 2015 rose to 78 per cent, as 32 convictions were obtained from the 41 trials conducted. SAPS noted that the #FeesMustFall protests especially had involved cases of arson. Yet, in the same breath, it noted that the number of arson cases reported more generally had decreased year on year, and in fact had declined 4.6 per cent from the previous year, before the student protests had started (South African Police Service 2016: 49). SAPS also noted that cases of public violence had increased, yet conflated these in their annual crime report with unrest incidents – a much broader category which records whether there has been police intervention in crowd incidents, itself a much broader category than protests. While it cannot be disputed that the number of community protests using turbulent means, including disruption and violence, is on the increase, the extent of the increase in the number of violent protests (the threshold of which is meant to trigger the security cluster's interest in protests) is almost certainly being overstated (Alexander et al. 2018).

The National Joint Operations Centre increased its capacity to coordinate and monitor all public order-related incidents 24 hours a day, seven days a week. SAPS also assigned dedicated detectives to focus on public violence-related incidents, and trained legal officers to ensure strict compliance with all by-laws and regulations applicable to traffic management. Dedicated crime intelligence gatherers were allocated to work closely with the Public Order Police (POP) units in the provinces (South African Police Service 2016: 153). Crime Intelligence generated a huge number of intelligence products despite disarray in the division, generating

Table 10.1 Number of Rica warrants, number of SAPS communication interception reports and number of SAPS communication analysis reports, 2014–2017

	2014/2015	2015/2016	2016/2017
Number of Rica warrants issued to SAPS (including new applications, reapplications, extensions and amendments)	386	422	*
SAPS communication interception reports	5 254	12 729	1 704
SAPS communication analysis reports	8 181	10 660	11 948

Sources: SAPS and Joint Standing Committee on Intelligence reports, 2014/2015, 2015/2016 and 2016/2017
Note: * Statistics unavailable

386 732 operational analysis reports during the 2015/16 period, well above the planned target of 158 283. The vast majority of these were intelligence analysis reports, with 10 660 being generated from communication analysis reports[1] and 12 729 being generated from communication interception analysis reports[2] (Table 10.1). They also generated more strategic intelligence reports than their target, including for the National Intelligence Coordinating Committee (Nicoc, a government entity that coordinates intelligence across the security agencies), citing an 'increased need for strategic intelligence reports due to the increased incidence of protest action at institutions of higher learning throughout the country' (South African Police Service 2016: 218).

LATER POLICE RESPONSES TO PROTESTS

In 2016/2017, SAPS's intelligence-led approach towards the protests matured. They continued to prioritise improvements in the investigation and prosecution of criminal and violent conduct in public protest. They set a new performance indicator of 47 per cent for detections, and underachieved slightly on this rate. SAPS explained the deviation by saying that protest incidents are usually committed in large groups and under circumstances that make it difficult to identify and arrest perpetrators, as many of the incidents are spontaneous and simultaneous. They also struggled with the poor quality of video footage to identify suspects, and the fact that members of the public were loath to come forward out of fear of retaliation. SAPS also set new performance indicators for prosecutions, to ensure trial-ready case dockets in

70 per cent of cases and a conviction rate of 71 per cent. In the case of trial-ready case dockets, it exceeded its new target by using focused investigations to finalise court cases and improving data integrity, but failed to exceed its target on prosecutions owing to the difficulties in identifying perpetrators (South African Police Service 2017a: 153).

The SAPS Crime Intelligence Division was also hard at work monitoring community and student protests, generating intelligence reports to counter 'an increase in the number of violent community protests, [as well as] protests at institutions of higher education, as well as an increase in violent and syndicated crimes ... [placing] a higher demand on the generation of tactical and operational intelligence reports' (South African Police Service 2017a: 220). SAPS also provided more strategic intelligence products to Nicoc as a result of what it claimed to be an increase in security threats, including 'an increase in the threats to the authority of the state' (South African Police Service 2017a: 221). In relation to that performance indicator, it overperformed significantly by producing 38 reports rather than its planned 22. SAPS also overperformed in producing operational reports, producing 278 187 tactical and operational reports against the planned target of 166 197 reports. Yet the number of communication interception analysis reports reduced massively to 1 704 over the same period (Table 10.1), suggesting that well-publicised instability in the Crime Intelligence Division had caught up with it. In spite of the overall increase in the number of intelligence products, SAPS was unable to meet its targets for convictions of those responsible for violence in protests and industrial action. While it set a target of 49 per cent for the detection rate, 44.55 per cent was achieved. A target of 70 per cent was set for the trial-ready case docket rate and 84.07 per cent was achieved, suggesting that SAPS was responding to considerable pressure to make these cases trial ready. Yet, of those cases, convictions were achieved in only 60.56 per cent, as opposed to the target of 71 per cent, representing the largest deviation from target of all categories of conviction. SAPS acknowledged that the difficulties in identifying suspects in protests led to mass arrests, in spite of evidence having to be provided in respect of each and every suspect – an onerous evidentiary requirement that led to many of their public order cases unwinding. Owing to the difficulties of achieving prosecutions in protest cases, going forward, SAPS decided to do away entirely with performance indicators relating to criminal and violent conduct in protests and industrial action (South African Police Service 2017a: 43). Tellingly, the one case SAPS defended with vigour involved the prosecution of 275 mine workers arrested in Marikana, who, bizarrely, were accused of the murder and attempted murder of their own comrades on the basis of the common purpose doctrine. These charges were withdrawn after public controversies.

By 2017, frustrated at the inability of government departments to address the issues giving rise to protests, SAPS requested that government departments find ways of reducing the number of protests. According to SAPS, 'Related departments are requested to ensure that service delivery protests are avoided through other means rather than end up in crime. These also put a strain on both our human and physical resources which are redirected to address crime caused by service delivery' (South African Police Service 2018: 19). However, in relation to the #FeesMustFall protests, SAPS pursued a unified command system and enforcement strategy at all the universities and further refined a strong evidence-gathering approach to its investigations in an attempt to ensure successful prosecutions. By then, SAPS had opened 51 cases and effected 207 arrests during the #FeesMustFall protests (Parliamentary Monitoring Group 2017).

This focused approach raised SAPS's performance slightly, in that while their detection rate decreased from 44.55 per cent in 2016/2017 to 42.73 per cent in 2017/2018, their trial-ready rate increased from 84.07 per cent in 2016/2017 to 86.36 per cent in 2017/2018. Nevertheless, SAPS's frustrations with the evidentiary requirements in these cases remained. The number of intelligence reports generated for early warning proactive interventions, as well as tactical interventions, including in relation to protests, was above the target, although the number of strategic intelligence reports was well below target. However, only about half of proactive and reactive intelligence reports were operationalised.

Possibly the most significant intelligence failure over this period was around the indisputably violent protests in Vuwani in 2016. In 2015, the Municipal Demarcation Board decided to demarcate eight wards into the Vhembe municipality, which caused great unhappiness in the area. Members of Vuwani challenged the decision in court, but the court dismissed the application, resulting in protests shutting down the area in May 2016 (South African Police Service 2017b). A total of 29 schools were burnt down, making it the single largest act of public violence in recent history, suggesting high levels of organisation on the part of those responsible. SAPS used the same four-pillar approach it had used in responding to the #FeesMustFall protests to respond to Vuwani. A total of 125 cases were opened in 2016 and, of 75 suspects, 23 were referred to the senior public prosecutor. In 2017, seven cases were opened, four of which were taken to court. To date, there have been no successful prosecutions of those responsible, despite former minister of state security David Mahlobo indicating a year before the protests took place that the SSA was aware of unhappiness about demarcation issues (Shazi 2017). The SSA and SAPS would no doubt also have been aware that protestors resorted to violence in neighbouring Malamulele, which attracted the attention of the authorities, and that it was likely similar tactics would be used in Vuwani as they had been shown to work. SAPS put their lack of success down to the fact that witnesses did not want to testify as they had been intimidated, but an intelligence-led approach should have yielded actionable intelligence. Given the obviously high levels of organisation of the arson attacks, coupled with the element of forewarning, it stretches the bounds of credibility for SAPS to argue that nothing could have been done to 'detect and disrupt' those responsible.

The above discussion shows that in spite of SAPS consolidating their intelligence-led approach during 2016 and 2017, there were clearly inefficiencies in the system. This approach failed to raise the conviction rates to their hoped-for levels, and failed spectacularly in relation to the most significant incident of organised public violence in recent history.

PROSECUTORIAL AND JUDICIAL RESPONSES

Despite instability and political meddling, the NPA achieved an extremely high overall conviction rate of 93 per cent by 2015/2016, so it was to be expected that it would only prosecute cases that it had high expectations of winning (National Prosecuting Authority 2016: 6). Like SAPS and in line with the JCPS cluster directive, the NPA also identified violent protests as one of the crimes for prioritised prosecution. However, according to the NPA, there have been hardly any prosecutions under the Regulation of Gatherings Act, a case involving the Social Justice Coalition, a Cape Town-based social movement, being an exception (pers. comm. Bulelwa Makeke). As shown in Table 10.2, in 2015/2016, 73 convictions were obtained in cases of violent protests and industrial action, with a conviction rate of 68.2 per cent, well below the overall rate (National Prosecuting Authority 2016: 30). By then, prosecutors were tracking violent protests as a special project for reporting (pers. comm. Bulelwa Makeke). In 2016/2017, the conviction rate dropped even further to 55.9 per cent or 57 cases (National Prosecuting Authority 2017: 26). In 2017/2018, the conviction rate improved significantly (68.8 per cent, or 88 cases), although it still remained under target. This could be attributed in part to the fact that prosecutors were assisted by advocates from the office of the Director of Public Prosecutions (National Prosecuting Authority 2018: 21).

The NPA claimed that it achieved notable successes in some #FeesMustFall cases, such as that involving Kanya Cekeshe, who pled guilty and was convicted of public violence and malicious damage to property after a SAPS vehicle was burnt. He was sentenced to eight years, imprisonment, of which two years were

Table 10.2 Conviction rates achieved by the National Prosecuting Authority, 2015–2018

Conviction rate in violent protests and industrial actions prosecuted	2015/2016	2016/2017	2017/2018
Number of convictions	73	57	88
Conviction rate (%)	68.2	55.9	68.8

Source: National Prosecuting Authority (2016, 2017, 2018)

conditionally suspended. After appealing to the Constitutional Court, Bonginkosi Khanyile was convicted of public violence, failing to comply with a police instruction and possession of a dangerous weapon; he was sentenced to three years' house arrest (Broughton 2019). Masixole Mlandu (University of Cape Town) was ordered to conduct community service (Evans 2018). Others making their way through the criminal justice system at the time of writing included Amla Monageng (University of Pretoria), who was put under house arrest for public violence and assaulting a fellow student, and Mcebo Dlamini (University of the Witwatersrand), who has made multiple court appearances.

Protestors who have legal representation generally find it much easier to navigate the police and prosecutorial system, and the experiences of public interest law clinics in representing those accused of assembly offences are instructive in this regard. According to the Right2Protest Project (R2P) – an advice and referral service representing a coalition of civil society organisations focusing on freedom of assembly – most of the cases they have dealt with involved public violence charges, followed by damage to property and contempt of interdicts. In its advice and referral work, R2P has noticed that the police often target conveners, as the most visible participants in protests. They have also noticed a tendency on the part of the police to keep accused people in jail for as long as possible, and to change charges depending on which ones have the greatest prospects of success.

According to the Socio-Economic Rights Institute's (SERI) director of litigation, Nomzamo Zondo, they have handled 40 protest-related cases since 2014, and only one of those led to a successful conviction. Most cases were withdrawn once SERI made representations to the NPA. Protestors who were not represented or who received inadequate representation were more likely to plead guilty (even if they were not), simply to bring the matter to a close given the arduous nature of the prosecutorial process. Like R2P, SERI has observed that the police use public violence as a nebulous, catch-all charge to justify arresting protestors, even if there is no cause to do so. In Zondo's experience, the police seem to consider protests per se as being public violence; they order a protest to disperse and then arrest those who run away. In one case, after a #FeesMustFall march on the Union Buildings, the seat of government, the police arrested seven people (six students and an informal trader who happened to be on the scene at the time) as the protest dispersed. After making representations to the chief prosecutor, they were released – this after the police had taken 20 hours to charge them, and the prosecutor had initially refused them bail (Zondo 2015). These trends in the policing and prosecution of protests suggest security responses to violent protests have been limited in their success. Nevertheless, these responses provide the pretext for overpolicing legitimate protests, thereby limiting spaces for the expression of dissent and practices of direct politics that use disruption to challenge and change how society is organised.

CONCLUSION

Contemporary society has seen a massive expansion of policing powers beyond crime control to cover all manner of social ills, including drug addition, sex work, migration and political dissent (including protests). Modern capitalist states have attempted to secure the consent of the policed, convincing them that the police's actions are necessary to secure the interests of the majority domestically. Yet, this expansion has made the overly political role of policing more visible as an institution tasked with maintaining social control, controlling dissent and reproducing inequality. The involvement of the police in political management more generally is particularly contentious, as the policed may come to experience policing as repressive and governments may lose whatever legitimacy they still enjoy. Consequently, political policing has benefited from reducing reliance on potentially controversial visible policing methods and incorporating more sophisticated, less visible (and hence less accountable) intelligence-based social control methods, including surveillance, infiltration of social and political movements, entrapment of protest leaders and targeted repression of protests. However, despite this expansion, a persistent and systemic feature of contemporary policing is its ineffectiveness in controlling crime, which can spiral out of control as the police busy themselves with disrupting movements that threaten the political and economic status quo, regardless of whether criminality is present (Vitale 2017: 197–201). In fact, in countries that consider themselves democracies, the expansion of policing into political management has been possible only through an intelligence-led approach. Typically, policing reforms have focused on increasing nominal accountability, but have largely failed to address the broader political role of the police under capitalism, and the massive expansion of policing powers more generally. This expansion is having a de-democratising effect, eroding even the narrow foundations of liberal democracy as these democracies take on more of the characteristics of dictatorships that spy on and harass their political opponents. It is also contributing to the rise of authoritarian nationalist populism by legitimising a more authoritarian state form in the name of protecting democracy and separating 'us' from 'them'. The rise of this form of populism is evident across the BRICS (Brazil, Russia, India, China, South Africa) countries in the wake of the 2008 global capitalist crisis, and involves the hijacking of popular dissent by charismatic right-wing politicians to gain legitimacy for a more authoritarian form of neoliberalism. While elements of authoritarian populism are apparent in South Africa – notably in relation to the state's treatment of foreign nationals – this form of neoliberalism is much more advanced in Brazil (see Saad-Filho, this volume) and India (see Nilsen, this volume). As things stand, though, there is no right-wing populist movement ascendant in the country to the point where there is an imminent danger of it taking over the levers of government. Nevertheless, elements of authoritarian populism are already worryingly visible in areas of the state and society, notably in the JCPS cluster. If the Left is not vigilant, then Brazil's and India's present may well become South Africa's future. In other words, we could see greater social acceptance of police violence and surveillance, and growing security powers more generally, as being necessary to secure the country from perceived 'foreign threats' and restore order domestically, as neoliberal accumulation strategies weaken more and more social institutions.

South Africa has embraced this expansion of policing powers, with the domestically focused security services playing a more explicit role in monitoring and policing protests. What has the JCPS cluster's framing and subsequent prioritisation of violent protests as serious crimes and domestic (even national) security threats led to? While the available evidence points to some successes overall, it also points to troubling patterns in the recent interventions of the cluster, and ones that are not politically neutral. Intelligence-led policing has led to a national police capability that is less rather than more publicly accountable for its actions than it was before Marikana, and one that still considers itself to be a force rather than a service. It has also led to lopsided priorities and a focus on the very politically charged domestic stability part of its work, at the expense of other serious crimes. It is no small wonder that in 2015/2016, SAPS failed to meet targets in relation to serious crimes and the contributors to them, including crimes against women and children, while achieving targets in relation to 'public incidents of a public disorder or security nature, which are not deemed to be "normal crime"' using their paramilitary and POP units (South African Police Service 2017a: 92). The justice and security cluster has also pursued a very narrow definition of social stability: one equated with crimes against the state. The police must focus on violent conduct in protests. According to Alexander et al. (2018: 31), a clear definition of violence should involve serious damage to buildings and/or injury to persons, but exclude disruptive tactics such as road blockades.

The elevation of violent protests, broadly defined by the security cluster, to the level of a priority crime has also occurred as priority crimes impacting on social stability more broadly recede into the background, with a disproportionately heavy impact on women and children. Intelligence-led policing can be particularly useful for detecting and disrupting organised crime, yet grand corruption on an industrial scale has blighted South Africa and organised crime continues to flourish. The large number of intelligence reports generated and the arrests effected have not translated into significant numbers of successful convictions, raising the question of what the intelligence has been used for. The inefficiencies in the criminal justice system – despite being intelligence-led – are difficult to ignore.

Those convictions that have been obtained from the #FeesMustFall protests have helped to identify some of those responsible for violent incidents, but the vigour shown in bringing these individuals to book has not been matched by the vigour shown towards policing other serious crimes. Several of these crimes have turned out to be not serious at all, evident from the fact that SAPS and the NPA have been willing to negotiate around these cases and agree to alternatives to incarceration. Yet there are cases of grand public violence that remain unsolved. The intelligence failures in relation to Vuwani need further investigation, as the arguments that have been given are difficult to fathom, and are even suspicious. It is difficult not to conclude that these blind spots are systemic rather than episodic. Certainly, they benefited former president Jacob Zuma and the corrupt networks around him at a time when they had captured the security cluster for their own ends. Commenting on these intelligence blind spots, Blade Nzimande, former minister of higher education and secretary general of the South African Communist Party, made the following observation:

> There are certain things that don't make sense to me, to us [South African Communist Party]. Why wouldn't you pick up the burning of so many schools in Vuwani? Even with the #FeesMustFall, some of the destruction that was happening. You know, in one of the universities, I was told that the people who were doing this damage and burning of things, including the library at one institution, were outsiders. They were not students. But they

did not pick it up. Does it mean, could it mean . . . Even now you can see now with the burning of trucks and the blocking of the toll road in Mooi River . . . I don't know, but you could hypothesise that the increasing capacity of state security has got more to do with issues of state security than the safety and security [of the people]. (Interview, Blade Nzimande)

As Alex Vitale (2017) has observed, perhaps the problem with the police is not the lack of training or weaknesses in oversight or other problems that require technocratic solutions, but a massive expansion of policing powers into areas that should not be policed. This expansion is leading to the overpolicing of racial and class inequalities, and administrative overreach designed to enforce austerity policies. Such policing can (and does) contribute to the reproduction of inequality as protests are a highly accessible means for the poor and excluded to voice dissent and challenge unequal wealth and power relations. This expansion of policing is having massive, negative consequences for any attempts to incorporate workers and the unemployed into the political system on their terms, thereby expanding democracy from below. Consequently, the conversation should not only be about the pros and cons of different policing models, oversight and internal controls. Rather, it should be about policing itself, and that is a conversation that has not even begun in South Africa. For a start, social (in)stability should not be a policing concern at all.

NOTES

1 Analysis of archived communication metadata acquired from communication service providers through section 205 of the Criminal Procedures Act.
2 Analysis of real-time communication-related information and communication content, intercepted in terms of the Regulation of Interception of Communications and Provision of Communication-Related Information Act, or Rica.

INTERVIEWS AND PERSONAL COMMUNICATION

Email correspondence with Bulelwa Makeke, Head of Communication, National Prosecuting Authority, 8 February 2019.
Interview with Blade Nzimande, South African Communist Party offices, Braamfontein, 14 May 2018.

REFERENCES

Alexander, P., Runciman, C., Ngwane, C., Moloto, B., Mokgele, K. and van Staden, N. 2018. 'Frequency and turmoil: South Africa's community protests 2005–2017', *South African Crime Quarterly* 63: 27–42.

Bezuidenhout, C. 2008. 'The nature of police and community interaction alongside the dawn of intelligence-led policing', *Acta Criminologica* 3: 48–67. Accessed 20 February 2019, www.repository.up.ac.za/bitstream/handle/2263/9445/Bezuidenhout_Nature%2820 08%29.pdf?sequence=1.

Branch, A. and Mampilly, Z. 2015. *Africa Uprising: Popular Protest and Political Challenge.* Cape Town: HSRC Press.

Broughton, T. 2019. 'Fees Must Fall activist Bonginkosi Khanyile sentenced to 3 years house arrest', *News24*, 28 January. Accessed 27 February 2019, https://www.news24.com/SouthAfrica/News/fees-must-fall-activist-bonginkosi-khanyile-sentenced-to-3-years-house-arrest-20190128.

Choudry, A. 2019. *Activists and the Surveillance State: Learning from Repression.* London: Pluto Press.

Cox, L. 2014. 'Changing the world without getting shot: How popular power can set limits on state violence'. In M. Lakitsh (ed.), *Political Power Reconsidered: State Power and Civic Activism between Legitimacy and Violence. Peace report 2013.* Berlin and Vienna: LIT-Verlag.

Della Porta, D. 2013. *Clandestine Political Violence.* Cambridge: Cambridge University Press.

Duncan, J. 2014. *The Rise of the Securocrats: The Case of South Africa.* Johannesburg: Jacana Media.

Duncan, J. 2016. *Protest Nation: The Right to Protest in South Africa.* Pietermartizburg: UKZN Press.

Evans, J. 2018. 'UCT #FeesMustFall activist to do community service, attend counselling', *News24*, 15 August. Accessed 27 February 2019, https://www.news24.com/SouthAfrica/News/uct-feesmustfall-activist-to-do-community-service-attend-counselling-2018 0815.

Farlam, I.G., Hemraj, P.D. and Tokota, B.R. 2015. 'Marikana Commission of Enquiry: Report on matters of public, national and international concern arising out of the tragic incidents at the Lonmin mine in Marikana, in the North West province'. Accessed 30 February 2019, https://www.sahrc.org.za/home/21/files/marikana-report-1.pdf.

National Prosecuting Authority. 2016. 'Annual Report: National Director of Public Prosecutions 2015/16'. Accessed 21 February 2019, https://www.npa.gov.za/sites/default/files/annual-reports/NPA%20Annual%20Report%201516.pdf.

National Prosecuting Authority. 2017. 'Annual Report: National Director of Public Prosecutions 2016/17'. Accessed 21 February 2019, https://www.npa.gov.za/sites/default/files/annual-reports/NDPP-Annual%20Report-2016-17.pdf.

National Prosecuting Authority. 2018. 'Annual Report: National Director of Public Prosecutions 2017/18'. Accessed 22 February 2019, https://www.npa.gov.za/sites/default/files/annual-reports/NDPP%20Annual%20Report-%202017-18.pdf.

Paret, M. 2017. 'Southern resistance in critical perspective'. In M. Paret, C. Runciman and L. Sinwell (eds), *Southern Resistance in Critical Perspective.* Oxon: Routledge, pp. 1–18.

Parliamentary Monitoring Group. 2017. 'Minutes of a meeting of the Portfolio Committee on Basic Education'. Accessed 22 February 2019, https://pmg.org.za/committee-meeting/24650/.

Savage, M. 2011. 'Police under fire as trial collapses over "agent provocateur" claims', *The Independent*, 11 January. Accessed 26 February 2019, https://www.independent.co.uk/news/uk/crime/police-under-fire-as-trial-collapses-over-agent-provocateur-claims-2181118.html.

Shazi, N. 2017. 'David Mahlobo clarifies Vuwani comments. We're still not sure what it means for State Security', *Huffington Post*, 5 July. Accessed 28 February 2019, https://www.huffingtonpost.co.za/2017/07/05/david-mahlobo-clarifies-vuwani-comments-to-huffpost-were-still_a_23016707/.

South African Police Service. 2014. 'South African Police Service Strategic Plan 2010–2014'. Accessed 14 February 2019, www.saps.gov.za/saps_profile/strategic_framework/strategic_plan/2010_2014/strategic_plan_2010_2014_2.pdf.

South African Police Service. 2015. South African Police Service Strategic Plan 2014–2019'. Accessed 14 February 2019, www.saps.gov.za/about/stratframework/strategic_plan/2015_2019/strategic_plan_%202015.pdf.

South African Police Service. 2016. 'Annual report 2015/16'. Accessed 14 February 2019, https://www.saps.gov.za/about/stratframework/annual_report/2015_2016/saps_annual_report_2015_2016.pdf.

South African Police Service. 2017a. 'Annual Report 2016/17'. Accessed 14 February 2019, https://nationalgovernment.co.za/department_annual/201/2017-south-african-police-service-(saps)-annual-report.pdf.

South African Police Service. 2017b. 'Briefing and status report on Vuwani: Portfolio Committee on Basic Education', PowerPoint presentation, 10 October. Accessed 19 February 2019, http://pmg-assets.s3-website-eu-west-1.amazonaws.com/171010SAPS.pdf on 19 February 2019.

South African Police Service. 2018. 'Media statement from the Office of the Minister of Police, 17 January'. Accessed 20 February 2019, https://www.saps.gov.za/newsroom/msspeechdetail.php?nid=14171.

Vitale, A. 2017. *The End of Policing*. London: Verso.

Zondo, N. 2015. 'Press statement: Sunnyside 7 released'. Accessed 28 February 2019, http://seri-sa.org/images/Sunnyside7Press.pdf.

11

PROSPECTS FOR A LEFT RENEWAL IN SOUTH AFRICA

Gunnett Kaaf

INTRODUCTION

Post-1994 South Africa is in the throes of a deepening political and social crisis. It is a political crisis marked by a decline of democracy, poor governance, corruption and lack of a development strategy. It is an economic crisis of stagnation, mass unemployment and widespread poverty. It is a crisis of development, manifesting in worsening township and rural underdevelopment. It is an ecological crisis in which natural resources are depleted and nature is destroyed in a manner that threatens the survival of human life on Earth.

Two outcomes seem possible from this deepening crisis: a resulting tragic impasse, or a responsive radical social transformation. The outcomes reflect very different forces. The first likely entails a deepening crisis of poor governance, poor public services, corruption, growing unemployment, massive poverty and inequality. The second entails halting the crisis and posing a social transformation that advances the social demands of the majority.

South Africa's political and social crisis is driven by two main factors: lack of meaningful social transformation following the 1994 democratic breakthrough, and worsening corruption within the state, led by the African National Congress (ANC). This corruption should be understood as an accumulation system of the ruling elites in terms of social class relations that formed after 1994, with the new black bourgeoisie playing a subordinate role to the established white bourgeoisie. Having been locked out of mainstream industries that are dominated by generalised monopolies, the black bourgeoisie resorts to looting state budgets and assets (see Von Holdt 2019).

The situation is exacerbated by the fact that there are no left alternatives to the ANC, despite the fact that the ANC is imploding. The Economic Freedom Fighters (EFF) are strategically limited and steeped in populist politics fraught with nationalist and racialist mobilisation, which is not helpful but rather worsens the crisis. The Democratic Alliance's (DA's) liberal vision, which focuses on fighting corruption without a social transformation agenda, has reached its limits. Mass movements, which have the potential to impose people's power from below, are weak. Hence, there are currently no viable alternatives on the horizon, begging the question: How will a Left be rebuilt?

The urgency of renewing left forces – buttressed by the social demands of the popular classes (workers, lower-middle classes, the unemployed, rural masses, township communities, youth and women) who make up the majority – is necessitated by the worsening crisis of liberal democracy in both the global North and South. In the absence of a formidable Left, far-right forces, neo-fascists or authoritarian neoliberal rulers tend to take the centre stage, as has happened in Brazil (see Saad-Filho, this volume). Neoliberalism has polarised societies through inequality and other exclusive outcomes of development such as unemployment, precarious labour, poverty, underdevelopment and squeezing the middle classes. This polarisation and the absence of a coherent development project as an exit strategy from the impasse of the deepening crisis of global capitalism have set the stage for far-right or neo-fascist forces that mobilise on the basis of social exclusion and blaming others, such as foreigners and other racial groups (see Shivji 2020; Solty n.d.).

POPULAR MOVEMENTS TOWARDS SOCIALISM

I use the concept of 'the Left' to refer to political forces that adopt an anti-capitalist dimension in their pursuit of social transformation to address the plight of the popular classes. These popular classes are largely black, reflecting the racist past of our country, the history of colonisation and apartheid, and how it continues to define the present social reality. The legacies of apartheid and colonialism manifest as part of the current social crisis due to the ANC's failure to effect meaningful social change in post-1994 South Africa.

The anti-capitalist dimensions of the South African Left fall into two broad categories. First, there are those from the various communist and socialist traditions who frame their visions and strategies around resolving the basic contradiction of capitalism between labour and capital and going beyond capitalism towards socialism. Second, there are those who fight for the immediate social demands of popular classes without going too far into the future. While their social transformation measures do not seek to replace capitalism outright, as in the case of communists, they still challenge the historical formation of South African capitalism, which has shaped society and social relations since the mining industrial revolution of the late nineteenth century. Activists and organisations that are part of this second category include liberation movements, feminists, environmentalists, and those struggling for radical reforms in community development in urban township and rural areas, and in other fields such as youth development, health and education.

There is growing evidence to suggest that we need to rethink the vision and strategy of the Left for anti-capitalist struggles and for building socialism. The starting point is to give up the old communist party line of conquering state power first and then building socialism. Instead, social and political conditions that allow for an advance towards socialism should be fostered. Hence, as in Latin America, we need to build 'movements towards socialism'. This entails abandoning an approach to building socialism derived from the Soviet experience, which focused on nationalisation and state planning. In contrast, a 'movement towards socialism' leaves open the question of methods to be used in socialising the modern economy and the ongoing democratisation of society.

Marx's ideas remain the most powerful framework for formulating this new vision and strategy for the Left, despite the distortions in Soviet and Maoist versions of Marxism. Beginning with Marx therefore means discarding the inadequacies and distortions of historical Marxisms, while developing Marx's line of thought to advance it in line with today's realities.

It is time for the Left to seriously integrate the ecological question into its socialist vision. The deepening capitalist crisis, based on the logic of endless capital accumulation, has brought about the destruction of nature and worsening climate change, which are now threatening the survival of human life on the planet. As a system based on exchange value rather than use value, capitalism is proving incapable of resolving the deepening ecological crisis. Taking into account use value means socialism must be ecological.

Some might object that attempts at socialism have failed and it is hence no longer an alternative. However, like the earliest attempts at capitalism in the Italian city-states of the Late Middle Ages, which were not strong enough to survive amongst the feudal societies that surrounded them, the failure of the first experiments at socialism presage nothing but its eventual rebirth in a new, more revolutionary, more universal form which examines and learns from the failures (Foster 2019).

UNITY AND DIVERSITY OF THE LEFT

We need to encourage diverse lines of descent in the formation and advancement of socialist thought and action. This should encourage unity in diversity among left forces. Karl Marx's experiences in the First International are instructive in this regard (see Musto 2015). The First International, founded in 1864, was the biggest movement of the working class in Europe. Its slogan was 'The emancipation of the working classes must be conquered by the working classes themselves'. Marx played a pivotal role in drafting speeches and resolutions for the First International, in which he sought to include the views of all tendencies within the nineteenth-century European Left, as well as workers' tendencies: the conservative British trade unions, the Chartists, Lassalle and his followers from Germany, Proudhon and his followers from France, Bakunin from Russia. The main policies of the First International were formed through integrating the points of convergence and synthesising the strong points. Marx clearly recognised the importance of the major tendencies of the European working-class movement and pursued an approach of true unity in diversity in practice.

The experience of the Third International (Comintern 1919–1949) contrasted with Marx's approach in the First International. The Third International placed more emphasis on unity to the detriment of diversity. The main criterion for affiliation was 'one country, one communist party', unlike the First International, which accommodated more than one working-class formation with varying tendencies from one country.

The legacy of this lives on among some in the Left, as witnessed at the South African Federation of Trade Unions (Saftu) Working Class Summit, held in July 2018 and attended by 145 organisations. Discussion of issues that concern the working class in the workplace, in townships and in rural areas was marked by a spirit of unity and shared perspectives. There was largely a shared understanding and a healthy, robust exchange of ideas on major policy questions around economic transformation, land reform, housing, education and health. Many of the resolutions adopted on key policy issues could easily pass as a unifying programme for the broad working-class movement. However, the debate on the left political party or the workers' party proved to be more divisive. The National Union of Metalworkers of South Africa (Numsa) and others did not treat the debate with a maturity depicting the spirit of unity and diversity.

Numsa argued that a workers' party is the most important political tool for the working class to conquer state power, smash capitalism and build socialism. Since the meeting was a working-class summit, endorsement of a workers' party was an essential requirement for Numsa. They were so preoccupied with achieving this endorsement that they did not appreciate the need for a thorough discussion of the issues involved: what character such a workers' party should assume; whether it should be a central vanguard party in the mould of communist parties; the historical experience of failed centralised parties; whether the name 'workers' party' excludes the unemployed; and how the party should link up with mass movements and mass struggles.

The Numsa comrades could not appreciate the necessity for the diversity that Marx warns about in the *Communist Manifesto*. Marx did not argue that the working class requires just one communist party. Instead, he said: 'Communists do not form a separate party opposed to the other working-class parties' (Marx and Engels 1990: 49). Why would Marx talk about 'other working-class parties' if workers needed only one communist party? Marx clearly emphasised the complementary relationship between unity and diversity of left forces in the *Communist Manifesto* and in his work in the First International.

The insistence by Numsa on the absolute need for the Working Class Summit to endorse their workers' party created unnecessary discord among left formations gathered at the Summit. There was a lack of maturity and appreciation of unity in diversity. For instance, Numsa could have launched the workers' party without insisting on broad support beforehand. If their model of a workers' party was viable, they would receive the support they needed from other left forces and mass formations, rather than demanding it at the Summit.

Numsa formed the Socialist Revolutionary Workers Party (SRWP), but it does not advance the creative Marxist emancipatory politics we need for a genuine left renewal. The SRWP is an attempt to mimic the old exhausted model of communist parties. However, there is much to learn from Prabhat Patnaik's (2009: 101) argument that the old centralised party form has to be abandoned:

> The idea of a centralized party running an economy and guiding society in the interest of a class, which in the process gets depoliticised, has to be abandoned. It is not enough to say 'democracy'; we need an activation of the people, which has to be institutionalised. Thus from this point of view, when we think of socialism today we have to think in terms of structure, parties and strategy, all of which really empower people to decide their own destiny.

FRAMING A LEFT CRITIQUE OF THE ANC CRISIS

The worsening rot and decline of the ANC looms large in the political and social crisis, given the ANC's dominance since 1994. A left critique of the ANC crisis is therefore essential in the development of a left renewal strategy. The basic premise is that the ANC crisis is mainly driven by two factors: lack of meaningful transformation since 1994, and corruption.

Even with Cyril Ramaphosa at the helm, the ANC does not look capable of meaningful renewal or of carrying out any effective social transformation project. The rot runs deep and Ramaphosa's limited power within the ANC makes him incapable of effecting the decisive measures necessary to halt and reverse the rot. Ramaphosa should be applauded for allowing the state capture commission and other similar investigations on corruption and maleficence. However, he will not achieve much without decisive political measures, such as removing all those implicated in the rot from his cabinet and disciplining Ace Magashule and his supporters.

Ramaphosa's close links to big business (he is himself a billionaire businessman) will not help the efforts of the ANC to make a genuinely radical turn. As evidenced in his policy pronouncements and foreign direct investment drive, he does not have a radical perspective but is rather pursuing a neoliberal 'business as usual' approach through the meek National Development Plan (NDP). The choice for the Left is therefore to transcend the ANC or to be trapped in the impasse of the worsening crisis.

There are no forces of renewal within the ANC fold; good comrades who still remain in the ANC are trapped in the inertia of the ANC crisis and factionalised politics. It is up to the Left and progressive forces outside the ANC to initiate a genuine renewal for the country, based on bottom-up democratic and emancipatory politics and a meaningful social transformation. There is a real danger that the whole country will be trapped in an impasse if we do not transcend the ANC, to a point where the main agenda is not set by the ANC, but instead the ANC becomes just one of the political players.

In terms of a left critique of the ANC crisis, the first point to bear in mind is that the betrayal thesis – that the ANC and the South African Communist Party (SACP) betrayed the working class – should be avoided. A limitation of this perspective is that it sees no fault with the ANC's National Democratic Revolution (NDR) strategy. In building alternatives, there is thus a tendency to replicate the failed models of the ANC and the SACP. Numsa's SRWP, for instance, replicates the models of old communist parties. Numsa and others on the Left see nothing wrong with the SACP's political strategy and argue that the working class was simply betrayed by the leadership of the SACP at the altar of government positions. The betrayal thesis is inadequate and lacks a nuanced analysis of the political and ideological weaknesses of the ANC and its NDR strategy.

The second pitfall to be avoided is the leftist criticism by Trotskyists and others of the Left outside the ANC that it was bound to fail and degenerate into a bourgeois comprador class party because it was always bourgeois. Such teleological arguments do not help us understand the actual forces that led to the ANC's crisis.

The ANC's political strategy, the NDR, proposes a popular national democratic project but is limited because it does not have a clear anti-capitalist outlook, which is essential for a radical revolutionary project. Without a consistent anti-capitalist approach, the ANC is politically and ideologically too weak to confront monopoly capital and shake the foundations of South Africa's historical capitalism, on whose base apartheid social relations were constructed. The ANC is aware of the impediments that South African and global capitalism pose to any meaningful social transformation that will bring about change in favour of the majority. Many ANC documents suggest that capitalism has to be challenged for the NDR to be realised (see ANC 1997: sec. 5; 2007: para. 57). However, the lack of a consistent anti-capitalist stance, combined with inconsistencies and ambiguous class positions, has led to an ambivalence around challenging capitalism and pushing ahead with meaningful social transformation.

The bourgeois capitulation of the ANC was born out of the dominance of nationalism at the expense of anti-capitalist forces. The nationalism of the ANC dominated over the socialist influence of the SACP, to the extent that even the SACP subordinated class struggles to the dominant nationalism. Hein Marais (2011) traces the subordination of class struggles to nationalism back to the 1950s. The inability to overcome inequalities in the post-1994 era is attributable to this dominance of nationalism. In world history, nationalism has never succeeded in bringing about meaningful social transformation with development outcomes for the majority and genuine economic redistribution. Since World War II, where meaningful social transformations have occurred in the global South (e.g. Russia, China, Vietnam and Cuba), anti-capitalist policies and struggles played a decisive role.

The SACP failed to add a meaningful anti-capitalist analysis to the ANC because it has no independent socialist programme that defines its independent role and character as a communist party, and that articulates the social demands of the workers and the poor that it claims to represent. If the SACP had such a programme, it could subject the NDR to the pressing social demands of the popular classes and the long-term socialist vision. It could effectively reject neoliberalism in the Alliance and insist on policies that are pro the popular classes and anti-capitalist. Instead, the SACP has been trapped in the NDR quagmire of the ANC.

Assuming an anti-capitalist stance is not to suggest that the ANC should immediately pursue a socialist construction. However, to stop at the bourgeois revolution, which is what the ANC's NDR has been reduced to, betrays the historically oppressed black majority. Post-1994, South Africa's historical capitalism was allowed to continue and restructure (by globalising and financialising) in terms favourable to big corporates (see Marais 2011). This betrayed the people because it did not provide acceptable responses to social problems stemming from the apartheid legacy. The basic components of the accumulation system of South African capitalism were left to continue: monopolies in the major economic sectors of finance, mining, energy, manufacturing, agriculture; cheap labour markets; and dependent integration into the global economy such that most capital is foreign owned.

The other key factor driving the ANC's decline is corruption. The Left has not been successful at exposing and waging struggles against corruption. Here the main challenge for the Left is to show how South Africa's monopoly capitalism created a comprador class out of the black bourgeoisie and small business classes after 1994, and how their vulnerability makes them prone to state corruption. The comprador class is particularly vulnerable at this stage of monopoly capitalism because monopolies dominate all major industries throughout the value chain. For example, as Samir Amin (2013) points out, the modern capitalist farmer is exploited by a generalised monopoly which controls the upstream supply of inputs and credit and the downstream marketing of products. These farmers have been transformed into subcontractors for dominant capital. This same logic applies to the black and small business bourgeoisie, which has been reduced to subcontractors of established monopoly capital. While mainstream liberal discourses proclaim 'state hands off the economy', the actual practice is the state in service of monopolies. This dynamic makes the black bourgeoisie and small business classes reliant on state tenders. The competition is unhealthy because it is not based on price, equity and efficiencies, but rather on connections with state officials, leading to all types of predatory looting of the state in the post-1994 period.

The challenge for the Left is not just to expose and fight corruption from a moralist point of view, as promoted by the liberal forces in the media and mainstream ideological discourses. If the Left does not go beyond the liberal moralist discourses, their strategies of fighting corruption will not offer a transformational dimension. The Left must therefore expose the symbiotic relationship between monopoly capitalism and neoliberalism, on the one hand, and corruption, on the other, in post-1994 South Africa. This relationship found expression through outsourcing basic public services to private operators in the name of efficiency, when in actual fact the opposite happened because of cost escalations resulting from corrupt relations. This proposed approach for the Left does not preclude working with liberal forces when corruption becomes widespread, as was necessary in the Zuma years. The challenge being thrown to the Left is to go beyond the limits of liberalism when confronting corruption, both in theory and in practice.

MASS MOVEMENTS FOR A LEFT RENEWAL

In this section I draw extensively from Samir Amin (2014) and Marta Harnecker (2016), who make interesting proposals about left renewal and strategic lines of struggle. Harnecker advocates against traditional forms of political parties, instead supporting turning mass uprisings into revolutionary advances. She argues that left activists should be in the service of popular movements, rather than wanting to replace them, and highlights the need to unite the political and social Left. She urges the Left to abandon their habit of wanting to build political forces (political parties) without a social base.

Mass movements are the nucleus of the strategy for rebuilding and renewing the Left in South Africa. They are needed to give solid organisational expression to political and social forces for meaningful social change in South Africa. Drawing on the experience of the last 27 years, the building of mass movements requires mobilisation, organisation, strategic vision, tactical sense, choice of actions and politicisation of struggles.

The starting point when rebuilding mass movements is to recall the radical traditions that were decisive in the victory against apartheid, particularly in the last 20 years of apartheid rule in South Africa. Labour unions organised themselves under the banner of the Congress of South African Trade Unions (Cosatu) labour federation, and students, youth, women, civics and other community organisations affiliated in the United Democratic Front (UDF). These key organisational expressions of people's power gained momentum in the 1980s and were decisive in the build-up to the democratic breakthrough in 1994. There is general consensus among historians and analysts that the hegemony of the ANC in anti-apartheid struggles from the 1980s, and its eventual ascension to power, were largely a result of the ANC being entrenched in the mass movements of the 1980s. Gail Gerhart observes that without the UDF, the politics of the contemporary ANC would have been completely different, its ascension to power would have been far more difficult, and the character of its subsequent actions would undoubtedly have been different and probably less successful (cited in Seekings 2000).

The mass movements of the 1980s and early 1990s were autonomous formations of the people in various sectors. They mainly pursued local struggles based on local demands but then linked these local demands with national political goals for ending apartheid. The ANC only succeeded in gaining control over these mass movements after 1994, by using the might of state power and offering employment opportunities in the state to many of the leading cadres of these movements, as well as other forms of patronage such as business opportunities through state contracts. Cosatu and the SACP were captured by the Zuma faction in the lead-up to the 2007 Polokwane ANC national conference. That marked the final destruction of any autonomy in these two formations, particularly Cosatu, which was at the time still a powerful mass movement.

In the post-1994 period, the Treatment Action Campaign (TAC) was one of the biggest mass movements, organised as a non-governmental organisation (NGO). It put pressure on government on a major public policy matter, the HIV/AIDS epidemic. TAC fought hard and succeeded in shifting government policy on antiretrovirals through a 2003 Constitutional Court judgment.

Many other social movements sprang up in the post-1994 period to take up the various social demands of the popular classes, ranging from better-quality public services, local development issues, local government demarcation issues, housing, healthcare and education, to jobs, electricity, feminism and environmental issues, as well as protests against extractive mining. These social movements have taken on various organisational forms, including autonomous mass movements, NGOs, and spontaneous community and worker protest movements. They have helped to hold to account corrupt local politicians, and have also constituted a form of counterpower against the power of monopoly capital, which continues along its path of accumulation based on ecologically harmful extractive mining and cheap labour.

Four key moments stand out in the period since 2012: the Xolobeni community protest against uranium mining in Pondoland, which is ongoing; the Marikana mine workers' strike in 2012; the De Doorns farm workers' strike in 2012; and the #FeesMustFall student movement of 2015/2016. The establishment of the United Front (UF) in 2013, an umbrella body of trade unions, NGOs and community organisations, was an appropriate response to the momentum generated by these events. The UF failed, however, because it was not a bottom-up approach relying on mass movements; rather, it was a centralised approach relying largely on the Numsa structures.

These mass movements also played a role in reducing the electoral dominance of the ANC, which fell from 69.69 percent in 2004 down to 57.50 percent in the 2019 general elections. The ANC's loss in metropolitan areas in 2016 was partly because these urban areas were storm zones of community protests against poor public services, since at least the early 2000s and with the number of protests growing significantly after 2004. The ANC lost Metsimaholo local municipality in the Free State in 2016 after community protests as a result of corruption in the municipality.

Pre-1994 mass movements such as the traditional trade unions in Cosatu, the student movements (Congress of South African Students, South African Students Congress, Azanian Students' Organisation, Pan Africanist Student Movement of Azania) allied with former liberation movements, and civics organised in the South African National Civic Organisation have been absent in key moments of revolt since 1994 that challenged neoliberalism and the social power relations dominated by monopoly capital. This highlights the importance of the task of building new movements for the post-1994 terrain and the twenty-first century, with the starting point being mass movements that already exist in local areas and in various sectors.

The left renewal strategy needs to respond to the current social formation in South Africa. Key features of this post-1994 social formation include the continuing legacies of apartheid, poverty, cheap labour and underdevelopment, all of which still have a racial dimension and a black face. However, there are also new features: an expanded black middle class and a class of black businesspeople (capitalists). Inequality has now widened within the black community. There has been no meaningful social progress for the black majority, despite the expansion of the social wage, and in many respects the living conditions in urban townships and rural areas have worsened. Declining infrastructure, high unemployment and increasing poverty are some of the main factors worsening the living conditions for the majority. Agriculture does not provide a source of livelihood for the people in rural areas in South Africa (Jara interview). Could it be that the disappointment and shock about post-1994 failures and the widespread rot have deeply offended the imagination of the popular classes, to the point of impairing them in taking up the political challenge and initiative to resist and fight for alternatives?

For much of the last 27 years the overwhelming dominance of the ANC was a barrier in building truly autonomous mass movements. The legitimacy of the ANC came from the heritage of the liberation struggle and the fact that mass movements of the 1980s and 1990s collapsed themselves into the ANC. It was thus the legitimate party of the democratic state with vast networks as a mass movement. Most political battles took place and were fought within the broad ANC fold. Even though post-1994 mass movements made an impact, they sometimes felt isolated because they were not close enough to Cosatu, a mass movement of workers attached to the ANC. Trever Ngwane (interview) recounts such experiences with respect to the Anti-Privatisation Forum and Soweto Electricity movements. The decline of the ANC, which has accelerated over the last ten years, opens up the space for building mass movements. Another weakness of mass movements and their struggles in the post-1994 period is that they did not fully appreciate the neoliberal dimension of the state and how the state is dominated (almost to a point of being colonised) by finance capital. Mass movements tended to demand services from the state without ever directly challenging the neoliberal fiscal and economic policies that shape the nature and delivery of public services. The Left must work with communities as they grapple with better ways of organising. The Left must also learn from and work together with the masses to strengthen mass movements to effectively push the social demands of the popular classes and offer an alternative form of social transformation, a point echoed by Ngwane (interview).

Trade unions remain important organisations of the working class, not only to fight for the immediate economic demands of workers, but also to advance meaningful social transformation. The decline of Cosatu in the mid-2000s marked a continuing decline of trade unions that has not been halted despite the launch of Saftu in 2017. The trade union movement faces many challenges. The majority of workers remain non-unionised, and only 31 per cent of the workforce was covered by collective bargaining in 2014 (Van der Walt 2019). Many unions do not have any meaningful worker control and suffer from serious corruption, elitism and bureaucracy. The neoliberalism of the ANC government has perpetuated apartheid-style cheap labour and even enlarged the sectors of precarious workers through various schemes of flexible labour markets. The tendency of 'sweetheart unionism' remains widespread in many sectors and is a serious blockage to building militant, effective unions that meaningfully advance the demands and interests of workers. Unions are not in touch with the actual reality of workers on the ground. The future of trade unions will be secured through building militant, worker-controlled unions that are effective and reach out widely to workers (Swart interview). New effective organisational forms of trade unions are therefore necessary to renew trade unionism in the twenty-first century and cover unorganised workers, many of whom are precarious workers. This could include smaller unions that are effective, with more internal democracy, operating in one industry across the value chain. Big unions tend to have less internal democracy, lack the necessary militancy and eventually become conservative. It is time to move away from the tradition of big unions dominating an industry and to drop the 'one union, one industry' slogan.

CONCLUSION

The Left's way forward out of the current political crisis is not to form a workers' party or a vanguard party that will contest elections with a socialist manifesto in the hope of winning parliamentary seats. Any preoccupation with a centralised party of the Left will be a serious distraction. Instead, the Left should work with the popular classes to build strong grassroots and sector movements to fight for the immediate social demands of these classes on health, education, housing, food, women, youth, sports, arts, culture, and so on. While the struggles should be about immediate social demands, they must have a clear anti-capitalist outlook and seek to go beyond the limits of the current capitalist society. They must express a yearning for a better society that is not capitalist. The struggles and mass movements must be connected through a coherent vision and political efforts to build an anti-capitalist and anti-neoliberal historic bloc in South Africa, and also connect with other struggles of popular classes in Africa and the wider world.

This is not to lose sight of political power, but rather to build popular power on the ground, on whose base genuine left political alternatives should be advanced. Rebuilding a New Left alternative political pole should be based on mass struggles and the vision of democratic eco-socialism. The mass political party or parties that come out of such efforts should be non-vanguardist, open-ended and long-term, and linked to mass movements without controlling them. A left electoral victory based authentically on a radical programme is only possible after the victory of popular struggles, not before.

Struggles for reforms in the here and now in order to ameliorate people's conditions are going to be essential in building the long-term momentum for a genuine left renewal. These struggles should be based on the constitution and other democratic rights and demands, including regulation of the private sector.

Struggles for alternatives and transformation will be essential in grounding the Left and mass movements in an anti-capitalist and anti-neoliberal outlook. The struggles should address matters concerning development in townships and rural areas, including issues such as seed banks; a solidarity economy; and public goods and services such as education, health, transport, housing, a social wage and renewables.

Popular struggles to characterise the left renewal must be made up of both protest and developmental work. Community development activities could cover art, culture, media (including magazines), poetry, cultural movements, people's heritage from below and knowledge production from below (including research, studies, publications of all types). These efforts should seek to build a popular movement for meaningful social transformation based on a coherent anti-capitalist, anti-neoliberal vision. However, none of this is possible without sustained activist development and political education in order to build a critical mass of conscious, confident, capable and effective activists who can carry out the tasks at hand.

The forms of activity and organisation proposed here, predicated on popular struggles and popular inventiveness, cannot be decreed in advance through a sanctified doctrine. Revolutionary advances are possible, on the basis of developing a real and new people's power to drive away the power of political elites and monopoly capital, which are responsible for protecting and reproducing the social inequality of post-1994 South Africa. Marx did not expound any theory of 'the great day of revolution and definitive solutions'; on the contrary, he insisted on an open-minded approach, believing that a revolution is a long transition marked by a conflict between social powers – the former powers in decline and the new ones on the rise. Let the power and organisation of the popular classes rise for a meaningful left renewal in South Africa.

ACKNOWLEDGEMENT

In revising earlier versions of this chapter, I benefited from criticisms, comments and encouragement from a number of people. I am particularly grateful to Sandile Fuku, Natalya Dinat and Mazibuko Jara. I am also indebted to the editors, Michelle Williams and Vishwas Satgar, for their guidance and useful suggestions.

INTERVIEWS

Jara, M., Marxist activist, active in rural movements, telephonic interview, 8 June 2019.
Ngwane, T., socialist activist, academic and author of *Makomiti: Grassroots Democracy in South African Shack Settlements*, telephonic interview, 19 June 2019.
Swart, K., Commercial, Stevedoring, Agriculture and Allied Workers Union, interview, Cape Town, 14 July 2019.

REFERENCES

Amin, S. 2013. 'China 2013', *Monthly Review* 64 (10) March.
Amin, S. 2014. 'Popular movements toward socialism: Their unity and diversity', *Monthly Review* 66 (2) June.
ANC (African National Congress). 1997. *Strategy and Tactics*. Johannesburg: ANC.
ANC (African National Congress). 2007. *Strategy and Tactics*. Johannesburg: ANC.
Foster, J.B. 2019. 'Capitalism has failed, what next?' *Monthly Review* 70 (9) February.
Harnecker, M. 2016. 'Ideas for the struggle'. Translated by F. Fuentes. Accessed 30 June 2019, http://www.oldandnewproject.net/Essays/Harnecker_Ideas.pdf.
Marais, H. 2011. *South Africa Pushed to the Limit*. Cape Town: UCT Press.
Marx, K. and Engels, F. 1990. *The Manifesto of the Communist Party*. Beijing: Foreign Language Press.
Musto, M. 2015. 'On the legacy of the International Working Men's Association after 150 Years: Interview with Marcello Musto', *Monthly Review* 66 (11) April.

Patnaik, P. 2009. 'Chapter 6: Interview Prabhat Patnaik, India'. In V. Satgar and L. Zita (eds), *New Frontiers for Socialism in the 21st Century: Conversations on a Global Journey*. Johannesburg: COPAC.

Seekings, J. 2000. *The UDF: A History of the United Democratic Front in South Africa, 1983–1991*. Cape Town: David Philip.

Shivji, I.G. 2020. 'Samir Amin on democracy and fascism', *Agrarian South: Journal of Political Economy* 9 (1): 12–32.

Solty, A. n.d. 'You can't have market polarization without political polarization! A tale of two siblings: Liberalism and fascism'. Accessed 2 August 2020, https://copac.org.za/you-cant-have-market-polarization-without-political-polarization-a-tale-of-two-siblings-liberalism-and-fascism/.

Van der Walt, L. 2019. 'Rebuilding the workers' movement for counter-power, justice and self-management', *Amandla!* April/May.

Von Holdt, K. 2019. *The political economy of corruption: Elite-formation, factions and violence*. SWOP Working Paper 10. SWOP Institute, University of the Witwatersrand, Johannesburg.

CONCLUSION

Vishwas Satgar

The term 'fascism' has become overused in the current context. From the standpoint of critical theory and Marxism, it has to endure a catachresis in the contemporary context to serve as a catch-all category for various shades of the new right wing. At the same time, old and new fascism are simplistically conflated. There is a second coming of fascism under way in the twenty-first century that cannot be understood through the conceptual apparatus of interwar twentieth-century fascism. While there is immense value in comparative perspectives on old and new fascism to highlight continuities and discontinuities, the expression of new authoritarian and fascist forces also has to be studied in the context of a new matrix of historic socio-ecological conditions. This volume provides a taxonomy to situate the new authoritarian and, in some instances, full-blown neo-fascist forces advancing deliberate reactionary class-based ideological projects. The geographic scope of this analysis spans the global level, the US, Brazil, India and South Africa. This is not an exhaustive study but certainly provides an optic to appreciate the political economy dynamics shaping the hard-right shift in world order, in the vanguard of liberal democracy (the USA), the largest democracy in the world (India), the largest democracy in Latin America (Brazil) and the most promising democracy in Africa (South Africa).

CRISES OF NEOLIBERAL CAPITALISM AND MARKET DEMOCRACY

Liberal theorists have declared the end of the third wave of democratisation since the early 1970s till the mid-2000s. Beyond this shared insight, Marxists and critical theorists have a very different explanation for the contemporary crisis of democracy.

This volume highlights several important historical conditions that need to be taken into account in thinking about the shift to a new hard-right neoliberalism. First, fascism has been a historical tendency within conjuncturally defined moments of systemic crisis of monopoly and transnationalising capitalism. The modern right wing has a history going back into the nineteenth century. In the twentieth century it has been the face of counter-revolution to ward off any challenges to capitalism. Its authoritarian defence of the institutions and social relations of capitalism has spawned the Ku Klux Klan, Italian Fascists, German Nazis and military dictatorships in the global South. Each of these reactionary social forces was also shaped by conjunctural and historically specific conditions. There are residues and resurgences of such extreme right-wing forces which we need to understand, but in terms of current realities. The Alt-Right in the US, for instance, is not the same as the Ku Klux Klan, but bringing the history of the Klan into view helps us appreciate what is new in the contemporary US context and how this is expressed by white nationalist Trumpian politics.

Second, the contemporary civilisational crisis of capitalism is caused by the unbridled financialisation and commodification of neoliberal capitalism on a global scale. The precariousness, inequality, social anomie and deeper systemic crises, such as global climate breakdown, are happening in a context in which global ruling classes are committed to defending and continuing the same rationalities of marketised rule. In this context, market democracy has become both constitutionalised in the interests of transnationalising capital and incapable of being responsive to citizens' needs. More of the same has given rise to the new authoritarian and neo-fascist forces on the march. The new anti-democratic forces are the progeny of financialised neoliberal capitalism.

Third, the Left has been in retreat, despite a few breakthroughs and important moments of resistance globally. Since the neoliberal class offensive of the 1980s, labour movements in both the global North and South have been dramatically weakened. The rise of the Workers' Party in Brazil and the African National Congress in South Africa portended prospects for transformative change. However, these forces were primarily halted by the loss of nerve and commitment to deepening mass-based logics of democratisation. As a result, market democracies in both these societies have created the conditions for authoritarian shifts. Brazil has moved to the hard neoliberal Right and South Africa's future is not certain, but can very likely end up in the same place.

Like the interwar years of the twentieth century, market democracies do not have the legitimacy to keep societies together. To defend the capitalist logics of these societies, liberals and conservatives also ended up siding with and strengthening the rise of fascist forces. This is also possible in the contemporary world, such that conservatives, liberals and centre-right neoliberals, caught in the twists and turns of electoral politics, embrace the discourses and practices of the new hard Right, or merely impose more market-based reforms and austerity which strengthens these forces. The world's ruling classes are poised to bury even the semblance of democracy as market democracy.

IDENTITY POLITICS AND NEO-FASCISM

The new hard Right clings to core tenets of financialised capitalism and its institutions, including globalised financial markets, international trade regimes, private property, corporate power and precarious labour markets. However, in this context harnessing discontent has meant a revanchism through reactionary identity politics. Neo-authoritarianism and fascism in the twenty-first century are deeply grounded in forms of exclusivist nationalism – from Britons who want their country back from the European Union, to right-wing Germans, Italians, Greeks and Poles, for instance, who want their countries expunged of refugees and migrants. White nationalism and supremacy is directly involved in exclusionary border regimes in the Euro-American world. Trump's USA gave this shift greater momentum. All of this connects with an eco-fascism bent on reproducing a carbon-based capitalism through climate denialism or, in some instances, using the climate crisis to build walls around societies rather than deal with the root causes of the worsening climate crisis. In South Africa, the Economic Freedom Fighters want a South Africa exclusively for Africans. Essentialised racial identities are at work in these nativist nationalisms. At the same time, fundamentalist religion is also constitutive of reactionary identities. Charismatic Christians in Bolivia are implicated in the coup against Evo Morales and the resurgent supremacist racism against indigenous peoples. In Brazil, similar convergences came together around Bolsonaro, and in the US, Trump effectively brought together socially conservative religious fundamentalists and patriarchal white nationalists. In India, Hindu fundamentalism is rolling out a neo-fascist project to achieve a purified Hindu society. Central to this is the disenfranchisement of its Muslim population, including preventing Muslims from entering India as refugees or migrants. Fundamentalist Zionism is no different.

Identity politics, with its emphasis on the particular, accentuation of difference, opposition to subaltern universals (or shared principles of solidarity) and rejection of structural social relations like class, has fed directly into the rise of neo-fascism. This is not to argue against respecting cultural diversity, secularism and pluralism.

However, the accentuation and constitution of obscurantist identities, as part of hyper-exclusionary nationalisms, is both anti-democratic and central to the making of neo-fascism. In the context of market democracies, anchored in deep inequalities and worsening climate crises, identity politics is the basis for antagonism and social polarisation. It is host for the seeds of Balkanisation and fractious politics. The dominance of postmodern identity politics in the academy, in the social media public sphere and now in the service of neo-fascism also contributes to explaining why citizens vote against their own interests. White male workers vote for Trump, or white Britons vote for Johnson, both of whom serve plutocratic class interests.

IMPORTANCE OF DEFENDING DEMOCRACY BY AND FOR THE PEOPLE

In this volume, the chapters collectively and individually illustrate the varying ways in which neoliberal capitalism undermines democracy. Corporate control of politics has reached fever pitch and its destructive forces are undoing the very states that made its rise possible. With the rise of authoritarian politics and neo-fascist parties, there is newfangled urgency. Democracy must be reclaimed but also remade. Modern democracy has always been part of a people's history of struggle and grew up alongside capitalism. Democracy has given us the basic freedoms, rights and powers we have accumulated and enjoyed over the past few centuries. At the same time, democracy is always subject to contestation; it is never complete and never fully arrives given the nature of class and popular struggle.

Rising mass movements defending democracy, advancing climate justice and challenging financialised inequalities face the challenge of advancing systemic alternatives that amount to new class and popular projects that can provide a new direction to societies beyond the impasse of market democracies. A post-neoliberal imagination is crucial. In this context, lobbying degenerate class-based power structures is inadequate and ineffectual. Moreover, mere crowd politics that is incapable of institutionalising the gains of struggle have also come short. A New Left orientation of constituting power from below, through building democratic alternatives controlled by citizens, is crucial. This includes commoning, solidarity economies, food sovereignty, democratic planning and more. The horizons of the twenty-first-century Left have certainly been about giving meaning and substance to the rallying call of 'transformation from below'. Now more than ever this has to be the frontier of grassroots activism. At the same time, international solidarities are absolutely essential. The global civilisational crisis of capitalism requires a global response.

A mass-based and institutionalised climate justice movement is crucial, as part of a larger, new internationalism of the Left that confronts the oppressions of the new authoritarianism and fascism in the world.

Rather than seeing the state, civil society and the economy as given, the balance of power among them must be scrutinised and analysed to push forward an expansion of democracy. Democracy has been transmogrified into anti-humanist, authoritarian politics that serves the interest of corporations, more intensive accumulation and ecological catastrophe. To reclaim a more expansive democracy, new state institutions must be created, ones that secure the public good and deepen the logic of democratisation from below. New forms of democratic political instruments need to be invented that enable citizens and movements to define political agendas and hold politicians accountable. A new generation of post-neoliberal, post-national liberation and post-social democratic left parties need to emerge on the world stage, deeply informed by the lessons of failed market democracies. Moreover, left politicians must serve the publics that elect them and practise an ethics of accountability, transparency and enabling citizens' power. Government officials and public servants must be reinspired and educated to serve the public. And most of all, states must once again regulate and advance democratic planning of the economy, such that corporate power is subordinated to the needs of human beings and nature. The democratic project in the twenty-first century still holds out promise and emancipatory possibilities. It must be defended and advanced, now more than ever, in response to the endgame of an eco-fascist carbon capitalism.

CONTRIBUTORS

Jane Duncan is a Professor in the Department of Journalism, Film and Television at the University of Johannesburg. She is the author of *The Rise of the Securocrats: The Case of South Africa* (2014), *Protest Nation: The Right to Protest in South Africa* (2016) and *Stopping the Spies: Constructing and Resisting the Surveillance State in South Africa* (2018).

Linda Gordon is University Professor of History and the Humanities at New York University. Her most recent books are *Inge Morath, Refugee Photographer: A Life* (2018), *The Second Coming of the KKK: The Ku Klux Klan and the American Political Tradition* (2017) and *Feminism Unfinished* (2014).

Gunnett Kaaf is a Marxist activist and writer based in Bloemfontein. Previously an activist of the African National Congress and the South African Communist Party, he is now active in community organisations in the Free State and explores New Left politics and alternatives. He works as a Fiscal Policy Research Manager in the Free State Provincial Treasury.

Dale T. McKinley is an independent writer, researcher and lecturer as well as Research and Education Officer for the International Labour, Research and Information Group. He is a veteran political activist who has been involved in social movement, community and liberation organisations and struggles for over three decades. He has written and published widely on various aspects of South African, regional and global political, social and economic issues and struggle, and is the author of five books.

Alf Gunvald Nilsen is a Professor of Sociology at the University of Pretoria. He is the author of *Adivasis and the State: Subalternity and Citizenship in India's Bhil Heartland* (2018) and co-editor of *Indian Democracy: Origins, Trajectories, Contestations* (2019).

Devan Pillay is an Associate Professor and former Head of the Department of Sociology at the University of the Witwatersrand. He has published on a wide range of topics, such as the politics of labour, the democratic transition, the media, ecological Marxism, globalisation and holistic development, drawing on his experience in the independent media, the trade union movement, government and as an activist.

Mandla J. Radebe is an Associate Professor in the Department of Strategic Communication at the University of Johannesburg. He is the author of *Constructing Hegemony: The South African Commercial Media and the (Mis)Representation of Nationalisation* (2020).

Alfredo Saad-Filho is a Professor of International Development at King's College London, and was a Senior Economic Affairs Officer at the United Nations Conference on Trade and Development. He has published extensively on the political economy of development, industrial policy, neoliberalism, democracy, alternative economic policies, Latin American political and economic development, inflation and stabilisation, and the labour theory of value and its applications.

Vishwas Satgar is an Associate Professor of International Relations at the University of the Witwatersrand, Johannesburg. He is also the Principal Investigator for Emancipatory Futures Studies in the Anthropocene project and a democratic ecosocialist. In his recent activism he co-founded the South African Food Sovereignty Campaign and the Climate Justice Charter process.

Ingar Solty is a Senior Research Fellow in Foreign, Peace and Security Policy at the Rosa Luxemburg Stiftung's Institute for Critical Social Analysis in Berlin. He is the author of *The Coming War: The US–China Conflict and Its Industrial and Climate Policy Consequences* (2020) and co-editor of *Literature in the New Class Society* (2020) and *On the Shoulders of Karl Marx* (2020), all published in German.

Michelle Williams is a Professor of Sociology and chairperson of the Global Labour University Programme at the University of the Witwatersrand in Johannesburg. She has published widely on democracy, development, gender, and South–South comparisons.

INDEX